The Invisible Man

The Invisible Man

Jay Dubya

·PUBLISHING·

ESTD. 2006

www.bookstandpublishing.com

Published by
Bookstand Publishing
Pasadena, CA 91101
4950_3

Cover design and front cover illustration by Al Margolis

ISBN 978-1-956785-48-7

For Dan

Other Books by Jay Dubya

Adult Fiction

Black Leather and Blue Denim, A '50s Novel
The Great Teen Fruit War, A 1960' Novel
Frat' Brats, A '60s Novel
Ron Coyote, Man of La Mangia
Pieces of Eight
Pieces of Eight, Part II
Pieces of Eight, Part III
Pieces of Eight, Part IV
The Wholly Book of Genesis
The Wholly Book of Exodus
The Wholly Book of Doo-Doo-Rot-on-Me
Thirteen Sick Tasteless Classics
Thirteen Sick Tasteless Classics, Part II
Thirteen Sick Tasteless Classics, Part III
Thirteen Sick Tasteless Classics, Part IV
Thirteen Sick Tasteless Classics, Part V
So Ya' Wanna' Be A Teacher
RAM: Random Articles and Manuscripts
Mauled Maimed Mangled Mutilated Mythology
Fractured Frazzled Folk Fables and Fairy Farces
FFFF&FF, Part II
Nine New Novellas
Nine New Novellas, Part II
Nine New Novellas, Part III
Nine New Novellas, Part IV
One Baker's Dozen
Two Baker's Dozen
Shakespeare: Slammed, Smeared, Savaged & Slaughtered
Shakespeare: Slammed, Smeared, Savaged & Slaughtered, Part II
Suite 16
Time Travel Tales
Snake Eyes and Boxcars
Snake Eyes and Boxcars, Part II
UFO: Utterly Fantastic Occurrences

Young Adult Fantasy Novels

Content Chapters

Introduction

The *Invisible Man* is adult satirical literature featuring adult language and adult situations. The setting is England in the late 1890s, just before the turn of a new century, and also, occurring right during the exciting advances evolving in modern science and technology, where new wonderful conveniences were dominant in the minds of people throughout the Western World whose lives were improving and changing almost on a daily basis.

Herbert George Wells (1866-1946) was born in England, and by the turn of the twentieth century, became one of the Founding Fathers of science fiction. Wells' most famous novels are *The Time Machine, War of the Worlds,* and *The Invisible Man,* which were written and published between 1895 and 1905.

H.G. Wells was a great student of history, and the author loved thinking about mankind's ultimate destiny. In his classic stories, Wells often tells through his characters what *he* believes is wrong with civilization, so that's why the author never ran out of characters for his popular novels.

By mentally taking his readers into the future, or by analyzing society in the present, Herbert George Wells skillfully demonstrated exactly where the human race would be evolving unless science, culture, and emotional growth would change their present courses. Herein lies a new adult-oriented satirical version of H.G. Wells' famous novel, *The Invisible Man.*

Chapter 1

"THE STRANGE MAN'S ARRIVAL"

The Stranger trudged down the frigid sidewalk early in wintry February, of 1896, arriving and walking several blocks from Bramblehurst Station in Iping Village, Sussex, England. The new arrival was slipping and sliding through a biting wind while encountering a driving snow, carrying a black portmanteau in his thickly-gloved right hand. Occasionally, the encumbered village newcomer would place his two-part leather handheld case upon the snowy pavement to rest his weary body from general fatigue, before resuming his onward 'Guest House' destination trek.

The sinister-looking Visitor was wrapped-up from his feet to the brim of his lowered soft-felt fedora, which hid every inch of his face except the shiny tip of his nose. In some places along the path, the snow had piled itself against his shoulders and chest, and the burdened fellow had truly gotten the drift of his extremely inclement, blizzard-like-environment.

The weary Traveler finally staggered into Iping's "Coach and Horses Inn", seemingly more dead than alive, and the New Arrival angrily flung-down his portmanteau. "A fire!" the Itinerant identified his immediate need. "In the name of human charity, I require a room and a fuckin' fire!"

Feeling quite cold and frustrated, the former Train Passenger stamped and shook the snow from off himself in the lodge's foyer, and followed Mrs. Edith Ethel Hall, the co-proprietor, into her guest parlor to negotiate a bargain for his stay. And with *that* almost-reticent introduction, the weird Fellow plunked-down three gold sovereigns upon the table, seriously indicating that the Stranger wished decent lodging would cost for a lengthy stay in the Iping Coach and Horses guest home.

Realizing that business had been terribly slow during *that* particular inclement winter season, Mrs. Edith Hall cordially lit the fire and left her peculiar guest inside the parlor, while the landlady stepped into the kitchen to prepare a substantial meal for her 'Guest'. A 'Lodger' to stop at the Iping Guest House in the wicked wintertime was an unheard-of piece of luck, let alone a guest who was 'no haggler or straggler', and then Mrs. Hall was resolved to show herself worthy of her good fortune as her covetous eyes closely examined the three shiny, gold sovereign down payment inside her right palm's grip.

As soon as the sizzling bacon was well under way on the stove, Millie, the Coach and Horses lymphatic maid, had been earlier brisked-up by a few deftly chosen expressions of contempt directed towards her by the inn's co-owners.

Mrs. Hall carried the cloth, plates, and clean glasses into the downstairs parlor and began arranging the specific items with the utmost care. Although the fire was burning briskly, the woman was immensely surprised seeing that her sullen Visitor still wore his hat and coat, standing with his back to her scrutiny, and staring-out the frosty front window at the falling snow, still accumulating in the front yard.

The Odd 'Gentleman's gloved hands were clasped behind his back in an awkward clench, and his mind seemed to be lost in deep concentration. The guest home's owner noticed that the melting snow that still sprinkled and melted upon the 'New Lodger's shoulders had been dripping upon her newly-purchased carpet.

"Can I take your hat and coat, Sir? I'll give them a good drying in the kitchen?"

"No," the surreptitious-looking Guest replied without turning his head or shoulders. "The wet clothes are nothing compared to my whet appetite! I need nutritional sustenance, now!"

Mrs. Hall was not sure that she had distinctly heard his peculiar mutter, and she was about to repeat and enunciate her question more distinctly.

The New Client turned his head and briefly stared at the concerned building owner over his shoulder. "I prefer to keep the clothes on!" the bizarre-looking Man emphatically stressed. "If I were a pirate, I would say, 'Shiver my timbers no more, Mrs. Jack Frost'!"

Upon further scrutiny, the perceptive landlady noticed that her Latest Tenant had been wearing enormous blue eyeglasses with sidelights, and had bush side-whiskers over his coat-collar that completely hid his cheeks and face.

'This Wacky Guest's glasses are making himself into a pathetic spectacle. This Outlandish Fellow appears to be an alien cross between a classic zombie and a wanderin' vampire. I'll try to jolly the Weird Shit a bit and see if I can learn something tangible about his background.' "Very well, sir; *As You Like It;* if I may quote the bard Shakespeare. I promise that the room will be warmer in a short bit. Winter seldom shows abundant mercy around Iping!"

The Laconic Guest made no answer, and had turned his face away from opinionated Mrs. Edith Hall, feeling that her conversational advances had been ill-timed and too personal for a first-time introduction. The surly-attitude Customer laid the rest of his loose items from his long coat's pocket upon the table, and grumbled some indecipherable mumbles muttered in a quick staccato, ventriloquist-type tone of voice. Mrs. Edith Hall, feeling under duress and also rather perturbed, whisked out of the room in mild embarrassment and consternation.

When the co-owner of the small inn returned to serve her Lodger's late breakfast, the Unusual Guest was still standing there, facing the street window, resembling a stone statue; his back was hunched; his collar turned-up; his dripping hat-brim still slanted-down, with the wet fedora completely hiding his face and ears.

Edith Hall gingerly put-down the eggs and bacon upon the parlor table with considerable adroitness, and boldly beckoned *his* preoccupied attention. "It's now time to *break* your *fast* sir. Your brunch is now served."

"Thank you," the Exceptional Visitor to Iping replied, but did not stir one inch until the landlady had been closing the parlor door. Then, the heavily-attired Fellow swung round, and possessing a large appetite to satisfy, approached the table with a certain eagerness, as if instantly governed by being extremely famished.

As Mrs. Hall proceeded into the kitchen, she heard a familiar annoying sound repeated at regular intervals. 'Chirk, chirk, chirk,' was audibly identified as the grinding of a spoon being rapidly whisked around a basin. "That dumb-shit bitch is clumsily making unnecessary, disturbing noises. There! I clean forgot it. It's her being so long unsupervised!"

And while the inn's co-owner herself finished mixing the mustard, Mrs. Hall gave Millie a few verbal stabs for the girl's excessive noise generations, which her critical boss mentally described as "lethargic slowness".

Motivated by profit and a decent work ethic, the landlady had cautiously cooked the ham and eggs; had carefully set the table, and had done everything required to impress her Newest Customer, while Millie had only succeeded in delaying the mustard mixing by attempting to kill a cockroach skittering around the floor, desperately searching for a safe refuge beneath the pantry's side wall. And "him" in the adjacent room, a New Guest, and wanting to stay; a Paying Patron, despite the assistant employee's general incompetence and slothfulness!

"Why are you such a lazy bitch?" Mrs. Hall rankled and complained to her helper. "Last week I caught you rubbing your clit with the rolling pin's end, and last summer, when the guest house was filled to capacity, I had entered the kitchen and found you with your dress raised and with your left hand sticking a large cucumber up your crotch with your right one! I think, Millie, that I'll buy you a king-sized dildo next Christmas, but you'll have to promise to use the son-of-a-bitch only in your servant's quarters when you aren't working, or aren't noticeable to me!"

"Sorry, Mam!" thoroughly unmodern Millie replied. "I know that I'm an ugly female with big tits, and regrettably, masturbation is my only real pleasure in my boring life! I crave sexual gratification!"

"Well, you aren't going to obtain any damned sexual gratification from me! You're lucky that good help is hard to find these days, so I don't have much fuckin' choice in the matter, now, do I? I must admit that I was once young too, and my husband had a nice-sized dingle on him, and was fairly good at using his erect tool from time to time, when Charlie wasn't as drunk as Dionysus. Ah, yes, Millie. Those were the good old days when sex was actually better than money!"

Recalling fond memories of getting laid three times a day with her once youthful husband, Mrs. Edith Hall filled the mustard pot, and, putting it with a certain stateliness upon a gold and black tea-tray as if it were the Queen's Crown, carried the item into the parlor.

Recognizing that her Eccentric Guest valued quiet and privacy more than oral communication, Mrs. Hall very deliberately and carefully rapped upon the door and entered promptly into the 'parlor lounge'. As the conscientious landlady did so, her Visitor moved quickly, so that her curious eyes received but a faint glimpse of a white object disappearing behind the table.

It would seem that the New Tenant had been picking something that had been dropped from the floor. Mrs. Hall, desiring to please her Newest Occupant, put down the mustard pot on the table, and then Charlie's wife noticed that the damp overcoat and saturated hat had been taken-off and placed over a chair in front of the fire, along with a removed pair of wet boots, then situated on the fireplace hearth.

Seeing the assorted items strewn about on the parlor chair and the table, the astute landlady gathered-up the chair garments in a resolute manner. "I suppose I may have them to dry-off, now. Don't worry, sir! I won't ask you for your wet underwear!"

"Leave the hat on the chair's shoulder," her eerie-looking Visitor imperatively stated in a low, muffled voice. And turning, the elderly woman noticed that the Drenched Gent had raised his head and was presently sitting and peering directly at her.

For a moment, the rather-astounded landlady stood gaping at him, as if he were an ominous ghoulish figure standing inside a dark cloud, making her so surprised to even utter either a syllable or a consonant.

The Unusual Man was holding a white cloth, actually his own serviette, which he had brought with him, and the neat linen had been covering-over the lower part of his obscured face, so that the 'Phantom', having his mouth and jaws completely covered and hidden, evidently explained why he had spoken in a very muffled voice.

'That's odd. This mental case is totally fucked-up! He brings his own mouth cloth to the table,' Mrs. Hall critically thought. 'I ought to shove one of Millie's slightly-used, unsanitary sanitary napkins down this son-of-a-bitch's raspy throat!'

But it was not only that observable serviette which startled Mrs. Hall. It was the fact that all of the New Tenant's forehead above his blue glasses was fully covered by a thick, heavy white bandage, and that another wide one covered his ears, leaving not a scrap of his face exposed, except only his pink, peaked nose. The Gent's exposed snout was bright, rosy, and shiny, just as it had been at his first entrance into the Guest House.

The weird fellow wore a dark-brown velvet jacket with a high, black, stiff, linen-lined collar turned-up about his neck. The thick head and black facial hair, escaping and protruded as it could through the bandage edges, had been exhibited below and between the cross bandages. And the tresses projected-outward in curious tails and horns, rendering the strangest appearance conceivable. The Man's covered and bandaged head was so unlike what the aged proprietor had ever anticipated or experienced in all her years, so *that* drastic departure from the ordinary, for a moment, made Mrs. Hall excessively rigid and paranoid.

"Leave the hat," the sinister-looking Guest explicitly ordered, speaking very distinctly above the white utilitarian napkin.

The hoary woman's nerves began recovering from the shock they had initially received. Edith Hall again placed the hat upon the chair by the fire. "I didn't know, sir," she began; "that—" and the woman stopped her commentary, rather embarrassed to finish her sentence.

"Thank you," the Bleak Guest grimly uttered, glancing from her to the door, and then at her again.

"I'll have them nicely dried, sir, at once." And with that abbreviated statement, the worried landlady carried the remainder of his soaked clothes out of the room. Edith glanced at his white-swathed head and blue goggles again as she was exiting parlor's portal; but his large napkin was still hanging in front of his concealed face, neck, and chin.

Shaking her befuddled head in confusion, Mrs. Hall quivered a little as she gently closed the door behind, and her face displayed a degree of alarm and perplexity. "I *never*," she whispered. "There now!" The Coach and Horses co-owner stepped quite softly into the kitchen, and was too preoccupied with her general analysis of the Stranger to ask Millie what she was messing-up *now*.

Meanwhile, the keenly-astute Visitor impatiently sat inside the tawdry parlor lounge and listened to her retreating feet into the inn's kitchen. Glad to be alone, the 'Phantom' glanced inquiringly at the front window before furtively removing his serviette, and soon resumed consuming his mediocre meal in utter privacy.

After each mouthful and hasty swallow, gulp by forced gulp, the very self-conscious Guest glanced suspiciously at the window, took another swallow of hot tea, then rose and, taking the serviette in his hand, rapidly paced across the room and pulled the blind-down to the top of the white muslin fabric, which had been purchased by Charlie and Edith Hall from the local militant Muslim Mosque and Farsi Fundraising Committee.

The rather dense curtain obscured the lower window panes, preventing any brave soul outside battling the wind and snow to ever spy-upon *his* presence, especially his unseen countenance. The room, because of the Man's suspect deportment, seemed to alter the parlor into a twilight condition. That objective being accomplished, the neurotic diner returned, with an easier disposition, to the table and continued eating his late morning meal.

'The Poor Soul has had an accident, or a major operation, or something akin to major surgery,' Mrs. Hall conjectured! 'I wonder if his aching pecker is bandaged, also?'

Feeling obligated to help *his* theorized medical condition, and not knowing exactly what to verbally communicate, Mrs. Hall deposited some more coal upon the low-glowing fire; unfolded the clothes-horse, and extended the Traveler's Coat upon the rack.

'And those queer-looking goggles that no self-respectable queer or LBGTQ fuck would ever wear! Why, he looked more like a nautical diving helmet than a human Peeping Tom-type voyeur!' the opinionated woman determined as Mrs. Hall hung his muffler on a corner of the horse. 'And holding that rather scary handkerchief over his mouth all the damned time. And talkin' plenty of nonsense and gibberish through it like a fuckin' ventriloquist! Perhaps his mouth had been hurt too, injured, and fucked-up; probably all the way to his tonsils. That mouth napkin he had brought along is quite a word muffler; I'm curious as to whether this Crazy Dolt has another muffler shoved-up his hairy asshole when he just wants to fart around!'

The Guest House owner turned-around, as one who suddenly remembers an important task to be completed. Mrs. Hall, feeling intimidated, rushed into the inn's kitchen without delay. "Bless my soul alive! My addled brain is going-off at a wild tangent. Ain't you done with them taters *yet*, Millie? You're gonna' rupture your pussy slit yet, with your overwhelming sex addiction! I hope you aren't using an enormous winter potato as an improvised summer cucumber substitute!"

When Mrs. Hall traversed again into the dim parlor to clear-away the Stranger's early lunch, her latest idea was that his concealed mouth must also have been viciously cut, or maybe radically disfigured, or perhaps involved in a major accident, which she had speculated her freaky Guest must have recently suffered.

Her theory was soon confirmed, for the "Kooky Gent" was seen actively smoking a pipe, and all the time that Edith had been standing and working inside the room, 'the Jerk' sitting in the dusty parlor chair never loosened the slitted silk muffler he had wrapped around the lower part of his face, in order to move and place the mouthpiece up to his invisible lips.

Yet it was not forgetfulness playing a role, for Mrs. Hall observed that the Erratic Nutcase sat in the corner with his back to the window-blind, and presently spoke more discernibly, having eaten adequate nourishment and having drunk hot tea, and seemingly being comfortably warmed, with less aggressive brevity than her Guest had demonstrated before. The reflection of the parlor fire lent a kind of red animation to his enormous, dark-blue spectacles, and almost dramatically, made the guest seem less morbid-looking, and more human.

"I have some heavy luggage still at Bramblehurst Station. Please tell me; how could I have my other cases delivered to here? Is Iping Village still functioning in the seventeenth century?"

'This freak of nature carries a lot of heavy baggage to go along with his heavy luggage!' "Er, Sir. It won't get here until tomorrow?" Mrs. Hall politely answered.

"I'm terribly disappointed with your' answer. Are there no common laborers available? There is no speedier delivery than by tomorrow? No ambitious asshole with a dolly or a *trap* to earn a decent tip?"

"No, Sir. Pardon my sense of humor, but it looks-like you're trapped here at the Coach and Horses like a doomed rodent!"

Mrs. Hall, endeavored to diplomatically provide explanations to his questions and concerns, and the pair finally developed the basis for a civil conversation. "It's a steep road by the down, sir," Edith declared in response to the question about 'a trap'. And then, snatching at the opportunity afforded during a silent interval, Charlie's obese wife remarked, "It was there, on such a winter day as this, that a carriage had become upset. A gentleman sitting inside the hansom had been killed, besides his unlucky coachman. Accidents, sir, often do happen in inclement weather?"

But the Visitor was not to be drawn so easily to superficial accounts. "They do," the Ghostly Guest agreed, nodding his weary head like a lazy dog, enunciating each word through his muffler, while eyeing his antagonist quietly through his almost-impenetrable dark glasses.

"But Sir, injured people take long enough to get well, don't they? They're entitled to have recuperation time. There was my sister's son, Tom, who just cut his arm with a scythe; the asshole tripped and tumbled onto the sharp blade in the hayfield, and bless me, it was during the poor lad's heyday! Tom, because of his stupid Tomfoolery, was three months tied-up lying in bed, sir. You'd hardly believe it. It's regularly given me a dread mourning of a lousy field scythe, sir. Injuring yourself with a scythe is far worse than getting syphilis!"

"I can quite understand that danger," declared the Visitor. "You didn't have to swing an imaginary scythe in the air to demonstrate your' point! You just looked really asinine and clownish performing *that* exaggerated gesture as a jester!"

"My good-hearted nephew Tom was afraid, one time, that he'd have to have an operation. Tom was that bad off, sir. Nobody likes to go under the knife!"

The Unique Visitor laughed abruptly, which sounded somewhat like a bloodhound's bark that the sinister Guest seemed to bite and kill-off inside his mouth. "*Was* Tom a transvestite Tom boy?"

"He was not, sir. And no laughing matter to them as had the doing for him when either insulted or bullied. However, Tom was a trifle on the gay side, more effeminate than a genuine homo, if ya' know what the hell I mean. There were bandages to do, sir, and bandages to undo, all freakin' day long. So, if I may make so bold as to say it, sir, but your facial wraps remind me of Tom's repulsive cuts to his forehead and to his cheeks; that is, the ones that made absolute craters and pock marks upon his face, sir!"

"Will you get me some matches?" requested the Unnerved Visitor, quite impulsively. "I want to pretend I'm a damned chimney! I don't give a shit about your fucked-up nephew Tom. My pipe is out."

'This narcissistic idiot is certainly an Impertinent Bonehead,' Mrs. Hall evaluated and concluded. 'He's just like petroleum. Always crude, and not refined. If the arrogant jerk-off hadn't already given me the three gold sovereigns, I'd kick him in the ass and rip the friggin' bandages right off his camouflaged face. I'll go and get his matches, only because I need to know how much more money he has to eventually frivolously spend before spring and the tourist season arrives!'

"Thanks for the matches", the Visitor replied, changing both his mood and his attitude. As Mrs. Hall placed a dozen matches upon the parlor room table, the macabre-looking Gent turned his shoulder upon her, and again suspiciously stared-out the front window.

'Our impromptu discussion involving the bandages apparently was altogether too discouraging for this ninny to sustain and endure,' the curious woman hypothesized. 'Evidently, this disguised Fellow is quite sensitive about the topic of operations and recovery. Has his skin been charred and severely burnt? But the mannerless Ignoramus his snubbed every courteous word I've so far uttered, and I feel like setting the imbecile and his spooky cloth wrapping on fire right this minute.'

Then, Mrs. Hall paused for a moment and smiled. 'Last February I had an eighty-seven-year-old geezer stay here, and as an impractical joke, Millie flashed her open beaver to the ancient codger, and the elderly coot immediately had a violent cardiac-attack and died before the doctor could get here. If Millie were to again flash her open beaver before this Distrustful Chap, who looks like a devious mortician, then this queer-looking bloke would probably ignore her kinky advances, and keep puffing-away on his treasured pipe!'

The Visitor remained seated inside the parlor until four o'clock that frigid February afternoon, without giving a hint concerning his secret life before arriving at Bramblehurst Train Station in Iping. For the most part, the dark figure was quite still and idle during that entire initial period; it would seem that the Lodger sat in the growing darkness, in the shadows smoking, his mind in sort of in a prolonged daze, perhaps occasionally dozing and snoring.

Once or twice Mrs. Hall or Millie might have heard him rise from his comfortable seat and engage in raking the fireplace coals, and for the space of five-minutes, his footsteps had twice been discerned pacing the dim and dreary room. The new arrival seemed to be talking to himself, angry and obsessed that his "important luggage" had not been delivered. Then, the armchair creaked, as the Restive Fellow again sat-down.

"I wonder what the hell he's contemplating?" Mrs. Hall asked Millie. "Why has he come to such a remote dump like Iping, arriving at Bramblehurst Station in the dead height of winter?"

"Well Madam; if the horny fuck wanted to shack-up and get a good piece of ass, any decent gentleman would've already made his move by now!"

"Well, Miss Millie. I keep ya' around basically because you're an avowed nymphomaniac, and please remember, I get to keep half your every trick. But if you do serious S and M with this New Weirdo, you might not come-out of it alive!"

Chapter 2

"MR. TEDDY HENFREY"

At four o'clock, when it was fairly dark and Mrs. Hall was ramping-up her flagging courage to go into the parlor and audaciously ask her Tedious Visitor if he would take some more tea, Teddy Henfrey, the local clock-jobber, came into the bar to perform one of his remarkable hand-jobs. "My sakes, Mrs. Hall. I see you've moved the big clock from your hall into the parlor room," Henfrey greeted the notorious Madam. "I gotta' tell ya' that this is terrible weather for anyone using thin boots, but I hear around Bramblehurst that you got a Flakey Guy with a sour puss stayin' here at the Coach and Horses."

"Yeah, Teddy. Business is slow with this big blizzard we're havin'. I'm no meteorologist, but the damned snow outside is fallin' faster than a speeding comet. Charlie and I are renovatin' the upstairs rooms, so my new Patron is temporarily stayin' down here in the parlor. Are ya' here to fix the clock? It doesn't work ever since Millie and I transferred it from the barroom. It was so damned heavy that I think I got a triple hernia! Now Teddy, that ordeal wasn't exactly a moving experience, if ya' know what the hell I mean."

"I won't charge ya' much for my indispensable services," Teddy sympathetically expressed. "Now-a-days, one needs a fat cash cow and a hefty sovereign-pound-money-tree to cancel-out the debt and mortgage pit a common citizen must have!"

"You got that right, Mr. Henfrey. The government needs someone with your practical brains sittin' in Parliament, yes, they do!"

"What's this New Stranger in town like?" Teddy inquired, briefly changing the subject out of general curiosity. "Word at the station is that he's a fucked-up weirdo with deep-rooted criminal tendencies!"

"He's sorta' like the grandfather clock you're goin' to fix," Mrs. Hall related. "He has two hands, but unlike my *Little Ben* in the parlor, you can't see his face."

"Great Westminster, Mrs. Hall. You made a funny! I'll be your manager and get you performin' on the alley burlesque stage over at Piccadilly."

"The clock's mostly going okay, and it strikes and chimes well; but the hour-hand won't do nothin' but point at six."

And leading the way for Teddy, Mrs. Edith Hall escorted the tinker across the hall to the parlor door, and gently rapped and waited with Teddy to stand outside.

"Well, Mrs. Hall. A broken clock, as they say, is right twice a day!" Henfrey weakly joked. "And I've been studying the dictionary and am masterin' my fuckin' cliches. Even a blind squirrel finds an errant acorn once in a while!"

"You're just like my broken grandfather piece in there," Mrs. Hall jested, pointing to the parlor. "You've already been right twice today!"

Opening the door, the landlady's Oddball Visitor was seated in the armchair before the fire, dozing, it seemed, with his bandaged head drooping-down upon his right side. The only light in the room was the red glow from the hearth fire, which subtly reflected off his eyes and goggles like adverse railway signals beyond Bramblehurst Station, but conversely, the dull glimmer left the Lodger's downcast face in shadowy darkness.

'Holy shit!' Teddy thought. 'Unlike the grandfather clock, neither of this guy's hands look broken, but the asshole sitting there also looks like he needs his clock cleaned along with his friggin' bell rung!'

To Teddy and Mrs. Hall, all of the scanty vestiges of the gloomy day appeared comparable to the dullness of the bleak parlor. Everything visible in the dimly-lit room was ruddy and fairly indistinct at initial impression.

'This is more eerie than when I had foolishly visited my cousin in Erie, Pennsylvania two summers ago. I should've gotten into one of

those barrels at Niagara Falls and ended it all with one huge plunge,'
Teddy recollected. 'This asylum nutcase sitting over there has more
bandages than King Tut, who I understand also wasn't wrapped too
tight!'

Mrs. Edith Hall meticulously lit the bar lamp, and whispered to
Teddy as the instant illumination brightened the parlor room. "I
believe he's still napping, but just gaze at his enormous mouth that's
wide-open, sorta' like the Thames Estuary, I reckon. His maw is as
big as a Great White Shark's! It's horribly vast and hideous."

"You're right Mrs. Hall. That open-mouth swallows-up his whole
lower face," Teddy concurred with his own mouth agape. "It's a
good thing I'm constipated, or else this New Tenant of yours would
have me crappin' a huge load on your new rug!"

The bizarre-in-appearance Guest was maintained as the
sensational topic of the moment: his mummy-like greyish-white
head; the monstrous thick-lens-goggle over his eyes, and also, the
rhythmic snoring, not to mention the wide yawning and trembling
below. Then, becoming aware of others entering inside the parlor,
the new Coach and Horses arrival stirred, started-up in his chair, and
put-up his hand to block the lamp's light, which apparently was then
affecting his limited vision.

When Teddy noticed the size of the serviette coving the waking
man's jaw, the clock repairman was momentarily petrified. 'I'll bet
that this son-of-a-bitch has cataracts, just like the Nile over in Egypt!
Maybe even bigger!'

"Would you mind, sir; this man came to look at the clock, sir?"
Mrs. Hall addressed the Perturbed Guest, who had been recovering
from the momentary shock of being intruded upon.

"Look at the clock?" you say, the Peculiar Sleeper articulated,
staring around in a drowsy manner, speaking over his open right
hand, and then finally, becoming more fully awake. "Certainly; but
really, a good idea at a bad time! Go right ahead, but make it quick."

"Good afternoon," Teddy politely greeted the roving, grumpy
itinerant. 'This asshole looks something like a gigantic ocean lobster,

and those colossal goggles! Oh my God!' Henfrey assessed. 'He's an underwater crustacean wearing a deep-sea diver's helmet!'

"I know you're not an American Indian, but do you have any reservations about my unique appearance?" the Traveling Stranger bluntly asked.

"No, sir, I don't. I hope," Teddy stuttered, "that it's no irritating intrusion or invasion, sir. But you'll have to excuse my rude manners. My ancient ancestors were obnoxious Huns and Vandals!"

"Do my bandages offend you in any way?" the inn's Latest Guest asked. Hearing no immediate response, the bizarre Fellow spoke again, turning to Mrs. Hall. "I presume that this room is really to be mine for my own private use. While here, if I wanted some company, I'd surely buy one off the stock exchange!"

"I had thought, sir," Mrs. Hall apologetically stated, "that you'd prefer the clock to be working properly in a timely fashion."

"Certainly," agreed the Estranged Stranger. "Most certainly but, as a rule, I like to be alone and undisturbed. I've always despised being uncouthly interrupted, even in my valued sleep. It ruins my ability to contemplate about more important matters."

"Then, you don't mind Mr. Henfrey working in the parlor room?" Mrs. Hall asked for clarification. "He really knows his shit, especially after taking a crap and lookin' inside the bowl!"

"But I'm really glad to have the clock examined and repaired," the Sinister Tenant disingenuously fibbed while perceiving a certain hesitation in Mr. Henfrey's uncomfortable demeanor. "Don't worry. I'm a mannerly Englishman, and not a temperamental Spaniard. No need to apologize for so rudely interrupting my siesta."

"Thank you, Miguel. Very glad to hear that vital knowledge while making your acquaintance, Mr. Cervantes," Teddy returned, trying desperately to make a funny statement in order to break the uneasy, tense social atmosphere that grossly dominated the parlor.

"Okay, Mrs. Hall. When Pancho Sanza here is done mending the clock and farting around, you can pretend being Dulcinea, and bring me some more delicious tea. But I advise, not until the clock-mending is completed."

'Holy Heaven!' Teddy evaluated. 'This visiting jerk-off really knows his literature. 'I'd better just shut the hell up and mind my 'p's and q's', just like I need to practice better drinkin' habits down at the pub with my pints and quarts of tasty draft! I dare not challenge this egocentric nutcase out of fear of me bein' humiliated by my lacking of quality academic education.'

Feeling unsettled at Teddy's reception by her outlandish guest, Mrs. Hall was about to leave the room without her accidentally making and contributing any additional awkward, conversational advances.

'I don't wish to be snubbed and indirectly ridiculed as Teddy had been. But if this Asshole dares to belittle me, he'll soon find-out I'm no Spanish pinata to be aggressively punctured!'

"Mrs. Hall," the bandaged-faced Patron asked. "Have you learned anything about my luggage registered at the train station?"

"I've mentioned the problem to the postman, and the carrier will deliver them tomorrow, once salt is put-down on the shoveled sidewalk. That was the earliest accommodation I could arrange. Although it's winter and 'autumn' has long past in December, the mail carrier can still *fall.* "

"I should explain," the Bandaged Guest added, "what I was really too cold and fatigued to reveal to you before, that, by profession, I am an experimental investigator of the highest caliber."

"Indeed, sir," Mrs. Hall declared, much impressed. "Do you know Sherlock Holmes and Dr. Watson?"

"Don't be so absurdly silly and ridiculously facetious," the Bandaged Man nastily replied. "I speak in terms of objective fact, and I seldom allude to preposterous fiction, or dumb-ass poetic metaphors. And so, I'm objectively disclosing right this minute that my baggage contains weighty apparatus and appliances that are quite relevant to my occupation. And naturally, I'm very anxious to continue with my significant research and related inquiries."

"Very useful things indeed they are, sir," responded Mrs. Hall. "You might be the most distinguished guest to ever stay at my humble inn."

"My reason for coming to Iping," the 'Mummy Man' proceeded to inform his hostess with a certain deliberation of demeanor, "was to function in solitude without any incidental distractions cluttering my thought processes. I do not wish to be disturbed during the execution of my work. As you might know, labor is a vital part of the word *labor*atory, and that's exactly what I intend that this inn's parlor will become; *my* laboratory. While I had been performing my essential experiments back in London, I had experienced an unfortunate accident that gravely interfered with the advancement of my principal crucial experiments."

'I thought as much,' Mrs. Hall reckoned to herself. "You do seem very professorial. Perhaps you're a tenured faculty member at Cambridge or Oxford?"

The Cryptic Stranger ignored Mrs. Hall's intrusive and interrogating commentary. "My physical condition necessitates a certain retirement and independence from all noise and diversion," the mysterious bandaged Guest divulged. "My eyes are sometimes so weak and painful that I have to shut myself up in the dark for hours without reading or studying my immediate environment, let alone my invaluable notes. Basically, I must lock myself up to avoid becoming mentally disrupted," the 'British Mummy' verbally conveyed. "Yes, at such times, the slightest disturbance, or even the unexpected entry of a person into the room, represents a source of excruciating annoyance to me. My mind loses its focus, so to speak, and I become excessively mentally and emotionally disheveled. It is quite advantageous for my welfare that these harmful reactions and difficulties I receive should be fully understood and avoided."

"Certainly, Sir," concurred Mrs. Hall. "I'm sorry to learn of your challenging disabilities. And if I might make so bold as to ask—"

"That, I think, will be all for now, Mrs. Hall," the Sitting Man tersely and succinctly answered. "You can keep and reserve your trite platitudes and sympathy for a better, and more satisfactory, occasion."

After Mrs. Hall had left the parlor room in a rather mental quandary, the Bandaged Occupant remained standing in front of the fire, glaring at the nervous clock repairman, suggesting that Teddy should get busy with his purpose for being there. So, Mr. Henfrey not only hastily removed the hands of the dysfunctional clock, along with its face, but extracted the entire inner works including the gears and pendulum, and then not wanting to make a mistake, tried working in as slow, as quiet, and as unassuming manner as possible.

Teddy, being extraordinarily nervous and working assiduously, with the mantel lamp shining-down close to his eyes, the mechanic also utilized the green lamp shade throwing a brilliant light upon his shaky hands, which also reflected upon the clock's frame and brass wheels. The general effect left the rest of the dusky and dusty room shadowy and rather ominous.

When Teddy glanced-up from his in-progress task, varied colored patches swam inside and were reflected in his eyes. Being constitutionally of a curious nature, the talkative repairman had diligently removed the inner works, which was indeed quite an unnecessary procedure, with the idea of delaying his departure, and perhaps initiating a conversation with the Stranger.

But the Bandaged Fellow simply stood there, perfectly silent and still. So still, in fact, that it got on Henfrey's already-frazzled nerves. Despite the presence of the Nebulous Guest, the tinker felt basically alone in the room, and as Teddy looked-up, there appeared, grey and dim, the bandaged head and huge blue lenses staring fixedly, with a mist of green spots drifting in front of the enormous spectacles. The visualization was so uncanny to the clock-man that for a minute, the two men remained staring blankly at one another. Then, feeling intimidated and terrified, Henfrey looked-down.

'I feel very uncomfortable!' Teddy worried and fidgeted. 'I would like to say something, but I'm absolutely tongue-tied. Should I remark something mediocre and common, such as that the weather is very cold for this time of year?'

Henfrey again gazed-up as if to take aim with *that* asinine perfunctory comment. "The winter weather has been rather abominable," Teddy began, attempting to break the prevailing cold atmosphere. "It's been positively atrocious! Ever since New Year's Day."

"Why don't you simply finish your easy responsibility and leave me the hell alone?" the Rigid Figure vulgarly criticized, evidently in a state of painful and suppressed rage. "All you've got to do is to fix the hour-hand on its axle. I could easily do that all by myself in a jiffy. You're simply humbugging, Mr. Henfrey, intentionally delaying your progress while still bothering me! I strongly suggest that you get both your ass and the clock in gear!"

"Certainly, sir, but only several minutes more I'll need. I had overlooked one vital feature. I'll leave shortly, even though I'm six-feet-eight inches tall!"

"I think that if you weren't so friggin' clumsy, you should go to America and play that new game everyone across the pond is raving about; basketball, I believe," the Bandaged Tenant ridiculed the garrulous clock workman. "I've been reading in the London papers that the novel sport had been invented back in 1891 in Springfield, Massachusetts by a physical education instructor, James Naismith, is his name, I recollect. If you venture several thousand miles across the *Atlantic,* your chronic and irksome pestilence will successfully be out of my hair, but more importantly, out of my damned life."

After completing his non-comical utterance, ten minutes later, Teddy rushed to gather his tools and hurriedly departed the premises feeling excessively annoyed. "Damn it!" the tinker bitched to himself, trudging down the village lane through the non-thawing snow. "A fellow must fix a clock at times, surely to earn a farthing or two. Can't an honest man even look at you? Ugly Deformed Asshole! He must have more craters than does the moon upon his pocked kisser! I mean, where the hell is the February masquerade party here in this primitive hick town?"

Then, Teddy recollected some more impressions his mind had received at Mrs. Hall's modest residence 'If the police had been wanting the Oddball Visitor for his bandit appearance here in Iping, the son-of-a-bitch would be easier to recognize than a 'Most Wanted' poster with an actual criminal face showing upon it!'

At Gleeson's Corner, Teddy rushed to get caught-up with Mr. Charlie "Horse" Hall, who had recently married the Stranger's hostess at the Coach and Horses, and chubby Mr. Hall now drove the Iping Stage Coach, when occasional people required coach transportation to Sidderbridge Junction, and also coming towards Bramblehurst on his return from that other miserable town.

Mr. Hall had evidently been "stopping a bit" at Sidderbridge, judging by his fairly intoxicated driving maneuvers. "How the hell ya' doin', Teddy?" Charlie greeted his regular tavern drinking buddy. "Last time I saw ya', you were on the floor after fallin' off your bar stool, ya' drunken lush!"

"Ya' got a rum-insane asylum psycho case stayin' at your disreputable place, yes you do!" Teddy anxiously announced. "The Asshole looks like one gigantic pregnant band-aid."

"What's that you say?" Charlie incredulously asked. "A new client staying at *our* house that's bein' renovated for the summer tourists?"

"Rum-looking Customer stoppin' at the Coach and Horses," Teddy confirmed. "My sakes! The Jerk appears to need heavy-duty electric shock treatments; a definite candidate for Bedlam, that's for damned sure!"

"Well, Teddy. Forget about good old St. Mary's of Bethlehem. I think that Millie will nurse him back to decent health with those solid tits and erect nipples of hers," Charlie laughed. "Remember, Teddy. Unlike in America, here in England there's a sucker born every fuckin' second!"

The neurotic clock tinker proceeded to provide Mr. Charlie Hall a vivid description of his wife's Grotesque Guest. "Looks a bit like a disguise, it does? I'd like to see a Man's whole face if I had him stopping to temporarily reside in *my* place," Henfrey emphasized and opined. "But women are too damned trustful, and also, so fuckin' naïve when it comes to a suspicious Man's secret proclivities, especially where Perverted Strangers into Iping are concerned. He's taken-over your parlor room, Charlie, and he ain't even given a freakin' name for identity, Hall. The suspicious bonehead is a complete enigma, I say!"

"You don't say!" Hall grunted and spit out a mouthful of saliva upon the pavement. The listening huge man of sluggish apprehension, finally comprehended Teddy's precise description.

"Yes," Teddy verified. "By the week he's been renting. Whatever he is, you can't get rid of him under seven days. And I've learned that he's got a lot of luggage coming-into your inn tomorrow, so the Queer Imbecile says. Let's hope it won't be quarry-stones in boxes, Charlie. We can steal half his loot from his suitcase if he's just robbed cash from a major bank."

"What's his personality like?" Mr. Hall asked. "Is he rough and despicable? If so, I'll kick his ass out of there in a London micro-second!"

"Let me tell ya' something, Charlie. My aunt over in Hastings had been swindled by a similar stranger carrying an empty, leather portmanteaux. The slippery crook quickly scurried hastily out of Hastings, over eight-hundred-years after William the Conqueror had raided the place from Brittany. In 1066 AD, if I accurately remember from my advanced kindergarten class."

"Get up, old girl," Hall yelled at his lazy horse before climbing back behind the reins. "I suppose I must see about this new interestin' development. If the Bloke annoys me, I'll give the punk a brass-knuckle ham-on-bread that'll make the infamous Earl of Sandwich quite jolly and humored!"

Teddy trudged on his way with his mind considerably relieved that Charlie Hall would efficiently solve *his* concern about the impudent fellow staying at the lackluster guest house.

But when Mr. Hall arrived home, instead of "seeing about the matter of concern," poor Charlie was severely reprimanded by his wife about the length of time he had spent in Sidderbridge, and his mild explanations were answered rather snappishly, and in a livid manner not to his immediate satisfaction about the New Lodger.

"Why have you been so long over in Sidderbridge?" Edith wanted to know. "Screwin' around with some lousy narrow-tunnel hussy, I suppose?"

Ignoring his wife's verbal assault, Charlie recalled the seed of suspicion that Teddy had germinated inside *his* jealous mind. "You gullible women don't know everything," Charlie equivocated to Edith, while attempting to resolve, and more accurately glean and ascertain basic information about *his* Guest's questionable character and personality. "I'll go into the parlor and examine what's there while the Creep is still sound asleep."

And after the Reclusive Stranger had gone upstairs to bed, which he did about half-past-nine, Mr. Hall stepped very aggressively into the parlor and looked very hard at his wife's 'medieval furniture', just to demonstrate to *his* ego that the New Occupant wasn't the master-in-charge at the Coach and Horses, and Charlie closely scrutinized, a little contemptuously, a sheet of mathematical computations which 'the Stranger' had inadvertently left upon the bureau. When retiring for the night, Mr. Hall instructed his mercurial spouse to look very intensely at the Parlor Resident's' luggage when it would be arriving the next day.

"Teddy told me over at Bramblehurst that there's nothing suave or genteel about our new, Reprehensible Renter! I imagine that he might even be a Wanton Killer or a Dangerous Felon!" Hall lectured to his wife.

"You mind your own fuckin' business, Charlie," insisted Edith, "and I'll mind mine. If you want a fairly decent piece of ass tonight, you might have to find a lousy donkey and carve its rear end off! The Stranger livin' in the parlor during the daytime is undoubtedly a strange kind of Stranger, and that's the long and the short of it!"

All that night, Edith Hall was by no means assured about the disposition of her sinister Guest, and *that* troubling apprehension had been dwelling deep inside her own mind. In the middle of a terrifying nightmare, the landlady woke-up dreaming of a bevy of huge white heads, similar to turnips, that were stalking and trailing after her, and at the end of their gruesome interminable necks, and with their vast black eyes craving her promiscuous body, were covetous arms. But being a fairly practical, sensible woman, Edith Hall subdued her phobic terrors, turned-over, and eventually went to sleep again, thinking about what might next 'turn-up' with the horrendous haunting turnips.

Chapter 3

"THE THOUSAND AND ONE BOTTLES"

A nd so, it was on that twenty-eighth day of February, 1896, at the beginning of the early thaw, that a singular 'Phantom' had arrived out of infinity into somnolent Iping Village. The next morning, his worn black luggage was being carelessly dragged through the mushy slush, and very remarkable and weighty baggage it certainly was. There were four bulky loaded trunks, such as any Irrational Man might need, but in addition, there was a massive box of books, big, fat books, personal journals of which some obscure scribbles had been just coarsely jotted-down in an entirely haphazard, incomprehensible, indecipherable handwriting that erratically approached something between primitive Egyptian hieroglyphics and ancient Sumerian cuneiform.

And included in the immense collection, there existed a dozen or more crates, boxes, and cases, containing perishable objects packed in wads of bundled straw. Charlie Hall, was ripping and tugging with a casual curiosity at the straw that surrounded the first of the fragile glass bottles. The eager Stranger, muffled in hat, coat, and gloves, impatiently exited the guest house to rendezvous with Mr. Henry Fearenside's overloaded cart, while Edith's bombastic husband was having a word or so engaging in preparatory gossip as to the amount it would cost to lug the cumbersome cargo items inside the Coach and Horses Inn.

Out the new excited Tenant came, not noticing Mr. Fearenside's ferocious dog, who was sniffing in a *dilettante* spirit at Hall's legs and smelling his raunchy testicles. "Come along with those boxes," the Stranger hollered at the newly-hired laborers. "I've been waiting long enough."

And the Inscrutable Fellow came down the steps towards the rear of the cart, as if to avariciously lay his hands upon the smallest crate, which the enthused Recipient seemed to value the most.

No sooner had Fearenside's fearsome dog caught sight of 'the Mummy', that the antagonistic cur began to savagely bristle and growl, and when the Odd Guest had foolishly rushed down the steps, the mangy canine gave an incisive hop, and then sprang its sharp teeth straight towards the luggage owner's left hand.

"Whup!" cried Charlie Hall, jumping back to avoid contact, for he was no hero who associated with fierce dogs. And old Fearenside howled, "Lie down!" and the wagon driver eagerly snatched his whip to tame the snarling beast.

Mr. Hall and Mr. Fearenside saw that the hound's teeth had slipped the hand, heard a soft kick, saw the dog execute a flanking jump, and administer a deep bite upon the Stranger's left leg, and then listened to the loud rip of his trousers. Then, the finer end of Fearenside's whip reached the wild animal's snout, and the cur, frightened of receiving more painful reprisal, yelped with dismay, and cravenly retreated under the wheels of the delivery wagon.

The whole episode had all elapsed and transpired in the short business of a swift half-minute. Being somewhat stunned and shocked, no bystander had spoken, and ten-seconds later, everyone began shouting hysterically.

The Stranger glanced swiftly at his torn glove and at his damaged leg, stooped-down to assess the injury, and then turned and swiftly hustled up the steps into the village inn. The assembled spectators heard the victim go headlong across the passage and up the uncarpeted stairs, directly into his newly-finished bedroom.

"You brutal brute, you!" Fearenside yelled, after climbing off the wagon with his whip in his hand, while the huge mutt watched his owner's delirious animation through the wagon's wheel spokes. "Come here, Tiger!" Fearenside vehemently bellowed. "You'd better behave, or else you'll really get the full-measure of this wicked whip in a Manchester Minute."

Hall had stood gaping at the in-progress saga, finally fathoming the full event that had just occurred. "He was bitten pretty bad," the co-proprietor worriedly stated to Fearenside. "I'd better go and attend to his wounds." And without further hesitation, Charlie trotted up the stone entrance steps, following the cryptic Stranger's path. The obese and fatigued husband soon met Mrs. Hall inside the inn's central passage. "The Carrier's dog had bitten your fucked-up Tenant, I think on the hand."

After the brief description to Mrs. Hall, Charlie dashed straight upstairs, and noticed right away that the victim's door was ajar. Hall forcefully pushed the entrance open, and without any formal ceremony or greeting, being of a naturally sympathetic turn of mind, reflexively moved his corpulent body inside.

The blinds were down and the room was dim, just as the morbid-looking parlor had formerly been. Soon, Charlie's pupils caught a glimpse of a most singular sight. His astute eyes perceived what seemed to be a handless arm waving towards his own visage, and a face comprised of three huge indeterminate spots, peering through the white muffler, the vague image seemingly similar to the face of a pale pansy.

Then, Charlie Hall was violently struck in the chest by the Stranger's clenched fist; his corpulent body hurled backwards, and next, the door rapidly slammed in his face, and Mr. Hall was immediately locked-out of the chamber.

The sequence of events all occurred so quickly that the incident afforded Charlie little opportunity to observe and interpret all of the pertinent details. First, the inordinate waving of inexplicit shapes; second, a vicious blow to the sternum, and third, a terrible concussion received to boot. The landlord stood there, breathing heavily upon the dark little landing, wondering what unearthly phenomenon he had just seen, confronted, and encountered.

A couple of minutes thereafter, Mr. Hall rejoined the little group that had formed on the cleared sidewalk outside the all-too-familiar Coach and Horses. Mr. Fearenside reiterated to the other assembled gentlemen about the bewildering and surreal event over and over again. Mrs. Hall came down the front steps, accusing that Mr. Fearenside's pooch didn't have any logical cause to bite her mysterious Guest's left wrist.

And then, there was hoary Mr. Gilbert Huxter, the general trading dealer and tobacconist from across the road, habitually pursuing his anticipated interrogatives; and Mr. Sandy Wadgers from the Village forge, also being abnormally judicial and opinionated; besides a variety of gossiping women and children, all of them saying dumb-ass fatuities: "I wouldn't ever let the beast near enough to bite *me*." "Isn't right to *have* or to own such a savage brute without the monster being tied to a strong leash and whipped every hour into submission."

"Why the hell did you bite the pitiful jerk's leg and hand?" Fearenside yelled like a court prosecutor at the guilty mutt, as if the skulking creature actually had a conscience and had been plausibly processing the wagoner's angry vernacular.

Mr. Hall, decoding the commotion below from the front steps, found it incredible that his eyes had seen something so very more remarkable happening from upstairs than a mere dog bite that had transpired down on the sidewalk. And besides, the portly man's astonished mental condition was truly preventing Charlie from vociferously cursing his regular litany of colorful expletives.

"He doesn't want any help!" Hall exclaimed in answer to his wife's inquiry about their Enigmatic Guest. "We'd better be-takin' his luggage inside before he either commits suicide, or attacks our asses and makes us both into homicide cases and obituaries."

"He ought to have his hand cauterized at once at Dr. Rehmann's place," Mr. Gilbert Huxter constructively recommended. "Especially if it's at all inflamed, or perhaps already infected. I do believe, and am willing to bet that *that* rabid mutt could easily deflate Millie's firm-solid tits with two decisive bites!"

"I'd shoot that insane hound right between the eyes, that's what the hell I'd do," screamed am out-of-control nosey female standing in the back of the chattering group.

Suddenly, the aroused dog began growling again, seemingly understanding that it was being publicly indicted by the biased crowd.

"Come along," cried an angry voice inside the doorway, and there stood, on the top step, the Muffled Stranger with his starched collar turned-up, and with his felt hat's brim bent-down. "The sooner you' bozos get those cartons inside, the better I'll be pleased. Start carrying this very minute, if you wish to be paid."

"Were you hurt, sir?" a concerned Henry Fearenside kindly asked. "Your trousers and your glove have been ripped. I'm really sorry that my pup...."

"Not a bit," the Mystic Stranger replied, without any notice of showing pain. "Never broke the skin. Hurry-up with those things before I have a French hemorrhage. I don't wish to hear any more dumb-shit doggerel about your damned dog!"

The first crate, as directed by the Stranger, had been unpacked with accordance and harmony as to *his* exact specifications, after of course, being cautiously carried into the parlor. The bitten Tenant flung himself upon the carton with extraordinary eagerness, and enthusiastically began identifying its contents, scattering the strands of straw wrappings with an utter disregard of Mrs. Hall's newly-acquired carpet.

And from the box's interior, the owner began to produce bottles; little fat bottles containing chemical powders; small and slender bottles holding colored and white fluids; fluted blue bottles labeled 'Poison'; bottles with round bodies and featuring slender necks; large green-glass bottles; even larger white-glass bottles; bottles with glass and cork stoppers, and finally, others having frosted labels. Next, there were bottles with fine corks as popularly exist with extravagant champagne containers; bottles with bungs; bottles with wooden caps; a dozen wine bottles; and also, nondescript salad-oil bottles.

The fastidious fellow then put the separate glass containers in rows upon the chiffonnier; on the mantel; on the table under the window; around the floor; and also, upon the bookshelf. The village chemist's shelves in his shop in Bramblehurst Station could not boast half that splendid array that had been so carefully organized.

Yes, quite a sight it was in its entirety. Crate after crate yielded a series of exquisite bottles, until all six trunks had been fully emptied, and the table was high with removed straw wrappings that had been heaped and accumulated. The only items that came-out of those sturdy crates, besides the myriad bottles, were a number of test-tubes, along with the plethora of other glass laboratory equipment.

Next, the Inimitable Stranger hurriedly paced to the window and set to work, not troubling in the least about the disgusting litter of straw strewn about; the faltering fire, which had expired; the heavy box of books remaining outside the inn, nor did his mind think about any remote consideration for the trunks and other second-in-importance luggage that had been conveyed upstairs into his awaiting room.

When Mrs. Hall took his dinner into his new upstairs living quarters, the Odd Client was already so absorbed in his devoted work, quite preoccupied while pouring little drops from bottles into various test-tubes. So engrossed was he that the Experimenter did not hear her entrance until Edith had swept away the bulk of the straw, and quietly placed the serving tray upon the wooden table, with some little emphasis perhaps, shaking her head in dismay at seeing the state of the debris still scattered upon the planked-wood floor.

Then, the Mystery Man half-turned his head and again, immediately rotated his noggin away from the landlady's scrutiny. But in the interim, Mrs. Hall had keenly observed that her non-conforming Guest had removed his horrendous glasses; and the unorthodox specs were lying beside him upon the table, and it seemed to Edith that 'the Ghoul's eye sockets were extraordinarily hollow, resembling 'little caves'.

The Guest Science Fanatic again donned his queer-in-appearance spectacles, and then turned and faced the totally exasperated woman. Edith was about to complain of the straw randomly scattered upon the floor when the 'Mad Scientist' anticipated her first salutation.

"I wish you wouldn't come in without courteously knocking," the Perturbed Experimenter maintained in the melancholy tone of voice that seemed so characteristic of his petulant demeanor.

"I knocked, but seemingly—"

"Perhaps you did, knock. But in my necessary investigations, I mean, in my really very urgent and vital important investigations, the slightest disturbance, even the slight jarring of a door distracts me. I must ask you to demonstrate discretion upon gently approaching me! Do I make myself clear?"

"Certainly, sir. You can turn the lock if your attitude is like that; you know, to make your room adequately secure from intolerant disturbances. Any time your whim so desires."

"A very good idea," acknowledged the Stranger. "You do show potential as an avid listener!"

"This straw, sir, if I might make so bold as to remark—"

"Don't you dare utter another word. If the straw makes trouble for you, put its removal down in the bill for future payment." And next, *he* coyly mumbled indiscernible nomenclature at her, articulating words that suspiciously sounded like coded, nasty curses.

The Investigator was so odd and yet, so dedicated to his obscure pursuit, standing there, yet so aggressive and explosive; with expensive bottle in one hand and fragile test-tube in the other, Mrs. Hall was so quite alarmed at the whole manifestation that her disbelieving eyes had been interpreting and witnessing. But Edith was a very resolute woman and adamant about expressing her thoughts. "In which case, I should like to know, sir, what you consider—"

"A shilling; put down a shilling to be recompensed for your silly inconvenience. Surely, a shilling's more than enough, isn't it?"

"So be it," Mrs. Hall conceded and compromised without negotiating. And next, the hostess adroitly took-up the table-cloth and began spreading it over the unkempt table. "If you're satisfied, of course—"

Being more than bored with the monotonous dialogue, the Laconic Visitor slowly turned and sat-down, with his coat-collar facing toward her.

All that afternoon, the on-a-mission Maniac worked with the door locked, and as Mrs. Hall later testified to Charlie and Millie, for the most part, 'the Fiend' toiled in silence. But once there was a distinguishable concussion upon the upper floor that had been heard downstairs, along with a sound of bottles ringing together as though the upstairs table had been impacted; and also, the discernible smash of a bottle being flung-down violently, apparently during a fit of rage; and later, a speedy pacing was rather audible meandering around the room. Fearing that "something crazy was the matter", Edith approached the upstairs door and listened, not caring to knock for fear of again being verbally disciplined.

"I can't go on with this shit!" the Upset Occupant was raving and exclaiming. "I *can't* go on. Three-hundred-thousand, four-hundred-thousand! The huge multitude! Absolutely cheated! All my life it may take me, just to solve this enormous conundrum! Patience! Patience indeed! Fool! Dumb-ass obstinate fuckin' fool! That's precisely what the hell I am!"

There was a distinct noise of hobnails upon the bricks in the room's inferior bar area, and Mrs. Hall very reluctantly decided to leave the rest of *his* enigmatic soliloquy to the distraught griever. When Edith returned, the parlor room was silent again, save for the faint creeping and squeaking of *his* rickety chair, and the occasional clink of a glass bottle. Much to her relief, his frenetic panic attack had terminated. The Stranger had passively resumed his secret work.

When the flustered landlady later took in his tea, Mrs. Hall noticed shards of broken glass in the room's corners, most of the debris lying beneath the concave mirror, along with a golden stain that had been carelessly wiped-away. Edith instinctively called attention to it.

"Put it down in the bill," snapped her again-incensed and interrupted Visitor. "For God's sake, woman; stop trifling me with minutia! Don't worry so much about a picayune money matter. If there's any substantial damage done to your property, write it down in the bill."

"I'll tell you something," Mr. Henry Fearenside addressed Teddy, sounding rather mysterious. It was fairly late in the afternoon, and the pair of alcoholics were conversing inside the little beer-shop sporting the swinging shingle "Iping Hanger".

"Well, Mr. Fearenside? What the hell is on your miniature mind?" Teddy Henfrey asked. "If anyone ever had a pea brain, it's definitely you!"

"This Chap you're speaking of, the one that my tame dog had accidentally bitten. Well, I ain't lyin' when I tell ya' that he's as black as the Ace of Spades; yes, he is; black as my bent chimney poker. Leastways, his skinny legs are also black. I saw his exposed knee through the tear of his trousers, and glanced at his hand through the tear of his glove. No blood on either, Teddy; no fuckin' blood whatsoever! You'd have expected a sort of pink pinky to show, now, wouldn't you? Well, dear Teddy, there wasn't any white or pink skin there, either. Just plain blackness. I tell you, he's as black as my hat and my recently-painted wagon. Might even be a convict from the African jungles. I hereby reckon!"

"My sakes!" Henfrey yelled, getting the attention of two barmaids along with three seated pub patrons. "He's a fucked-up Rummy Case, altogether. Why, Hank; I observed that his nose is as pink as a pussy tunnel!"

"What I've shared with you is strictly confidential, but it's all true as Gospel," Henry Fearenside insisted. "I know *that* particular truth for being an indisputable fact. And I'm tellin' you now, Teddy, exactly what the hell I'm thinkin' and revealin'. That Man's a piebald, Teddy. Black here, and white there, in different patches. Some kind of freaky foreign mongrel, he is. And he's obviously ashamed of it," the wagoner convincingly claimed. "The creep's a kind of half-breed, and the color's come off patchy, instead of mixing, if ya' know my stark depiction. I've heard of such things before in remote parts of the world like China and Africa. And it's the common way of nature that often happens with pinto horses, and with ordinary stray calico cats, as anyone with common sense can easily see. Barmaid. Set-up two more brews for my good pal and me!"

Chapter 4

"DR. CUSS INTERVIEWS STRANGER"

I have thoroughly explained the odder-than-fiction circumstances of the weird Stranger's arrival in Iping, with a certain fulness of detail. But with the exception of two separate incidents, the particulars of his lengthy stay, until the extraordinary day of the annual crab festival, may be passed-over, just like Passover in this biased Christian community, in a very cursory manner.

There were a number of verbal skirmishes with Mrs. Edith Hall on conflicts of domestic discipline in regard to arbitrary house rules, but in every case until early May, when the first signs of winter poverty were beginning to lift, the wily Newcomer over-rode Mrs. Hall by the expressed pledge of paying extra sovereigns in order to continue staying within her good graces well into the summer months.

Charlie Hall did not like his 'abominable Tenant's' general deportment, and whenever Mr. Hall dared conferring with Edith about the advisability of getting rid of the outlandish 'Impostor', the husband usually concealed his animosity and rancor in deference to his wife's totally-dominant opinions, and then, to avert further disharmony within the rocky marriage, as a viable alternative, Hall chose to chiefly avoid his dysfunctional Visitor as much as possible.

"Charlie, just wait till the summer," Mrs. Hall sagely predicted. "That's when the screwball artists are beginning to come back for the hot months. Then, we'll see what materializes in terms of our cash flow. I agree that our Eccentric Tenant may be a bit overbearing, but bills settled punctually are indeed bills settled punctually, whatever you'd like to maintain or argue. We need his abundant money supply, at least until mid-June."

The Stranger did not ever attend Sunday church services, and in his convoluted mind, determined no difference between Sunday and the six other irreligious week days. On some auspicious mornings, the 'Phantom Experimenter' would come downstairs early to breakfast, and then be continuously busy for hours on end inside his recently-renovated laboratory room. On other cloudy and more dreary mornings, 'the Psycho-Case' would rise late, pace his room like a frenzied caged lion, fretting audibly for hours-on-end about unknown esoteric subjects and sophisticated scientific formulas; then smoke incessantly; and relentlessly sleep for hours in the armchair by the fireplace.

The Lodger's communication with the outside world, beyond and inside the village, was rather negligible. The fellow's temper continued to be very mercurial, and constantly vacillating; for the most part, the all-too-prudent Guest's puzzling mannerisms were that of a tortured man, especially suffering under almost unendurable sacrifice, and seemingly plagued by perpetual societal rejection. And once or twice, certain articles of his weatherworn clothing were snapped, torn, crushed, or broken after the 'Madman' had enacted spasmodic gusts of violence.

The intriguing academic dreamer always seemed to be under a chronic irritation of the greatest magnitude. His habit of talking to himself in a low voice grew steadily upon his suspect ego, even when walking the dark streets of deserted Iping after midnight all alone. But though Mrs. Hall had listened conscientiously to the narrow-minded, garrulous town critics and cynics, the coy woman could make neither heads nor tails of what her ears had heard, because deep inside her greedy heart, Edith Hall needed the source of *his* infinite money to sustain her household through the late winter months.

The 'Odd-Bird' rarely ambled around the vicinity of Main Street by daylight, but at twilight, occasionally he would saunter-out into vacant lanes, with his hands all muffled-up, and with his face tightly wrapped in cloth and heavy bandages, whether the weather was particularly cold or not. And the insular 'Night Trekker' chose the loneliest paths and those remote alleys most overshadowed by trees and banks in which to hike all alone.

The "Churlish Professor's" goggling spectacles, along with ghastly covered face, under the protection of his broad hat, came with a disagreeable suddenness on several occasions when the "Midnight Ambler" had exited out of the darkness upon one or two home-going laborers.

And Teddy Henfrey, stumbling and tumbling with Mr. Fearenside out of the "Scarlet Coat Pub" one night, at half-past nine, was instantly and shamefully scared by the Meandering Stranger's skull-like head (he was walking with hat in hand), where *his* sudden appearance had been illuminated by the instantaneous light emitted from the opened inn door.

Such irreverent children of the exclusively Christian community, who had an occasional opportunity of incidentally viewing the 'Bandaged Bandit' at nightfall, dreamt of "monstrous bogies and a roving bogie-man" who was actively searching for innocent pedestrians to either slay or assault. And it seemed doubtful whether the anonymous evening Trekker disliked boys more than the obnoxious lads disliked him, or the reverse; but there was certainly a vivid-enough dislike on either side, with much of the town gossipers insisting that the wandering Tenant of Mrs. Hall's respectable inn was either a child predator, or an ever-dangerous kiddy pedophile.

It was inevitable that a person of so remarkable an appearance and bearing should naturally synthesize into a frequent topic in such a retarded and antiquated village as Iping, Sussex County. Public opinion was greatly divided about his arcane occupation and his foreign behavioral propensities. Mrs. Hall was quite sensitive on those exact points, strongly wanting to retain his financial assistance into the early summer.

When abruptly questioned by local church-going connivers on Sunday mornings, Edith explained very carefully that the Lodger was in reality an "important experimental investigator", her words gliding gingerly over each specific syllable as one who dreads experiencing oral pitfalls and verbal contradictions.

When asked exactly what an "important experimental investigator" was, and precisely prescribed by dictionary definition, the challenged landlady would state with a touch of superiority that only university educated professors knew complicated erudite knowledge such as *that* advanced subject required, and would thus explain that he "has discovered amazing things like rare atoms and incredible molecules".

"My Visitor had had a terrible accident, which temporarily discolored his face and hands," Mrs. Hall elaborated when questioned by worried churchgoers. "And being of a sensitive disposition, my wonderful Guest has been personally averse to any negative public skepticism about his serious medical disability. He's truly here in Iping to fully recuperate from his malady!"

"He's a full-blown Asshole," the church choir director accused Mrs. Hall's renter up in the religious edifice's chorus loft. "He might even be a full-blown Asshole without an actual asshole!"

"Go rub your rectum in the rectory Baptism Fountain," Edith angrily countered. "My fabulous guest is a fantastic gentleman of the highest caliber, who only has a temporary skin infection that'll gradually heal in time. But I doubt if he'll get any special empathy or miracle cure from a sanctimonious, fucked-up shithead like you!"

Out of Mrs. Hall's perceptive hearing of public opinion, there was a pessimistic view that was largely entertained in downtown Iping that the "Nutjob at the inn" was a vicious criminal on the lam, trying to escape from the jaws of justice, with his infamy being done by wrapping himself up so as to hide himself altogether from the scrutiny of the police. This highly-speculative idea sprang from the brain of regularly intoxicated Mr. Theodore Henfrey. However, no major crime of any heinous nature, dating from the middle or the end of February and early March, was known to have occurred.

"The Jerk-off's so clever and shrewd that his plethora of felonies, let alone his innumerable misdemeanors, cannot be either traced or detected," Teddy disclosed to Charlie and to Mr. Fearenside inside the decadent Scarlet Coat Pub. "It's almost as if the devious Culprit is invisible to the long arm of the law! The cops have never found the Phantom cop-out immorally copulating, or salaciously masturbating in public!"

Elaborated in the imagination of Mr. Frederick Gould, the probationary assistant in the National School, Teddy's radical conspiracy theory took the form that the "Peculiar Itinerant" was an Anarchist, and also an avowed Atheist, dressed in a highly-queer disguise, clandestinely preparing powerful explosives inside his mysterious, designated upstairs laboratory at the inn, and it was conjectured that the grouchy maniac had resolved to undertake such national "criminal detective operations" as his limited time in Iping permitted.

"But to public knowledge around the village, the Freak-of-Nature has detected or discovered nothing, which in regular layman's language, does mean *no-thing!*" Charlie Hall argued. "I should ask Dr. Connor Cuss to cauterize his asshole and make the weird fuck shit out of his nostrils!"

"Yes, Mr. Hall," Teddy eagerly admitted. "However, you happen to be tremendously wrong. Your fucked-up upstairs Guest has detected that you wholly loathe his existence, and the science guru is quite aware that Mr. Fearenside here, also absolutely despises his unworthy guts. So therefore, your uncouth Tenant has indeed both *discovered* and *detected* certain things, even outside his inn laboratory room! Does that information give you an element of fear-inside, Mr. Fearenside?"

"It makes me want to shit bricks and piss cement," the wagon-master laughed as the lush guzzled-down some more delectable Scarlet Coat Pub ale.

Another school of opinion that prevailed throughout the neighborhood barber shops and hair salons followed Mr. Fearenside's tenable conclusion, which was the notion that citizens should accept and endorse the wagoner's piebald view of "the reckless Recluse", or some fundamental modification of *that* designation.

Another prominent town savant, Mr. Silas Durgan, the village's top accountant, was heard to assert that "If the side-show freak chooses to show himself at the July Carnival and Festival, he'd make a blasted fortune in no time, standing next to the bearded lady and the tattooed Arab sword-swallower."

And being a bit of an encouraging amateur theologian, Dentist Paul Douglas compared the innocent Stranger to a very special man possessing one singular brilliant talent, similar to Martin Luther of Germany. Yet another view, espoused by the Greg Jensen, the gay guidance counselor at the elementary school, explained the entire matter by regarding the "very different and falsely-condemned Stranger" as being nothing but a "harmless lunatic seeking safe asylum and refuge from straight sex Anglicans".

Between these Main Street doubting Toms, there were myriad waverers and compromisers living within the Iping village borders. Caustic Sussex County folk tend to have few superstitions, and it was only after the events of early April that the thought of supernatural intervention, including the devil's satanic influence, had been first whispered inside the village square. Even then, it was mostly given credence about Lucifer's influence among the "more vocal bitchy witches suspected of commuting with demonic mediums at diabolical Iping secret seances".

But whatever the scuttlebutt that the more ignorant residents preferred discussing, people in the village, on the whole, agreed in resenting and hating *his* nightly strolls. "The Ogre's" irritability, though it might have been comprehensible to a London urban brain, had constituted itself as an amazing deviation to the quiet and reserved Sussex County residents.

The populus often described "the Night Grump" passing down the village's side streets, and when "the Nutcase Professor" was passing by, juvenile delinquent hooligans would-turn-up their stiff coat-collars, and fold-down their hat-brims in a pompous and snooty fashion, and after mimicking *his* unorthodox behavior, go pacing nervously after him in sheer imitation of what the insubordinate punks considered *his* obscure, occult disposition.

At that time in local history, there was a song popularly sung at parties and at funeral viewings, appropriately titled "The Bogey Man". Miss Peggy Stachell, the whoring music teacher and horny church organ player, sang the ditty at the school concert amateur night, and thereafter, whenever one or two of the Iping dipshits were gathered together, and the Roving Stranger appeared in their midst, several bars or so of "The Bogey Man", more or less in something *sharp* or in nothing *flat,* was egregiously whistled to facilitate their noxious levity and despicable insolence.

And also, this defiance of human decency had influenced the conduct of little children, who would call-out "Boogie Nights, Bogey Man!" at the lonely hiker, during his nightly midnight patrol, shouting the derogatory phrase from their open bedroom windows.

Dr. Connor Cuss, happy that he was a human with a single life and not a nine-life house-cat, was devoured by intense curiosity. The Iping surgeon actually admitted to Charlie Hall inside the Scarlet Coat Pub that the "Midnight Wanderer's horrendous bandages" greatly excited *his* professional interest, and that the rampant reporting of the "thousand and one bottles' psychosis" had irresistibly aroused the physician's jealous regard.

All through April and May, Dr. Cuss coveted the opportunity of privately speaking with the "fucked-up" Stranger, and at last, towards Whitsuntide, according to Biblical tradition, the second Sunday of Pentecost that corresponded with the tongues of fire that had descended from Heaven to bless Jesus's loyal disciples, the village doctor could not resist his overwhelming fascination no longer.

While pretending to be collecting donations to hire a new town nurse as a viable excuse to visit the noble Coach and Horses Inn, Dr. Connor Cuss was surprised to find-out that neither Charlie nor Edith knew their kooky guest's first or last name.

"He gave me a name on his initial day arriving at my inn," falsely testified Mrs. Hall. "But I didn't rightly hear it in its entirety. Charlie and I just usually refer to him as Mr. Incognito!"

* * * * * * * * * * * *

Dr. Connor Cuss, being a true democratic apostate, rapped at the parlor door and casually entered to exchange scientific ideas with the "Segregated Isolate". There was a fairly audible "Pardon my intrusion, sir," when the intrepid brain surgeon cordially addressed his targeted mark. And then the door closed, and the swift shutting cut Mrs. Hall off from eavesdropping on the rest of the 'furtive conversation'.

Edith could barely hear the low murmur of voices for the next ten minutes, but then a boisterous cry of surprise arose from Dr. Cuss's throat; which was followed by a wild stirring of feet; and subsequently, a chair being wildly flung aside; and afterwards, a chilling bark of laughter; and next, quick steps tramped all the way to the outside door; and then, a beleaguered Dr. Cuss's anatomy appeared in the foyer, his horrified face pale and ashen, with the surgeon's blinking eyes staring over his shaking shoulder.

Cuss left the door wide-open behind him, and without ever looking at Mrs. Hall standing in the foyer, strode past her presence like a flash, across the narrow corridor, and virtually sprinted down the stone entrance steps. And Edith soon heard his fleeting feet hurrying, tripping. and scurrying along the road.

The horrified fellow carried his hat in his hand during his hasty departure. Mrs. Hall stood behind the door, looking at the hectored sawbones desperately running like an Olympic Champion, energetically endeavoring to save his mortal life. Then, Edith heard the Stranger laughing fairly quietly, and next, his footsteps came traipsing across the room. Mrs. Hall could not see "the Ogre's" face where she had been standing. The parlor door slammed behind the "Ostentatiously Daffy Scientist", and once more, the parlor inside the inn was again relatively silent.

Dr. Cuss, whose bad habit was perpetually cursing expletives, went straight up the village to Reverend William Bunting's residence, the village Vicar. "Am I fuckin' mad?" Cuss began abruptly, as the human cursing machine entered the shabby little rectory library like a raging barbarian. "Do I look like a dumb-shit sane person to you?"

"What's happened, Connor?" the somewhat-appalled Vicar requested knowing, putting the held ammonite upon the loose sheets of his upcoming sermon. "I'm trying to take care of my crabs!"

"Crabs, you say? Forget this ammonite shit! Did you, my dear Vicar, just state a sexual allusion to the polysemantic, colloquial nomenclature, uttering the fuckin' word 'crabs'? At this propitious time, Vicar Bill, I have always thought that you had fuckin' syphilis and gonorrhea instead of sufferin' from a minor crab infection! That dirty fuck-headed Chap over at the inn!"

"Well, Connor? Describe your unique predicament more in detail. What about *that* unfortunate individual living at the guest house? Where's your sense of mercy and benevolence? You've always struck me as being a trifle morally deficient!"

"Give me something that doesn't fuckin' taste like cat piss or skunk urine to drink," Dr. Cuss desired and requested, and then the tempestuous surgeon finally sat-down to gather his depleted wits.

When Dr. Cuss's frayed nerves had been steadied by a full glass of cheap sherry, the mild intoxicant that was the only liquor which the good Vicar had available, the vulgar town physician told the very pious Reverend of the "fucked-up" interview he had just had with the "Hall Jerk-off from another planet".

"First, Reverend Bill, I stepped inside the foyer, and boldly marched up to Mr. and Mrs. Hall's parlor," Dr. Cuss cleanly reported and clearly gasped. "And next, I demanded from the Nutjob a hefty donation. I had desired to obtain from the Itinerant Bastard a goddamned meager subscription for the needy Nurse Fund, which the demented pricks and strumpets sitting on the Village Council have been fuckin' soliciting pounds from the citizens of Iping for the past half-year."

"Well, now, Connor; that's a good beginning to your marvelous narrative!" Reverend William Bunting, whose haggish wife daily sewed bland banners and flags to supplement the Vicar's diminutive church income, complimented and related. "Even St. Peter, also known to Biblical scholars as the admirable Apostle Simon Peter, had to work hard to supplement the apostles' Jerusalem expenses."

"Cut the fuckin' bullshit, Bill, and let me continue my story!"

"Yes, Connor. Good old St. Pete was the thrifty and parsimonious money collector for Lord Jesus. Peter had persuaded the rich disciples Joseph of Arimathea and Nicodemus to finance the dinner expenses, along with the other outstanding money debts, for the extravagant Last Supper! If you analyze the exact word, Doctor, you can almost-plainly see the term 'Parson' along with the name 'Simon' in the context of the linguistic etymology of the elusive dictionary terminology *parsimonious.*"

"Shut the fuck-up about your Last Supper analogy!" Dr. Cuss shrieked. "Now then. The Coach and Horses Tenant stuck his hands in his pockets as I came in, and the Freak sat-down like a lump of feces inside his chair," continued Dr. Cuss, ignoring Reverend Bill's irrelevant academic bullshit. "Next, the loony Pecker-head incessantly sniffed like a snuff addict. I told the A-hole that I'd heard that he took an interest in exploring scientific theories. He said 'Yes'. Then, the Retarded Asshole sniffed again. The inane Jerk-off kept on sniffing all the g. d. time; evidently, the Stupid-Shit had recently caught an infernal cold. No wonder, wrapped-up in cloth like that Egyptian transgender bitch, Cleopatra!"

"I take it, Doctor, that you had no immunity to protect yourself against this obscenely Grotesque Personage, staying at the parsonage, er, I meant to instead say, residing at the Coach and Horses?"

"I had creatively developed the Nurse Solicitation idea, and all the while, kept my eyes open studying *his* filthy room. Bottles, test tubes, and chemicals were in disarray everywhere. "Would you subscribe to this vital need?" I requested. "The "Freak of Nature" expressed that he'd consider it."

"I'm becoming intrigued," Reverend Bill admitted. "Please resume your story."

"I asked the evasive Jerk-off, point-blank, if he was actively performing a secret research project. He answered in the affirmative. Are you engaged in enacting a very long research project?" I additionally inquired. "Then, the nasty Cunt-lapper became quite cross and irritated."

"How did he respond to your aggressive interrogation?" the fascinated Vicar questioned.

"A most damnable, very long research," the 'Frightening Fiend' acknowledged, hesitating before blowing the cork out of another bottle, so to speak. "Oh," I enunciated. "And then Reverend Bill, out of his mouth came the fucked-up grievance that's' haunting my vulnerable brain. The maniac was just simmering on the boil, and my question had obviously boiled him over. He had been given a prescription, a most valuable prescription, from a prominent London doctor, exactly for what singular purpose he wouldn't say."

"Was it medical? Damn you, Connor! Answer me!"

"What are you fishing after?" I apologized to the sinister, coughing, fucked-up 'Village Night Stalker'. I had astutely been observing that the vulgar Shit had been industriously working in a confined room with an open fireplace. My eyes noticed a dull flicker, and there was the London doctor's prescription burning and lifting chimney-ward. I rushed towards the brick hearth, just as the note whisked up the shaft. So, Reverend Bill! just at *that* pivotal point, to illustrate his fucked-up story, out came his arm."

"Well, Connor? Why are you so baffled? Haven't you ever seen an arm come out of a sleeve before *that* fairly extraordinary occasion?"

"There was no deformed hand showing; just an empty sleeve. 'Lord!' I thought. *'That's* a horrible deformity! The Bastard's got a cork arm, I suppose, and he's taken it off.' Then, I worriedly thought to myself. 'There's something odd in that fucked-up mystical occurrence I've just witnessed. What the devil keeps that sleeve up and open, if there's nothing in it like an arm or hand'?'

"Are you certain as to what you had seen? Were you inebriated?"

"Absolutely not," asserted the insulted brain surgeon. "There was nothing inside the empty sleeve, I tell you. Nothing inside it, right down to the joint. I could see right down it to the elbow, and there was a glimmer of light shining through a tear of the cloth. 'Good

God!' I fearfully imagined. "Well, Wild Bill," vindictive Dr. Cuss continued his vociferating tirade. "Then, the mummy-like Fuckhead stopped doing his rehearsed experimental activity, and the crazy Dickhead stared at me with those enormous black goggles, and then I fuckin' noticed his left sleeve."

"Well now, Connor? I can't determine precisely what is responsible for producing your current diatribe!" Reverend Bill politely challenged.

"That's not fuckin' all, Reverend Bill, that my keen and wary eyes incredibly saw. The reticent Shithead never said a g. d. word; the laconic Fuck just glared at me like Medusa's stone-cold face, and then self-consciously, the Wise-shit quickly put his left damned sleeve back inside his pants pocket. The Stupid Shit had thought I had said "Prescription" instead of the generic reference 'Subscription'."

"Did the Queer Tenant say anything else?"

"How in the devil can you fuckin' move an empty sleeve like that?" I fuckin' asked the 'Space Alien'. Where's your dumb-ass left hand? Are you a fucked-up unemployed Magician, or what? And your' freakin' right sleeve shows no hand being evident inside, either! How the hell do you ever Jerk-off?"

"How could you say that this oddball fellow over at Halls' place can have a hand in committing crime when the fellow has no hands in which he could commit an unlawful act, as all of the macho men among the village people claim?" Reverend Bunting argued and asserted.

"Well, Reverend Bill. The Sleazy Prestidigitator stood-up right away, and I fuckin' stood up, too. The deranged Freak-show soon paced towards me in three very deliberate steps, and the imbecilic Shithead was sniffing snuff rather voraciously. I didn't flinch a cunt hair, but I was certainly alienated by his accursed blinkers, which the stupid Cocksucker wears to scare the living and dead shit out of gullible townsfolk!"

"'You said it was an empty sleeve?" the venerable Vicar incredulously desired knowing. "You're an ornery daft bird, indeed, most certainly, Connor. What the hell happened next?"

"Then very quietly, the mangy Bastard pulled his sleeve out of his pocket again, and the Motherfucker raised his arm towards me as though the incensed Shithead would show it to me again. He did it all very, very slowly, just like my wife gets her rocks-off orgasming three times with her dildo each and every night. The bitch won't let me do it to her, but I'm fuckin' allowed to watch!"

"Well then, Connor. Did this interesting fellow make any *off the cuff* remarks when the Son-of-a-Bitch Bastard showed you his empty sleeves?"

"I'll swear on a stack of Korans, Reverend, that the empty cuffs were at least six inches from my fuckin' face. Queer thing to see an empty sleeve come at your countenance like that! And then, something analogous to an invisible finger and thumb nipped at my nose."

Reverend Bunting began laughing rather indulgently. "Oh now, Connor; a tremendous fucked-up sleight-of-hand trick, I am sure! You'd better gain immediate absolution from the Lord, or else I'll need to perform a fuckin' exclusive exorcism on your vulnerable, most sinful ass! When's the last fuckin' time you've been seated in the confessional? Confidentially, that's how I learn all the damned sex secrets of all the promiscuous whores, hookers and pimps in town, ya' know!"

"There wasn't anything tangible there!" exclaimed Dr. Cuss like a raving maniac, with the brain surgeon's staccato voice running-up into an absolutely frightening shriek. "It's all very well for you to chuckle and snicker, Reverend Bill, but I'll tell you the truth; I was so startled and traumatized from the whole unsavory experience. I instinctively hit his cuff hard in self-defense, and swiftly turned my ass around, and hastily cut-out of the extremely unpleasant room."

"I've read where there's a new innovative technique called plastic surgery on the horizon that might just help this unfortunate Fellow recover from his horrible, fucked-up disability!" the Vicar suggested.

"That method of hospital remediation will not be implemented for many decades!" Dr. Cuss informed Vicar Bill. "It's just in its goddamned experimental stage!"

With those incredible words being exchanged, Dr. Connor Cuss ceased his dramatic elucidation. "Well, Reverend Bunting. I believe that I need a second tall glass of your terribly-inferior sherry. When I had hit *his* cuff," Dr. Cuss paused and then emphasized, "I tell you, Bill, it felt exactly like hitting a physical arm. And there wasn't any observable arm, bones or physical flesh! There wasn't even the ghost of an arm, on either invisible hand!"

Vicar William Bunting deeply thought the whole matter over, and then, the austere Reverend looked strenuously and suspiciously at Dr. Cuss's pallid face. "It's a most remarkable story, you've expressed, Connor. Remarkable indeed! That's for damned sure. It's really quite unique," Mr. Bunting resumed his extensive disbelief with judicial emphasis. "It's positively a most noteworthy oral rendition. Now tell me the gospel truth, Connor. Are you certain that you weren't having a lousy fucked-up vicarious experience over at Halls' Guest House," the extremely impressed Vicar hooted and scoffed. "Now, fuck-off, Connor. Stop aggravating my delicate ass with your constant trivial bullshit!"

Chapter 5

"THE BURGLARY AT THE VICARAGE"

The documented facts of the burglary at the vicarage came to the village's attention chiefly through the medium of the Reverend William Bunting and his wife, Jezebel's exaggerated testimonies. The robbery had occurred in the wee-small hours of Whit Monday, the religious day devoted in Iping to the Club and Crab Festivities designed to honor Pentecost Monday. The celebration of ammonite, delicious crabmeat, is served in the form of 'a tongue of fire' crab slab upon a flat soft bun.

Mrs. Bunting, it seems, woke-up suddenly in the spooky stillness that comes just before dawn, with her nightmare-oriented, deranged brain possessing the strong distinct impression that the door of their bedroom had surreptitiously opened and closed on its own. Jezebel did not arouse her snoring husband at first, because the Vicar had been suffering from extreme erectile dysfunction, and loudly breathed and exclaimed whenever she endeavored arousing his myriad subconscious fantasies.

But then, the wife anxiously sat-up in bed, listening intently, trying hard to interpret a foreign sound that smacked of a possible burglar engaged in illicit trespassing. Jezebel then distinctly heard the pad, pad, pad of bare feet coming-out of the adjoining dressing-room, and a queer sound maneuvering along the hall passage leading towards the staircase. Immediately, Vicar Bill was abruptly awakened by his neurotic spouse.

"What is it dear?" the Reverend Bill asked, half-drowsy and yawning. "Did you drink too much sherry last evening and have an upset stomach? I know that you'll always be faithful to me, unlike that licentious Jezebel in the Bible who was a depraved, sex-hungry prostitute. And also, if I may add, an avowed schizomaniac! Thank the Lord dear wife that we've both pledged to be celibate!"

"But Bill; I think I hear strange stirring being conducted in the house," Jezebel whispered. "It's coming from outside this bedroom!"

"Trespassing, you say? Doesn't the intruder, if indeed it is an intruder, know the Golden Rule. I shall forgive a trespasser as the Bible teaches, and I shall not trespass against the trespasser!"

"Bill: be the man of the house and venture downstairs, and if you don't wish to arrest the trespasser, then notify the Iping constable, Mr. Jaffers!"

"I'll go and see what or who it is," Reverend Bill promised and answered in a very low, raspy tone. "Why Jez; why the heck do you have your hands being held together over your crotch?"

"Because William; the noise I heard might be a mouse, and mice always run to the nearest hole!"

Reverend William rose from the comfortable bed, but dared not strike a match to alert the possible intruder of him being on the prowl. Next, the feckless Vicar donned his furry slippers and kept his investigative movements quiet and cunning.

The Vicar did not strike a light, but putting on his dependable spectacles, along with his wife's heavy dressing-gown, the amateur detective awkwardly creeped-out into the hallway to investigate anyone trespassing and breaking into the 'holy vicarage'. A fumbling sound coming from below had been detected, which was also heard quite audibly by Jezebel.

'Holy Moses! There's someone searching through the study desk downstairs, and my ears just detected a rather violent sneeze! This really could be a brazen robber on the loose!' the jittery Vicar speculated.

Governed by his instinct to survive a possible violent home invasion attack, the venerable minister returned to the master bedroom, and slowly grabbed his most suitable and available weapon, the trusty fireplace poker. Then, very stealthily, revered Reverend William descended the squeaky steps to further investigate the true source of the unexplained noise.

The hour was about four in the morning, and the ultimate darkness of the night had already passed. There was a faint shimmer of light being emitted from the hall, but the study's doorway entrance was apparently pitch black, and seemingly opaque. Everything appeared normal and still, except for the faint creaking of the loose stair-steps underneath Mr. Bunting's deliberate tread, and also, the curious and inexplicable slight movements heard originating from the dark study.

Then, something snapped inside the library; the desk drawer was opened, and there was a rustle of important papers belonging to the church being frenetically shuffled. Next, a match was struck, and instantly, the study soon became flooded with yellow light.

Vicar Bunting was now furtively approaching the library/office from the downstairs hall, and through the tiny crack of the door, the frightened and out-of-his-wits craven observer could see both the desk and the open drawer, and also, a votive candle burning upon the cherrywood desktop.

But the assumed robber was not visible, whatsoever. As the Vicar stood frozen and petrified in the hallway, undecided what to do, Jezebel Bunting, her face white and intent, slowly crept downstairs. One thing had kept Mr. Bunting's courage buoyed; the persuasion that this burglar was more-than-likely a resident of the village, and as a result, the instigating culprit's crime against a man-of-the-cloth would swiftly be brought to justice by Constable Bobby Jaffers.

The almost-delirious Buntings next heard the chink of coins, and quickly realized that the burglar had found the housekeeping reserve of gold ready for tomorrow's bank deposit, which amounted to six pounds, ten-in-half sovereigns altogether. At that familiar clinking sound, Reverend Bunting amassed sufficient bravado to initiate abrupt action. Gripping the poker firmly, the incensed Vicar rushed into the vicarage's office, closely followed by a half-traumatized Mrs. Bunting.

"Surrender!" Mr. Bunting fiercely screamed, holding the iron poker a foot above his bald head. But much to Reverend Bill's utter astonishment and chagrin, the office/study was perfectly empty.

"Did you see anything?" Bill asked his petrified wife. "This seems like one of those paranormal experiences to the 10th degree that the local juvenile delinquents read about in sinful science-fiction magazines!"

"I heard sounds, of clinking coins, I believe William, but I never saw any robber rummaging around inside your library. There's only one doorway inside your study, and obviously, there's only one way out. And the side window is evidently still shut and locked."

"If it's a demonic evil ghost," Reverend Bill wildly conjectured, "I'm certain that it's not the Holy Spirit robbing us in the middle of the night during this sacred week of Pentecost."

For half a minute, the knee-knocking couple stood gaping, but then, garnering enough courage, Mrs. Bunting very cautiously ambled across the study and hastily searched behind the window screen, while Mr. Bunting, by sharing a kindred impulse, keenly peered under the wooden desk. Feeling more relieved, Jezebel folded-back the window-curtains, and bending over near the narrow hearth, Mr. Bunting's eyes scanned up the chimney stack to evaluate the shaft as a possible robber escape route.

"Well, Jez. It's certainly not Christmas Eve, and I don't think that Santa Claus is a wanton criminal worthy of imprisonment. I mean, I even wholly trust his very reliable and loyal elves as being God-fearing!"

Feeling more confident about no one being an imminent danger inside the office, Mrs. Bunting soon scrutinized the waste-paper basket, and simultaneously, Reverend Bunting opened the lid to the coal-scuttle. Puzzled and befuddled, the pair came to a full stop, and stood with helplessly-confused eyes, blankly staring at each other.

"Even though I'm not under oath, I could have sworn—", Mrs. Bunting declared. "Yes William; I could've sworn that—"

"The candle!" said Mr. Bunting. "Who the hell lit the damned candle in the office?"

"William; I absolutely resent your new-found cursing. I realize that you've been unnerved, but please stop uttering and muttering your foul language immediately. Have you been hanging-out with Connor Cuss, Mr. Hank Fearenside, Teddy Henfrey and Charlie

Hall?" Jezebel turned-prosecutor indicted. "Have you been drinking liquor and ale with those four lushes over at the Scarlet Coat?"

"The drawer!" said Mr. Bunting, intentionally ignoring Jezebel's accusations. "And the money's gone! Stolen! Heisted! Pilfered! Purloined!" complained the Vicar, exhausting his litany of synonyms. "Is this some sort of enigmatic aberration? Has Satan or one of his Fallen Angels entered our lives and is attempting to disrupt and usurp our happy home?"

"Of all the strangest of occurrences," Mrs. Bunting concluded and remarked. "And the church's Sunday Pentecost collections and our parishioners' generous holiday donations have all been stolen by a most clever thief and con artist!"

Much to the couple's worry and dismay, a violent sneeze was then heard, originating from the downstairs hallway. The Buntings rushed-out of the library, and as the scared pair did so, the kitchen door slammed shut.

"Bring the candle," whispered Mr. Bunting, and the cowardly Vicar, believing that Heaven was on his side and that the host of saints would protect him, carefully led the way to the scene of disruption. The intrigued husband and wife were immediately startled. Chills ascended up their spines as both listeners heard the distinct sound of door bolts being hastily shot back.

"The noises are coming from the scullery," Bill lowly declared. "Yes; the thief is in the small kitchen alcove where we nightly wash and dry the dishes. He's probably eating all of our leftovers kept in the icebox!"

As Reverend Bill very cautiously opened the kitchen door, the self-appointed detective noticed through the rear scullery that the back exit was just opening, and the faint light of early dawn displayed the dark masses of the rose garden beyond.

The clergyman was certain that nothing or no one had any opportunity to exit out of the back door without ever being noticed. The formerly locked portal had amazingly opened all on its very own, and the scullery door had mysteriously remained open for a moment, and then the portal swung upon its rusty hinges and closed with a jolting slam.

After studying the lock, Reverend William said to his terrified wife, "Someone had unlocked the scullery door and then abandoned the vicarage. But who?"

As the semi-traumatized Vicar described the cryptic scene, the votive candle that Mrs. Bunting had been carrying from the study flickered and flared from the mild draft caused by the slammed door. It was a minute or more before the distraught couple gathered sufficient audacity to fully enter the now-normal-looking kitchen nook.

The cooking and eating areas were completely empty and devoid of any noticeable disturbance. Showing major distress, and in total befuddlement, perplexed Reverend Bill refastened the back scullery door; closely examined the kitchen cabinets and table; thoroughly inspected the pantry, and at last, being enormously superstitious, descended down into the cellar to further investigate what his apprehensive mind had evaluated as "the supernatural intervention".

Even though Halloween festivities had passed six months before, there was not a soul, ghost, specter, apparition, spirit, burglar, or robber to be found anywhere inside the Vicar's 'haunted house'.

Daylight found precocious Reverend Bunting and promiscuous and pretentious Jezebel still prodigiously marveling about the disappearance of their gold coin bank deposits, and the two wondered what kind of brazen felon had the guile and the audacity to commit such an unearthly crime, which had been enacted upon a distinguished clergyman in the community, along with his rodent-fearing wife.

Chapter 6

"THE FURNITURE THAT WENT MAD"

Now it so happened that in the early hours of Whit Monday, Charlie and Edith Hall were at wits end with surviving their own individual ghostly encounter. Before thoroughly unmodern Millie had been rented-out for the day to work her vital services at the prosperous Iping S and M Parlor and Body Mutilation Shoppe, Mr. and Mrs. Hall both rose from their diminutive bed and silently stepped noiselessly down into the cellar to survey the remainder of their Coach and Horses beer and whiskey inventory, with their intent and purpose being to order more brew and liquor for the upcoming Iping Lobster, Sausage and Sex Bun Festival.

"Holy crap, Charlie," Edith cited, breaking the temporary silence with her husband. "I forget to bring down a bottle of sarsaparilla from the joint-room. And I'd like you to go and fetch the commodity for me to hide down in the cellar so that the Weird Fuck upstairs doesn't accidentally discover it in the medicine cabinet and drink-down the entire amount in one guzzle."

"I don't know where your mind is wanderin' now-a-days," the husband snapped-back and rankled. "Your brain is deteriorating into a big fat zero, and ya' don't drink half as much rum and brew as I do. Truthfully, Hon. I don't know whether you remember to forget, or if you forget to remember!"

"Fetch me the bottle of sarsaparilla right now, or you'll stay soft all night long, and your wiener will be just as big as the tiny sausages that'll be served at the annual Lobster and Bun Festival. I even understand that Vicar Bunting is importing several new edible products this spring; hot dogs from Frankfurt, and hamburgers from Hamburg, Germany."

"What about baloney from Bologna, Italy?" Charlie laughed and snickered. "And I've heard it through the grapevine, although their ain't no grapes growin' anywhere in Iping, that the kind Reverend is getting some tasty Limburger cheese from Belgium to smear onto the smelly Hamburgers from Germany. I can't wait to sample the fuckers!"

"Everything involvin' that whore Jezebel Bunting is poisonous sour grapes," Edith Hall remarked. "That raunchy bitch is in direct competition with our Millie every Sunday afternoon, to see who could make the most money over at the scurrilous S and M Parlor and Body Mutilation Shoppe over on Delilah Shady Lane."

To accommodate and avert his wife's developing wrath, Mr. Charlie Hall very improperly climbed upstairs to locate and confiscate the alluded-to bottle of sarsaparilla from the medicine cabinet before their 'Fucked-up Renter' could roam around the premises; incidentally find the treasured liquid, and then avariciously imbibe its contents. On the landing, Charlie was surprised to discover that the 'Queer Stranger's' door was ajar, and after briefly peering inside the crack, the curious landlord noticed that *a jar,* which was empty, had been lying upon the ancient table. Hall then paced into his own room and found the sought-after bottle in the joint-space medicine cabinet as had been directed by Edith.

But returning and staggering about the upstairs hall with the confiscated sarsaparilla, the chronic alcoholic noticed that the bolts of the Tenant's door had been shot back, and that the wooden frame was in fact simply separated from the latch. And with a flash of divine inspiration, Mr. Hall connected *that* specific irregularity with the suggestions and scuttlebutt of Mr. Teddy Henfrey's theories concerning the Coach and Horses Stranger being a most reprehensible and heinous wanted criminal.

'I think I'm burnin' the candle at both ends,' Charlie imagined. 'Although I'm still a trifle soused, I recall that last night I was holdin' the candle while Edith shot these same bolts into their slots.'

At the sight of the ajar door along with a jar that had been placed upon the room's singular table, Charlie, in a convoluted state of mind, stopped his gaping, and then, gaining sufficient fortitude, Hall intrepidly rapped at the Stranger's door. But ironically, there was no answer to his pounding. Being frustrated, Charlie rapped again; becoming rather livid, the pissed-off, irate landlord forcefully pushed the door wide open, and sweating profusely, entered the small quarters, finding the bed and also, the small chamber empty.

The most peculiar aspect of Mr. Hall's observation was the fact that the "Weirdo's" stench-laden garments had been scattered upon the bedroom chair, and also along the rail of the bed, and even the oddball Tenant's big slouch hat had been jauntily cocked over the bed-post.

'Where is the connivin' son-of-a-bitch hiding?' Hall pondered and wondered. 'The Bastard's got to be cavortin' around naked, because the only clothes I'm ever seen the deplorable Asshole wear are now scattered all the hell over his room! What the fuck kind of repulsive pervert is this zany Ignoramus?'

As Mr. Hall stood there rather astounded, his sensitive ears pricked-up when he heard Edith's soprano voice coming out of the cellar depths, imperatively yelling a catalog of syllables and interrogatives as fat and perturbed women in that remote Sussex village are wont to do when indicating their mounting impatience. "Charlie! You got the damned sarsaparilla I commanded ya' to find?"

"Yeah, Edith. Don't worry about the bottle. It's still filled to the cork. But let me tell ya' somethin' pretty germane; what Teddy Henfrey says about our Perverted Guest is the gospel truth. He's nowhere inside or outside his room. And the front door is now bolted, so the Wily Shithead has not left the property," Mr. Hall very comprehensively reported, shaking his head in disbelief. "And what's boggling my pea brain the most is that he's gotta' be runnin' around somewhere in the area stark naked, because his only clothes are strewn all over, without his ass nowhere to be seen either, inside or outside his two rooms."

At first, Mrs. Hall did not understand her husband's depiction, and as soon as she had fathomed its essence, the wife resolved to see the empty room all for herself, thinking that Charlie was having a drunken relapse from his last night's libations at the Scarlet Coat.

Half-intoxicated Hall, still-holding the acquired bottle, bravely went first towards the "forbidden door". "If the impostor ain't in there, he's gotta' be somewhere close-by. And what's he doin' without wearin' his stenchy clothes? It's a most curious business, Hon. It is, I mean, Edith. We're tryin' to run a respectable business here, and not be promotin' a dumbass nudist colony!"

"Well Charlie, let me tell ya' my opinion. Something's happenin' here, but what it is, ain't precisely fuckin' clear! I just hope we ain't being fuckin' buffaloed by this demented itinerant Bison this time around! If needed, we'll seize the Stupid Shit's glass bottles as collateral, if he doesn't pay us more gold sovereigns! I suspect that the Buffoon might me running-out of dough. In fact, he says his next monthly installment will be done in half-sovereigns instead of in whole ones."

The wary husband and wife then fancied they heard the front door open and shut, but seeing it closed and nothing tangible being observed there, neither of the two uttered a word about their ears perceiving the inordinate sound. Feeling motivated to resolve the current departure from the ordinary, Edith passed her husband in the downstairs hall and in a rush, was the first to clamber upstairs.

"What the hell's that?" the wife mentioned to Charlie with her right hand over her mouth. "Someone just sneezed? I'll bet the Asshole is stark naked in there, and he's havin' a severe spring allergy attack!"

"I heard the sneeze, too," Charlie lowly replied. "I think that our anonymous Tenant's name might really be Nostril-damus!"

"This is no time for amateur comedy night at the Scarlet Coat," Edith harshly admonished. "I'll go inside first. I want to see what the hell his dinky pecker looks like if he's still naked. Probably looks like an inchworm, I'm willing to wager!"

Edith, pretending to be an accomplished sleuth, flung-open the door and alertly stood enthralled, carefully regarding the room's contents. The landlady heard a sniff and a snuffle originating close behind her head, and quickly turning her noggin out of dire curiosity, was surprised to see Mr. Hall a dozen feet off.

But in another moment, the hung-over husband was actually standing directly adjacent to his unnerved wife. Edith bent forward and put her hand upon the pillow, and then felt under the pile of clothes.

"Quite cold," she wonderingly announced. "The Freak's been up this hour, that's for sure. If the Bastard gets caught roamin' around nude on Main Street by Mr. Jaffers, then the ambitious constable will certainly arrest the insane deviate, and the local gazette will accuse the Coach and Horses of being a disreputable business specializin' in caterin' to guiltless pedophiles and child molesters."

Suddenly, a most extraordinary event happened. The bed-clothes magically gathered themselves together, leapt up into a sort of triangular peak formation, and then jumped and leaped several times over the bottom rail, dancing around like a dizzy taproom ballerina. It was exactly as if a supernatural hand had clutched the discarded attire, and quickly and whimsically, hurled the garb aside in an arcane, playful manner.

Immediately after, the Stranger's hat hopped-off the stationary bed-post, and the fedora participated in a whirling, circular flight through the air, and soon propelled straight at Mrs. Hall's face. Then, just as swiftly came the sponge from the washstand, flopping and hopping around the ceiling; and next the chair, becoming activated, abnormally and recklessly flinging the Stranger's coat and trousers carelessly aside.

A familiar voice, quite similar to that of the dreaded 'Impostor', boisterously laughed, which was instantly accompanied by incessant farting from an unidentified Asshole cavorting somewhere else in the room.

And next, the occult chair turned itself upside-down with its four legs threatening to violently impact Mrs. Hall, as it took particular aim at her breasts, and mischievously, savagely charged at her stunned presence.

"What the fuck's goin' on here?" Edith screamed at her louse of a spouse in what constituted a spellbound yell. "This friggin' room is haunted; yes; the cursed place is indeed under an evil spell! This sort of shit never happened before 'the Mad Professor' had arrived!"

"Let's get the hell outta' here before I gotta' change my underwear and wipe my ass four times!" Charlie loudly urged. "I've already pissed myself twice! This room's much-more-dangerous than Mr. Fearenside's four snarling bloodhounds, I'll tell ya' that!"

Mrs. Hall dashed-out of the 'haunted room' as if experiencing a sudden diarrhea attack, huffing and puffing, her head almost-evolving into a serious fainting condition. It was with the greatest difficulty that Mr. Hall and Millie, who had also been roused by Edith's ear-shattering scream, succeeded in getting Mrs. Hall downstairs, and with Charlie providing the restorative strong rye whiskey remedy, the customary emergency medicine, usually utilized in such critical attack scenarios, was competently administered.

"He's conjuring-up the Devil's diabolical evil," Edith Hall alleged and claimed, breathing rather heavily. "I've read all about how a witch or a wizard can transfer restless spirits trapped inside a regular liquor bottle directly into a bed, into clothes, or even into a hat. I've also read in the popular London tabloids of tables and chairs radically leaping and dancing about rooms, after coming under the control of demonic influences."

"Take another large gulp, Edith," Mr. Hall suggested. "From the immense wisdom I've received over at the Scarlet Coat, whiskey is the best remedy to escape either dangerous reality or perilous fantasy!"

"Shit, Charlie. My latest orgasm was unexpectedly interrupted by Edith's chilling, shrieking tirade," Millie contributed to the inane conversation. "According to your crazy stories, it's a good thing the London Tax Bureau wasn't in the room to wildly throw the big dresser at both your asses!"

"If we was livin' across the pond in the States, some charity organization would've thrown the Community Chest at our personals!" dumbfounded and flabbergasted Charlie Hall exclaimed, feigning black humor. "And I ain't exaggeratin', either! My filthy drawers would've been scared right the fuck out of the bureau's dirty drawers!"

"Lock the Evil Magician out of his room," Mrs. Hall commanded Charlie. "Don't let the Bastard come in again, with his repertoire of nasty pranks and tricks. I'm sure that he's one of those hedonistic, immoral cretins who teach Alchemy at either Oxford or Cambridge, those evil dens of *inequity*. I should've known better that the Jerk is a lousy charlatan of some sorts, wearing them goggling eyes, and sportin' that bandaged head, and never goin' to church on Sunday, or never seeking divine absolution inside the Vicar's confessional. Not to mention that huge bottle collection he's suspiciously put together; more fuckin' bottles than exist at the Scarlet Coat Pub."

"Oxford and Cambridge are definitely dens of *iniquity,*" Charlie earnestly contributed to the dialogue, academically correcting his dominant wife's aberrant nomenclature. "In fact, Millie told me that her best customer, Mr. Gilbert Huxter, the bullshitting village huckster, had told our maid last week, inside his thriving tobacco and marijuana shop, that our unsavory Guest is some sort of Evil Prestidigitator. And Mr. Huxter really knows his shit. He sells more drugs across the street in tobacco-land than Mr. Raymond Canfield's Chemist and Apothecary Emporium does over on High Street."

"I believe you're right," Charlie agreed with Edith, mostly to be compatible and to again avoid her impulsive scorn. "Our Weirdo Tenant has transferred the evil spirits from a hidden liquor bottle, and gotten them absorbed into the furniture; *your* good old furniture! And Edith, the very chair in which your poor dear mother used to sit when you were a little girl, well, the invisible Dickhead threatened your head and face with the haunted seat."

"I think you're sobering-up fast," the wife observed and declared. "You're no longer drunk as a skunk, or soused as a louse."

"Here now; take another swig of potent rye to calm-down your frazzled nerves," Charlie recommended. "I find that sex is better when we're both drunk and only imagine it happenin' in our sleep."

Millie was soon dispatched across the street to rouse-up very practical Mr. Sandy Wadgers, the brawny, muscular village blacksmith, for the expressed purpose of determining why the uncanny furniture in the Coach and Horses guest room had been behaving in a most extraordinary manner.

"Mr. Sandy Wadgers is quite very resourceful and professional at his chosen trade," Charlie mentioned to Edith, after Millie urgently left to fetch the needed services of the local Hephaestus. "Wadgers can nail-down the chair's legs to the planked floor so that you won't have to again worry about being mugged by the accursed flying chair. If Millie's not back with the blacksmith in half an hour, I'll bet that she's earnin' a nice stipend on the side with her legs wide open."

Upon arriving at the Coach and Horses Inn a half-hour later, Mr. Sandy Wadgers, with his pants still wide-open, assessed quite a grave view of the "fictional case" being discussed. "Witchcraft belongs centuries in the past," Mr. Wadgers opined. "You want horseshoes, well, I got 'em! You want an exorcist, then fuckin' hire that dumbass flake Vicar Bunting!"

"Well, Sandy; can you simply nail-down the furniture so that it doesn't attack either Charlie or me!" Edith begged. "I've never before ever been assaulted by a crazed chair, and in the future, I don't want to ever be knocked cold by something like a wingless flying sofa or zooming ottoman!"

"I'm in no hurry to prove your ridiculous *hall*ucinations," Sandy joked out of character. "I'm reluctant to venture up to his room, but if you insist, I'll be on my way. But I'm no qualified expert when it comes to ghosts and spirits. I only know hammers, anvils, the blazin' furnace, and iron horseshoes."

Over the way, across the lazy lane, Mr. Gilbert Huxter's apprentice came out of the local tobacco store and began taking-down the shutters protecting the front window. The young fellow had been called-over by Millie to join the ongoing discussion as a possible witness to eventually initiate a legal eviction notice. Being curious and valuing the thrill of gossip, Mr. Huxter naturally followed his assistant over to the Coach and Horses, all in the course of a few seconds.

Mr. Gilbert Huxter, who regarded himself as a gnostic genius in the very scholarly study and history of Anglo-Saxo parliamentary government procedures and law, assumed the philosophical position that Mr. Sandy Wadgers should knock down the "evil door", and that the Halls should then burn the diabolical object immediately in order to extricate any remaining malicious demons that might still be inhabiting inside its panels.

"Let's have all the pertinent facts first," Mr. Wadgers advised. "Let's be sure we'll be acting perfectly right in bustin' *that* supposedly haunted door open," the burly blacksmith advised. "A door on bust is always open to bustin', but ya' can't un-bust a door once you've busted it. Just like spring is bustin'-out all over. Ya' can't un-bust spring after it's been busted-out!"

And suddenly and most wonderfully, "the possessed hellish door" to the Stranger's upstairs room magically opened of its own accord, and as the shocked spectators looked-on in sheer amazement, the stunned audience saw, descending the stairs, the muffled figure of the Alien Stranger staring more blankly than ever, and his blue-tinted goggles featuring those unreasonably large azure lenses that were truly emblematic of his obscure personality. The inimitable no-name Stranger descended the steps, stiffly and slowly, staring straight ahead all the time; like a roving nomad, the "Stalker" sped past his awed audience, stepped across their standing positions, momentarily stared backwards, and then stopped his forward progress.

The Mystical Tenant entered the downstairs parlor room, fully dressed, and definitely not nude. His queer demeanor in passing his petrified bystanders appeared to be casually arrogant, but also nonchalant.

Not a word had been spoken until the last echoes of the parlor door's loud slam had died away. The fazed and horrified eyewitnesses incredulously stood in silence, consciously staring in wonder at one another.

"If I were either of you two idiots," Mr. Wadgers addressed Charlie and Edith, "I'd go and ask the Freak all about these fucked-up shenanigans he's employin'. I'd demand an immediate explanation, or else I'd evict the Dumb-Shit from the Coach and

Horses in a fuckin' heartbeat. Honestly; I've seen less bullshit in Farmer Joe Cromwell's big cow pasture, that's for damned sure!"

"Aren't ya' goin' to nail-down the furniture?" Charlie pleaded. "We really need your expertise!"

"Well, if that don't lick everything except my dick!" Mr. Wadgers exclaimed, and then, the confounded blacksmith, being quite disenchanted with the entire evolving situation, rapidly abandoned the premises, with his extremely stressed mind swimming in a total quandary.

"But Sandy!" Charlie Hall screamed in the wake of the village blacksmith's hasty departure. "Edith and I can be killed by a flying chest or bureau if the furniture isn't nailed-down to the floor!"

Chapter 7

"THE STRANGER'S UNVEILING"

The obscure "Lecherous Stranger" entered into the little parlor of the Coach and Horses Inn about half-past five in the morning, and there, the Walking Enigma remained until near midday, brooding with the blinds down; making the door shut, and no one in proximity even daring to venture anywhere near "the Shithead Scourge". All that time, the "Manipulative Menace" must have fasted, being so dedicated to his undefined pursuit as he was. Thrice he rang his service bell, the third time quite furiously and continuously, but no one answered his summons out of fear of experiencing unforeseen reprisal.

"He can go to the devil and shovel shit, volcanic ashes and molten lava down below, for all the hell I care!" Mrs. Hall confided to Charlie. "He's without a doubt Satan's apprentice, that I'm certain. I'd like to poison his tea with hemlock and arsenic; that's what the hell I'd like to do!"

"Ya' know, Edith. We've been assholes ever since we bought this pathetic dump," Charlie confessed. "There's a wise sayin' that goes, 'You can't put the cart before the horse', and just look at the shingle above our humble inn. The Coach and Horses is ass-backwards."

Presently came an imperfect rumor of the "insane burglary" that had recently occurred at the vicarage, and two and two had been slowly put together within the very active Iping gossip community.

Charlie Hall, assisted by Mr. Wadgers, strolled-off to find Mr. Clark Shuffleboard, the county magistrate, and objectively discuss his advice about achieving a viable solution to the Halls' Tenant dilemma. No one at the inn had audaciously ventured upstairs, and noticed exactly how the "Nefarious Stranger" had occupied and conducted his secret affairs, and the "Satanic Genius's" daily habits were still greatly unknown. Now and then, "the Witchdoctor" would stride violently up and down the steps like an obsessed sprinter, and twice his vocal cords released a powerful outburst of belligerent curses, and once, "the Incensed Moron" came downstair tearing quantities of papers, and there was always a violent smashing of glass bottles inside the confines of his off-limits room.

The little group of scared-but-curious townspeople increased in number as the legend of "the Freak at the "Coach and Horses" proliferated throughout all of isolated Iping Village.

Mrs. Alice Huxter came over from the tobacco shop to offer her sentimental support to Charlie and Edith, and then, some gay transvestite young fellows, resplendent in black, ready-made jackets, accentuated by *piqué* paper ties, appeared upon the scene to celebrate Whit Monday, and soon the elite Cambridge College punks joined the agitated citizens' group by asking a litany of confusing, smart-assed interrogations.

Young Archie Harker, a haughty college-bound pseudo-intellectual, distinguished himself by going up the yard and trying to peep under the window-blinds to watch the "screwball magical act" in progress. The idealistic idiot could see nothing noteworthy, but gave reason for supposing that he had accurately observed something significant, and then, other snotnose egocentric assholes of the Iping Socratic Youth Organization presently verified the bonehead's totally exorbitant claims.

It was the finest of all possible Whit Mondays imaginable, and down the chosen village street stood a row of nearly a dozen commercial booths, a shooting gallery, and on the grass by the forge were three yellow and chocolate wagons, and then, some picturesque strangers of both sexes were preoccupied putting-up on an improvised-clothesline holding a variety of nude drawings displaying the sizes of each other's genitalia.

The participating gentlemen wore blue jerseys that had been deftly manufactured on the Isle of Mann, and the more genteel Iping Ladies Civic Club were adorned in white aprons along with quite fashionable flowered hats, gorgeously accentuated with heavy plumes.

Mr. Marcus Codger, old fart owner of the "Purple Fawn Inn", a third-class establishment grossly inferior to the pedestrian Coach and Horses, along with Mr. Jaggers, the babbling stone cobbler, who also sold old second-hand rusty bicycles, were stretching a string of union-jacks and royal ensigns (which had originally celebrated the first Victorian Jubilee) across the narrow festival entrance road.

"Hoary Mr. Marcus Codger kept yelling at and cursing a hired vacationing painter making cursive letters on his overhead festival shingle bellowing, 'It's called Purple Fawn, you dumb fuck; not Purple Faun'!"

And inside the artificial darkness of the lackluster Coach and Horses parlor room, into which only one thin jet of sunlight penetrated daily, the "Sinister Stranger", hungry and fearful, stayed alone and hidden in his uncomfortable hot wrappings, poring through his dark glasses upon his writing paper, and out of sheer boredom and monotony, occasionally chinked his dirty little bottles, persistently swearing rather savagely at the pre-pubescent boys below, who were meanly mocking his presence through the parlor's open window. In the corner by the fireplace lay the fragments of half-a-dozen smashed bottles, and a pungent twang of chlorine both tainted and saturated the room's air.

About noon, the ailing Tenant suddenly opened his parlor door, exclusive to only his use, and stood glaring fixedly at the three or four people drinking potent liquor at the inn's bar. "Mrs. Hall," the distressed resident client yelled.

Some neighboring whiskerando chugging-down a double straight shot of bourbon departed his laughing company and sheepishly scurried-off to call for Edith Hall.

Charlie's wife begrudgingly appeared after a brief interval, a little short of breath, but all the fiercer for that short trip back to moderate her business. Edith was very formally holding a little black tray with an unsettled inn bill laid upon it. "Is it your bill that you're wanting, sir?" the landlady suavely asked. 'Well then, sir, here is the exact balance of your settlement!"

"Why wasn't my breakfast laid-out as was our original oral agreement? Why haven't you prepared my meals and responsibly answered my bell? Do you think I live without eating? I don't go into hibernation like bears or hedgehogs do, and I don't shit in the woods like bears do, either!"

"Why isn't my bill paid?" countered Mrs. Hall. "That's what I want to fuckin' know. I think you're goin' bankrupt and are deeply in debt; that's what the hell I actually do believe."

"I told you three days ago I was awaiting a huge remittance from my—"

"And I told you two days ago that I wasn't going to wait for no fraudulent remittances from your imaginary London bank. You can't grumble if your mediocre breakfast waits a bit, if my bill's been waiting these five overdue days, can you?"

The Stranger swore briefly in a muttered mumble, which Mrs. Hall could not vividly interpret.

"And I'd thank you kindly, sir, if you'd keep your swearing to yourself, sir," Mrs. Hall austerely admonished. "My dear husband and I are of decent Christian upbringing, and we despise vulgarity and all obscene *illusions!*"

The stranger stood looking more like an angry deep-sea diving-helmet than ever before. It was universally felt among the regular patrons at the inn's bar that Mrs. Hall had gotten the better of "the Psychopath" with her expert usage of authoritarian lectures. The inn's only guest's next words showed as much subordination on his part to her overwhelming dominance.

"Look here, my good woman—"

"Don't 'good woman' *me,*" Mrs. Hall chided. "Don't expect me to lick the weeds out of your skinny gaunt asshole! I'm no fuckin' bottom of the food chain insect, ya' got *that* special message, Pal!"

"I've told you my remittance hasn't arrived yet. It's merely en-route from the London post office! It'll be here in a few days."

"Remittance indeed!" Mrs. Hall rather vociferously chastised. "If ya' don't come clean in another day, I'll be reportin' your ass to the local constable, who'll send your balls and pecker to the famous area hanging judge, for a scheduled rendezvous with the county workhouse for deadbeat debtors."

"Still, I daresay, in my pocket—"

"You had told me three days ago that you hadn't anything but a sovereign's worth of silver upon you. If you was as good as that no good traitor Judas Iscariot, you'd have at least thirteen pieces of silver in your damned pocket."

"Well, I've found some more—"

"'Where? Under the bar? In an overflowed storm drain? Up Vicar Buntings smelly asshole? Inside Jezebel Bunting's V.D. infected pussy? Where I ask?"

Edith Hall's emphatic response seemed to greatly annoy the Stranger very much, sending "the A-hole" into a tyrannical rage. The embarrassed and humiliated Tenant promptly stamped his foot upon the planks, rattling the floor. "What do you mean by speaking such vile impertinence to an honorable man without attempting to mitigate our disagreement?"

"I have wondered from the start where you would ever find your free money source," Mrs. Hall indirectly accused her debater of being a phony and a crook. "And before I take any coins from your greedy fist, or fetch you any breakfasts, or do any such servile things for your convenience, you got to tell me, for my own satisfaction, one or two relevant facts I don't understand; and what nobody else around this fucked-up inn don't understand, and just what everybody in the vicinity of this fucked-up village is very anxious to understand."

"And what the hell do you wish to learn from me?"

"I want to know what've you been doing to my chair upstairs, and I want to know how it is that your room had been empty, and how you ever got into it again with me and Charlie standin' like soldiers at the portal. Whoever fuckin' stops by this inn uses regular doors to enter and exit rooms, and that's the goddamned rules of the house that my husband and I strictly enforce, and quite obviously, you *didn't* do that simple thing. And now, what I want to know is how you *did* come-in like a veritable escaped ghost, flying your lousy butt straight out of Hell. And I want to know—"

Suddenly the "Mortified Stranger" raised his clenched gloved hands, wildly stamped his foot, and boomed, "Stop your nonsense!" with such extraordinary violence that the exasperated and stunned listeners standing and eavesdropping at the bar immediately became silent.

"You don't understand the half of it," the "Ogre" pleaded. "You'll never fathom who I am, or what I am. But I'm prepared to show you the truth, By Heaven! I'll show and convince you of the magnitude of my supreme omnipotence."

Then, without any further notice, the non-paying patron put his open palm over his face and quickly withdrew it. The center of his visage frightfully and instantly became a black cavity. "Here," he resumed his bizarre demonstration. The "Crazed Mage" stepped forward and handed Mrs. Hall something which she, staring at his metamorphosed, cave-like, very hollow countenance, automatically retreated backwards in a state of absolute shock.

And next, when Edith fully recognized what the manifestation truly was, Mrs. Hall screamed quite loudly, almost collapsing upon the floor and entering into a deep coma. The "Male Medusa" dropped a facial organ, and staggered back with a spine-tingling shriek. The nose; it was the Stranger's Nose! pink and shining— horrifically rolling like a marble upon the dusty barroom floor.

Then, the "Voodoo Conjurer" roughly removed his spectacles, and everyone at the bar immediately gasped in horror. "The Evil Wizard" next removed his felt hat, and with a violent gesture, aggressively tore and ripped at his whiskers and bandages. For a moment, the, half-drunk bar clientele resisted watching the remainder of his evil anti-miracle. A flash of horrible anticipation zoomed through the bar area.

"Oh, my God!" Mrs. Mabel Maloney, a brothel Madam, shouted. "I'd rather look at the eyes of two hurricanes."

It was worse than anything imaginable in the ultra-predictable Sussex County daily Iping world. Mrs. Hall, standing open-mouthed and horror-struck, shrieked at the instances of supernatural chicanery that her besieged pupils had recently observed, and the vexed woman made a hasty exit towards the door.

Everyone at the bar began to fearfully move-away from the "Black Magic Sorcerer" as if he had contracted advanced leprosy. The regular inn-goers were prepared to receive scars, disfigurements, tangible horrors, but short of nothing less than resembled immediate death! The bandages and false hair flew across the counter onto the inn's serving bar, making a somersault-type jump to avoid *their* shocked physical presence. Each and every standard patron became petrified, and soon tumbled onto everyone else into a heap of bodies, with their forms swiftly rumbling-down the front stone steps and ultimately landing in a cluttered pile of vanquished humanity, lying in a section of mud.

People down in the village proper heard a variety of shouts and shrieks, and looking-up the normally quiet street, stared in the direction of the now-infamous "Coach and Horses". The witnesses, still with their mouths agape, saw Mrs. Hall fall down atop Mrs. Mabel Maloney, and Mr. Teddy Henfrey was seen jumping like a bullfrog to avoid tumbling over *her* obese butt. And then the appalled bystanders heard the frightful screams of Millie, who, forgetting about her next self-induced orgasm, had emerged suddenly from the kitchen at the noise of the tumult, and had regrettably and unfortunately, come upon the headless "Stranger Strangler" from behind.

Every gawker and hawker, all down the street, including the sweet-stuff seller; the shy and nutty coconut proprietor and his goofball assistant; the dildo vendor, and the masochistic and transgender little boys and girls, all became excited and commenced running towards the rustic inn. And in a miraculously short space of time, a crowd of perhaps forty rubbernecks, and rapidly increasing by the minute, swayed, hooted, inquired, gossiped, and were exclaiming a plethora of insipid vulgarities and uncharitable curses.

Everyone involved in the chaotic mix seemed eager to talk at once, and the ongoing result was somewhere between the Tower of

Babel and a cacophonic chicken-coup. A small bevy of Iping citizens supported Mrs. Hall, who was picked-up off the street's sidewalk, with buckling knees, in a state of total mental and physical fatigue.

There was an impromptu conference convened on the pavement, and the incredible evidence of a vociferous eye-witness. "Bogey Man!" "What's he been doin', then?" "Ain't hurt the woman's tender ovaries, has he?" "Run at the faceless Bastard living inside the parlor room with a sharp knife or sword, I do believe should be done."

In the volatile crowd's struggles to see into the inn's interior through the still-open door, the restive maniacs formed into a straggling battering ram; a sort of military phalanx, with the more adventurous apex nearest the inn. "A pedestrian, who happened upon the tumultuous scene, stood and solemnly testified for a moment, "I saw her skirts whisk-by, and the Faceless Fiend was dashing after her. Didn't take but ten tiny seconds to occur. Back comes the crazed Dipshit with a sharp carving knife in his left hand, and a clever in the other; the creep just stood there staring, randomly deciding who exactly he meant to kill first. It all happened but a mere moment ago. I Think that the Instigator became flustered and went back inside that inn door. You other latecomers missed all of the fucked-up action!"

The speaker, a tourist from Leatherhead, stopped his phony oration to step aside and allow a small procession of angry men marching very resolutely towards the now-defamed Coach and Horses Inn.

First Mr. Hall, who appeared very florid-faced and determined, not to mention bellicose; then Mr. Bobby Jaffers, the no-nonsense village constable, and next, the wary Mr. Sandy Wadgers, the brawny "Vulcan" carrying his heavy sledgehammer. The trio had come fully armed for action with an official warrant from Magistrate Clark Shuffleboard to arrest and jail the egregious "Debt Owner".

People shouting all around the scene were yelling conflicting information about the recent confusing and contradictory developmental circumstances along with the corresponding uncanny events. "Oxford professor or no Oxford professor," Constable Jaffers vehemently declared. "Where is the evasive Bastard? He's gotta' be served and taken into custody."

Mr. Hall marched up the steps, ambled straight to the parlor door and flung it wide open. "Constable," Charlie adamantly demanded. "Perform your sworn duty."

Bobby Jaffers instantly marched inside the Coach and Horses to serve his warrant. Charlie Hall next followed, and Mr. Wadgers entered last. The Iping triumvirate gasped in the dim yellow light. The Headless Figure was facing their' intruding countenances, and the "Specter" was gnawing on a stale crust of bread in one gloved hand, and soon the "Mad Mage" alternated biting-off a chunk of cheese with the other.

"That's him!" Hall exclaimed. "He's been eating Edith and me out of house and home ever since he's parked his ass at the inn. For each pound he's gained, it's cost me two pounds in return."

"What the devil's this?" came an interrogative voice emitted from the collar of the Charon-like figure. "Haven't you' craven jerk-offs ever seen the Grim-Reaper before! But anyway, thanks for barging-in on my parade without needing to cross the River-Styx!"

"You're a damned rum-head customer, Mister," accused Mr. Jaffers. "You're really part indigent, and part mendicant, and you'll be under arrest unless you can balance your debts owed to Mr. and Mrs. Hall."

"Keep off!" warned the ominous-looking Figure, starting back. "I'm not wearing a damned disguise! I have the power to easily annihilate the whole mess of you if I'm either challenged or injured!"

Abruptly, the Faceless Apparition whipped-down the bread and cheese he had been eating upon the floor, and Mr. Hall lunged forward and defensively grasped the knife lying upon the table, just in time to save the weapon from the Raving Lunatic. Off came the Stranger's signature left glove, which then was used to briskly insult and slap Jaffers' face three times.

In another moment, Constable Jaffers, cutting short some lengthy legal statement concerning the proper administration of an arrest warrant, had firmly gripped the perpetrator by the invisible wrist, and next luckily caught "the Transgressor's" invisible throat. The obstinate constable soon received a sound kick on the left shin that made him shout and wince, but the determined policeman kept his grip by using the long arm of the law.

Hall sent the knife sliding along the table to Mr. Wadgers, who acted as goal-keeper for the offensive move, so to speak, and then Charlie valiantly stepped forward as Constable Jaffers and the "Inane Insane Stranger" swayed and staggered towards him, clutching and hitting his opponents with damaging uppercuts, left hooks, and right crosses. A chair stood as an obstacle in the way, and the seat flew aside, with no one apparently throwing it, and the hurled seat landed with a loud crash, as the obdurate combatants came-down in a ridiculous heap upon the floor, all together.

"Get the feet," Constable Jaffers commanded between his gritting teeth. "Get his fuckin' feet!" the policeman hollered to Charlie. "I've never wrestled with a Slippery Ghost before, and I never wish to grapple with one ever again."

Mr. Hall, endeavoring to promptly act on Jeffers imperative instructions, received a sounding kick in the ribs that disposed of his fighting ability for a moment, and surly Mr. Wadgers, seeing that the "Decapitated Stranger" had rolled-over and had gotten the upper side of Jaffers neck, fearfully retreated towards the door, knife in hand, and so collided with Mr. Gilbert Huxter and the recently deputized Sidderbridge carter, who had been coming to the rescue of Iping public law and order.

At almost the same moment, down came three or four bottles from the chiffonnier, and their shattering shot a web of contaminating pungency into the fight zone's already-drab air.

"I'll surrender," cried the exhausted Stranger, though at that moment, he had tough-guy Jaffers pinned-down. The Defeated Pugilist stood-up panting, a strange figure indeed, both headless and handless. The Militant Tenant had pulled-off his right glove, as well as his left, and his arms were completely invisible. "It's no good," the Invisible Freak conceded, as if sobbing for breath. "I need to mitigate an honorable truce!"

It was the strangest thing in the world to hear *that* screeching high-pitched voice coming as if out of a fully empty throat, but the Sussex peasants are perhaps the most matter-of-fact people living under the sun. Constable Jaffers got-up from the grimy floor, dusted himself off, and expertly produced a pair of shiny handcuffs.

"I say, you fucked-up Scoundrel!" Jaffers exclaimed. "Damned it! You'll use these babies as only I, Bobby Jaffers, can see fit to apply them onto your filthy wrists. You're under arrest for at least earning seven major violations!"

The Subdued Stranger ran his arm down his waistcoat, and as if by a secret other-world miracle, the buttons to which his empty sleeve pointed popped and became undone. Then, the "Possessed Magician" reached about his skinny shins, and acrobatically stooped-down. The Handcuffed Prisoner seemed to then be neurotically fumbling with his shoes and socks, since only his thumbs had been cuffed.

"Why of all the condemned shit accumulatin' in Hades! Go to Hell!" Mr. Gilbert Huxter yelled. "That's not a man at all. It's just some empty tawdry clothes. It might be some sort of manikin, or maybe a weirdo fuck like Pinocchio over there in Italy. Look! You can see down his collar and notice the linings of his clothes. I could put my arm—"

Mr. Huxter extended his right hand; it seemed to meet something solid in mid-air, and the tobacco and illegal drug storeowner drew his arm back with a sharp exclamation. "I wish you'd keep your fingers out of my eye," said the aerial voice at nose level, in a tone of savage vengeance. "The fact is, I'm all here, right in your midst; head, hands, legs, penis, testicles, epididymis, and all the rest of me, but it so happens that I'm invisible and have total impunity from your frivolous town rules of law and order. It's a confounded nuisance for all you dimwits to ever comprehend, but here I am. There's no valid reason why I should be poked to pieces by every stupid, self-important bumpkin in Iping, now is there?"

The suit of clothes, now all unbuttoned and hanging loosely upon its unseen supports, stood-up, with its flaccid arms pointing akimbo.

Several other curious men folk had now entered the mayhem and havoc room, so that then, the inn's bar was extremely crowded.

"Invisible, eh?" Mr. Huxter screamed and questioned, ignoring the Stranger's accelerated verbal abuse and braggadocio. "Whoever heard the likes of such pure bullshit?"

"It's strange, perhaps, but it's not a crime to be invisible. Why the hell have I been assaulted by a dick-headed policeman and his deputies in such an unruly fashion?" the Invisible Man objected.

"Ah! Now that's a different matter," Jaffer maintained. "No doubt you're a bit difficult to see in this peculiar room light, but I got a warrant for your immediate apprehension, and it's all worded correctly by Justice Shuffleboard. What I'm really after ain't no crazy, hard to prove, invisibility charge; it's blatant burglary at the vicarage, and it's you not satisfying your massive debt obligations to the Halls. And there's plenty of evidence of a nearby house been broken into, and money taken."

"Well? That's not even circumstantial evidence being expressed!" the Invisible Man objected. "I demand to be liberated by a quick judgment from an impartial jury. Until then, I'll be out on bail, as soon as my dividends from the prestigious London bank arrive here in Iping."

"Forget that circumstantial evidence bullshit," Constable Jaffers argued. "And my circumstances certainly point and indict—"

"Stuff and nonsense!" the Invisible Man boldly articulated. "You have no absolute proof; only weak speculation! You better watch your forked tongue, or else, I'll have you busted-down to town dog catcher!"

"I hope so, sir; but I've got my explicit instructions from Magistrate Clark Shuffleboard himself."

"Well," replied the obstinate "Criminal", who had been born with a stub-head. "I'll come. I'll *come*. But with no handcuffs worn upon my sensitive wrists."

"It's the regular thing," Jaffers insisted. "Derbies are part of the process, even in fuckin' Kentucky!"

"No handcuffs," stipulated the beleaguered Stranger. "I promise that I'll voluntarily accompany you to the local jail."

"Pardon me," interrupted Jaffers. "You have to follow the exact established procedure; we do not have the liberty to deviate one iota from rules that's been in effect from past practice."

Abruptly, the central figure being arrested sat-down, and before anyone could definitely realize what was being done, the leg slippers, socks, and trousers had been kicked-off under the table by the Irascible Trickster. Then, the Invisible Man sprang-up and flung-off and tossed his wrinkled coat into the air.

"Here, stop doing that shit," Constable Jaffers commanded, suddenly realizing precisely what was happening. The overwhelmed law enforcement officer gripped and frantically tugged at the Elusive Magician's waistcoat; it effectively resisted his surge during the dramatic struggle, and the cotton shirt slipped-out of Jaffers palms, and left its tattered remains empty inside his limp hand. "Hold him!" Jaffers instructed very loudly to all those gawking cowards in attendance. "Once he gets the things off—"

"Hold him!" cried everyone else, male and female, but refusing to get involved in the phenomenal arcane battle. And in seconds, there was a mad rush at the fluttering white shirt which was now the only remaining visible part of the Sinister Stranger, with the now-gallant retrievers wanting to own a piece of the trophy from the spectacular bar altercation.

The twirled shirt-sleeve had planted a shrewd crater in Charlie Hall's face that naturally halted his open-armed advance, and the impact sent Hall backward into old Toothsome Tim, the Vicar's sexless sexton, and in another moment, the enchanted garment was mystically lifted-up and became convulsed, vacantly flapping about its lifeless arms, acting solely as an empty shirt that would be unexpectedly thrust over a man's head.

Constable Jaffers futilely clutched at the whirling garment, and his impotent effort only helped to pull it down; a clenched fist from his invisible opponent struck the already-hurting constable directly in the mouth, and in desperation, Jaffers fiercely threw his truncheon, which accurately smote Teddy Henfrey savagely upon the crown of his head.

In the midst of the wild wrangle, Charlie reached for the "Invisible Asshole's" legs, and in the heap of flaying arms and bodies, instead, picked-up Constable Jaffers by mistake, lifted the arm-flailing cop onto Halls' shoulders, who quickly applied the use of a clever, whirling propeller spin, and Edith's husband frenetically flung the screaming policeman onto the inn's front steps."

"Look out! It's gotta' be a demon from Hell! Iping is doomed to disaster!" yelled a fully-inebriated, panic-stricken woman. "Hall and Jaffers are fencing and swinging at random, and hitting absolutely nothing."

"Hold him! Shut the door! Don't let the dirty Bastard loose! He can't escape our clutches! I got something! Here he is!" Jeffers screamed, without having any deputy assistance being rendered.

Everybody, it seemed, was being hit all at once in the massive Iping imbroglio, and Sandy Wadgers, knowing that his drunken wits had been sharpened by a frightful blow to the nose, reopened the door and led the rout of outside barbarians into the bawdy Coach and Horses. The other pugnacious deputy fighters, being reinvigorated, followed the blacksmith's stellar example.

The incessant hitting and pummeling continued. Phipps, the Unitarian, had a front tooth broken, and Teddy Henfrey had been injured in the cartilage of his left ear, and now possessed a swollen groin, yelling and complaining of a massive "my groin headache".

Constable Jaffers had been brutally struck under the jaw, and, turning, the brawling policeman, by sheer luck, caught at something that was intervening between him and Gilbert Huxter during the culmination of the incredible mêlée.

"I got him!" gleefully shouted Jaffers. "I've finally gotten this sleazy snake! Yes; the wriggling Asshole is now securely in my custody!"

"But remarkably, despite the power of strong men like Constable Jaffers, Charlie Hall, and doughty blacksmith Mr. Sandy Wadgers, the Iping arrest team truly failed in their vital mission, and the Invisible Man had successfully accomplished his great escape.

Constable Jaffers rose from his ailing right knee and proceeded to pessimistically comment to the totally spent Iping blacksmith, "Well, Mr. Wadgers. It's not a wonderful day in the neighborhood after all!"

Jay Dubya

Chapter 8

"IN TRANSIT"

Gibbons, the amateur naturalist of the somnolent village, while lying-down upon the spacious open downs with nary a soul breathing any oxygen within a mile, and almost enraptured in the dozing phase of marvelous deep sleep, heard a close-by sound, as of a man coughing, sneezing, spitting, and then swearing savagely to himself. But looking around his immediate environment, Gibbons beheld nothing except an empty pasture, even devoid of cows, sheep, pigs or horses.

Yet the voice his ears had discerned was indisputably human. The beckoning continued to hostilely swear with that certain breadth and variety that distinguishes the cursing of a cultivated Man, but in fact, resembled that of an uncivilized barroom asshole like Teddy Henfrey, Mr. Henry Fearenside, Dr. Connor Cuss, or volatile Charlie Hall.

The mysterious alto inflection grew to a climax, diminished again, and died away in the distance, going as it seemed to Gibbons, originating in the direction of Adderdean. The tone lifted to generate into a spasmodic sneeze, and then abruptly ended. The listener, a superstitious nincompoop, actually thought that he was being haunted and stalked by a demon from Hell.

Gibbons had heard nothing of the morning's occurrences at the Coach and Horses Inn over in Iping, but the "odd voice in the pasture" phenomenon was so striking and disturbing that the napper's philosophical tranquility, and relaxing reverie, instantly vanished.

'Something is giving me a bum steer,' Gibbons reckoned as the fellow drowsily couldn't interpret the meaning of the un-angelic voice. 'I think I'll just take the bull by the horns and run the fuck out of this fucked-up haunted pasture!'

Gibbons rose quite hastily, and being wholly intimidated by what his inferior brain could not fathom, scampered down the steepness of the hill heading towards the nearest village, as fast as his skinny legs could go in order to avoid a diabolical, possessed demon, for some obscure reason, summoning his undivided attention.

Chapter 9

"MR. THOMAS MARVEL"

Mr. Thomas Marvel, is defined as being a doltish youth of flexible visage, a liquorish, sample of non-licorice humanity, possessing a fluctuating mouth, and sporting a black beard of bristling eccentricity. Mr. Marvel's splendid figure features short limbs, a long narrow neck, and an acne countenance. Thomas wore a furry silk hat, and the frequent substitution of twine and shoe-laces for shirt buttons, apparently implemented at critical points of his costume, all the marks of an aimless punk bumpkin not at all ready for matrimony, and essentially a non-eligible, indolent, worthless bachelor, who despised the likes of screaming children.

The big Sussex County fracas had occurred outside the Coach and Horses Inn over in Iping, where Constable Jaffers' clumsy and his totally incompetent, dumb-ass posse of loyal-but-discriminating, blundering, and moronic sycophants had valiantly battled the almost invincible Invisible Man. The inept deputy dunces consisted mainly of Charlie Hall, Mr. Henry Fearenside, Teddy Henfry and Mr. Sandy Wadgers, the rough and tough blacksmith; the four of whom had been soundly thrashed and vanquished by the incredible Invisible Man. The Unseen One, along with Master Thomas Marvel, were sitting with their feet in a roadside ditch over the down facing Adderdean, about-a-mile-and-a-half out of metropolitan downtown Iping, England.

Tom Marvel's massive feet, save for socks of irregular open-work, were bare and stinking; his big toes were exceptionally broad and pricked as are the ears of a watchful hound-dog. In a leisurely manner, Tom, whose last name should have been Foolery, did everything in a lazy, mediocre-but-nonchalant manner.

That day in that year, the idealistic hillbilly had been contemplating trying on a valued pair of boots. The selected foot gear represented perhaps the soundest boots the idiot had ever come across, but the clodhoppers were simply too large for his prodigious feet; whereas, the ones the junior clown had been wearing at the time, being worn in dry weather, were a most-comfortable fit, but the boots were too thin-soled for accommodating a fairly damp environment.

Mr. Thomas Marvel hated roomy shoes with a passion, but then the young fellow had animosity towards damp weather, too. The fastidious asshole had never properly thought-out which he loathed the most, roomy boots or bad climate, but that morning was a pretty pleasant day, and there was nothing better for the lazy scumbag to do than to daydream his life away.

So, Tom decided to put the four articles of footwear into a graceful, circular pattern upon the wet turf, and intensely scrutinize both pairs for hours on end. And seeing the four boots lying there among the majestic green grass blades, it suddenly occurred to the bogus examiner that both pairs were exceedingly ugly in appearance. But amazingly, preoccupied Tom Marvel was not-at-all startled by an alien voice beckoning and distracting his attention from behind his back.

"They're boots, anyhow," the self-centered Gnostic Voice announced. "What the hell are ya' deciding! Stop actin' like an asshole if you don't want to shit your tawdry pants three times!"

"They are, I suppose, charity boots," Mr. Thomas Marvel explained in a semi-trance with his head on his left shoulder negatively regarding his un-treasured possessions rather distastefully. "And which is the ugliest pair in the whole blessed universe; by Jupiter, I'm damned if I know! Now my name is Thomas Marvel; who the hell are you?"

"H'm," the Foreign Voice evaluated and uttered. "Jupiter most-certainly *mars* your day. You oughta' become patriotic and fuckin' join the British Army, and go to boot camp, just like the asshole Americans do!"

"I've worn worse boots, in fact," Mr. Tom Marvel quietly admitted, "and sometimes I go barefooted and have worn none. But all of my footgear was so bodaciously ugly, if you'll allow for my impertinent trite expression. I went cavortin' around barefoot because I was sick of wearing *them*."

"Look Jerk!" the Mystic Voice criticized. "Pretend that you're a cesspool and get your shit together. If you want my empirical opinion, you're wasting-away your fucked-up life foolishly evaluating for hours two pairs of boots. All your stupid energy is being used deciding which pair you're gonna' wear. I suggest Tom, that you keenly read the children's book *Puss and Boots,* and then forget all about the damned boots, and do some muff-divin' and pussy lickin' to a young girl's hairy eager beaver."

"My boots are sound enough, of course," Tom all-too-honestly attested. "But a gentleman or tramp sees such a thundering lot of his boots, and soon becomes tired of his favorite walking arrangements. And if you'll believe me, sir, I've raised nothing of significant importance in the whole blessed country, try as I would, but have earned and valued these mothers for the last five years. Just look and fully admire 'em! But listen Stranger," Thomas Marvel continued. "It's just my promiscuous luck to own the beautiful suckers. I've been struttin' my boots around this county at least five years or more. And then the shrinking fuckers treat me disrespectfully like this."

"It's a beast of a county, and it's a monster of a country out there," the Voice metaphorically and philosophically expressed. "And pigs are for people, because most people are pigs behaving like hoggish gobblin' hobgoblins!"

"Ain't it so?" Mr. Thomas Marvel wondered and questioned the mysterious Foreign Voice. "I just gotta' say that these here boots are made for walkin'! That's just what I'll say! And Mr.; I worked hard on a cattle farm for five-long-years, and after getting paid, I got five shiny gold sovereigns as a bonus to boot! Ha, ha, ha! Life is good!"

"Well, Thomas; hardly working is not the same as working hard!" the Magical Voice summarized, even though it was still springtime.

Finally, being immensely curious, Mr. Thomas Marvel turned his head over his right shoulder, specifically to glance at his Interlocutor's boots, all the while obtaining an advantageous view of his own for comparisons. But much to Tom Marvel's utter consternation, above where the boots of his Interlocutor had their physical existence, his astonished eyes perceived neither hairy legs nor hairy thighs.

Young Tom appeared to be having a miraculous Epiphany, or some sort of Road to Damascus Biblical moment. "Where *are* your damned legs?" Mr. Thomas Marvel gasped over his shoulder, and then came crawling over to the alluring Voice on all fours.

Marvel's keen and insightful eyesight spotted a stretch of empty downs, with the gentle wind swaying the remote green-pointed furze bushes, and soon the lackadaisical lad had become miraculously inspired by what his sentimental blue eyes had just interpreted.

"Am I drunk? What the fuck is happenin'!" Mr. Marvel spoke to the Elusive Voice. "Have I had visions? Was I freakin' talking to myself during a whim? What the—"

"Don't be alarmed," the ethereal-sounding Voice advised. "Stay cool as a ghoul in a cess, er, I mean swimming pool."

"None of your ventriloquizing is interesting *me* in the least," Mr. Thomas Marvel stubbornly retorted, rising sharply to his bare feet. "Where the hell *are* ya? Alarmed, indeed! Show your face and laugh at me, and I'll beat the livin' shit and intestines out of your ugly ass. I'll recklessly wreck your rectum!"

"Don't be alarmed," sternly repeated the Voice. "I'll not harm you, at least not just yet."

"*You'll* be alarmed in a *minute* minute, you' silly Fool," Mr. Thomas Marvel threatened his latest adversary. "Where the hell *are* ya? Let me get my mark on yer...

"Your attitude is too grave!" the Unseen remarked. "I do believe that your mind is dead, and that your locked in a mental mausoleum without ever achieving anything big in your paltry existence."

"Are you *buried* in a *cementary,* or are you still alive?" Mr. Thomas Marvel strangely answered, playing word games with what he considered to be his newest shill to be verbally exploited.

"Please tell me, Tom. Do you confuse the words 'diary' and 'dairy', or 'trail' and 'trial'? What about 'exasperate' and 'exacerbate'? And also, Mr. Marvel; make sure that your personal writing paper is 'stationary' before you begin jotting-down crucial words on the 'stationery'! And one more thing, Tom. Did you know that because of serious economic inflation, pirates in New England have to buy corn at a 'buck an ear'?"

There was no viable answer forthcoming from Mr. Thomas Marvel, who simply stood bootless, his lackluster jacket nearly thrown-off from profusely sweating from the Unseen's intensive interrogation.

"Peewit," the Voice alleged and accused. "You have what is called out here in the hinterlands a peewit!"

"Peewit, indeed! You falsely think I'm an airhead birdbrain, do you?" Mr. Thomas Marvel challenged the Voice's impolite commentary. "This ain't no time for oral deception. If ya' wanna' *fuel* around, go fuckin' work in the damned kerosene industry!"

The grassy down had been barren and desolate for weeks, both east and west, and also north and south; the road, with its shallow ditches and white bordering stakes, ran smooth and empty north and south, and, save for that lone chirping peewit, the blue sky was basically empty and devoid of life, too.

"So, I'm begging you to help me about my boots' debacle," Mr. Thomas Marvel guiltily admitted, shuffling his coat onto his shoulders again. "It's the friggin' drink! I should've known from past experience; if ya' like to booze, ya' fuckin' always lose."

"It's not the drink," the Voice objected. "Intelligent folks keep their nerves steady with rye, scotch, beer, ale, gin, rum, bourbon, wine, vodka, brandy, tequila, champagne, and obviously, decent sex."

"Ow!" Mr. Marvel conceded, as his face grew white amidst its florid patches. "It's the drink, I think!" his lips repeated, almost-noiselessly. The befuddled youth remained staring about his confused existence, rotating his neck slowly backwards and forwards. "I could have *swore* I heard a foreign Voice," Tom whispered.

"Of course, you did. A Voice is like a sign. It's a stark signal to get your fuckin' life together, and achieve something great before ya' die and evolve into empty infinity."

"It's there again," Mr. Tom Marvel said in a hushed tone, closing his eyes and clasping his hand upon his brow with a rather tragic gesture. The disoriented lad was suddenly taken by the collar and shaken violently by a grasp, and with his senses left more dazed than ever. "Don't be a fucked-up Fool," the Stern Voice instructed and demanded.

"I'm off my blooming chump," Mr. Marvel un-marvelously marveled. "It's no good. My addled brain is fretting about them blasted boots that destroyed and infected my long dirty toenails. I'm off my blessed blooming chump. Or it's the devil's demonic spirits in the form of *you* bein' sent to demolish my completely vulnerable ass and head."

"Neither one thing nor the other," the Irritating Voice corrected. "Listen!"

"Chump," Mr. Marvel annoyingly replied, "Chump!" the unsophisticated classic knucklehead reiterated.

"One minute," the Venerable Voice countered with confident self-control. "You're a loathsome chump because you've spent your entire worthless life working for chump change, and worrying about something totally insignificant, like your' damned two pairs of boots!"

"Well," Mr. Thomas Marvel defensively remarked as if the ignoramus was experiencing a queer sensation of having been dug in the chest by the stiff middle-finger of fate.

"You think I'm just pure imagination, don't you? Just pure imagination?"

"What else *can* you possibly be?" Mr. Thomas Marvel incredulously declared, rubbing the back of his neck and then swatting at an annoying green-headed fly. "I ain't never communicated with a ghost, specter or spirit before."

"Very well," the Uncanny Voice responded in a tone of relief. "Then I'm going to throw flints at you until you think differently. You're acting like a baby king still sitting in his high chair, and then pouting while lying in his crib."

"But where the hell *are* ya' inside those splendid boots of yours?" Thomas Marvel questioned.

The Illustrious Voice made no direct answer. Whizz came a thrown flint, and to Tom, apparently and inexplicably, the heavy mineral zipping out of thin air. And the rock just missed Mr. Marvel's shoulder by a hair's-breadth. Being distracted from his lengthy reverie, Mr. Marvel turned, and incredibly, witnessed a flint jerk up into the air; and the object traced a complicated path directly toward his kisser; the stone hung, suspended in space for a moment, and then again aimed at his Marvel's bare feet with enviable rapidity.

The bearded adolescent was too amazed and so impressed to successfully dodge the impact. Whizz, the rock came around Marvel's head again, and wonderfully ricocheted from his bare big right toe, and then zoomed smack into the ditch.

Mr. Thomas Marvel jumped a foot off the damp ground and lustily howled aloud. Then, the post-pubescent Jerk-off started to run; tripped over an unseen obstacle, and tumbled head-over-heels into a sitting position.

"You aren't 'allowed' to yell 'aloud'," the Voice joked. "You need more 'patience' than Dr. Cuss over in Iping has 'patients' sitting in his lackluster waiting room. Ha, ha, ha!"

"Stop bustin' my balls!" Thomas Marvel hollered to the wind, in what constituted absolute disdain. "Please forgive me! I get testy when it comes to my testicles."

"Ha, ha, ha, Tom Marvel," the Exquisite Voice mocked the young dreamer. "You oughta' know the difference between how to 'wind' a watch when the 'wind' is blowing, or how a 'bow' on a boat is not (knot) like a 'bow' tie. And let's not forget that 'kayak' and 'repaper' are spelled the same, both frontwards and backwards, just like 'racer' 'level', 'rotator', 'civic', 'peep' and 'poop'."

Mr. Marvel, by way of lacking an esoteric-like quality reply, struggled to his bare feet, and was immediately rolled over again by a powerful, mysterious, Unseen Force. The young man lay quiet for a moment, evaluating his recent negative supernatural experiences.

"If you struggle and resist anymore," the Voice firmly predicted, "I shall throw the largest flint at your head, and split your empty noggin wide open, just like it was a used coconut shell."

"It's not a fair punishment to do to an innocent victim like myself," Mr. Thomas Marvel protested, sitting-up, taking his wounded toe in hand, and fixing his eyes on expecting the third arriving flint missile. "I don't understand it. Stones flinging themselves at my skinny body. Stones talking. Put yourself down. Rot away. I'm done with *your* fucked-up black magic bullshit."

The third flint fell from a cliff, and honoring Newton's gravity, dropped to the ground. "It's all very simple, Thomas," the Omnipotent Voice's Echo orally conveyed. "I'm an invisible man."

"Tell me something important that I don't already know," Mr. Marvel sincerely requested, gasping with pain. "Where you're hiding—how you do it—I *don't* know. I'm beaten and quite soundly defeated."

"Well, you mentioned the word *sincere,* so I'll tell you all about it. Sincere is a combination of two Latin words, *sine* meaning without, and cere, meaning wax. Roman sculptors often labored and toiled carving marble statues, and when the artists made mistakes, and there were many, the sculptors would fill in the holes with wax. Hence Tom, if a statue was formed perfectly, it would be carved and finished *without wax.* So, if you're always honest and truthful, your character will be without wax, or plain and simple, you'll be perfectly *sine-cera,* or positively sincere."

"Anyone could see that you are decently literate and that I lack essential academic education. There is really no need for you to be so confounded and coy, Mister. *Now* then. Give me a notion; a clue; a vital hint. How are you so hidden that I don't know where the fuck you are?"

"I'm invisible. That's the great point you have to fathom. And what I want you to understand is this—"

"But whereabouts?" Mr. Marvel interrupted, going on a self-inflicted tangent. "Do you smear yourself with vanishing cream? If so, why the hell aren't most women invisible, too? Are you fuckin' gay? Perhaps even some kind of naked transgender Asshole?"

"You do know about polysemantic words, don't you, Tom? Here! I'm only 'six yards' in front of you. And I don't mean either front or back yards, either!"

"Oh, come now? I ain't 'blind', Mister, and I've never been to Venice. The next lie you'll be tellin' me is that you're just a mass of thin air, and that you're on a strict diet, and need to gain weight. I'm not one of your ignorant tramps—"

"Yes, Tom. Presently I *am* thin air. You're looking right through me with your magnificent peepers. Speaking of 'air', I do think that your retarded life needs more 'atmosphere', ha, ha, ha!"

"What! Ain't there any ordinary stuff to you like blood, bones, sweat and tears?" the questioner asked. "What is it that compels you to continually annoy my ass with jabberwocky. Is it that? You're loaded with ridiculous jabber! Is it all nonsensical poetic nonsense, or what?"

"I'm just a regular human being. I'm solid when I want to be; I need and require food and drink, and I need to wear clothes in public, too. But the truth is that I'm invisible. You' see? Invisible Man. Simple idea. Got it down pat? Totally Invisible. Now Tom; are you merrily daffy like candy and taffy? Forgive me for being a little daffy, too, because right now, Tom, I'm a bit laughy! Ha, ha, ha. That was two-thirds of a pun, Tommy boy. p.u. Ha, ha, ha!"

"Let's have a hand of you," Marvel zanily requested, "if indeed you *are* 'real' and are not a talking 'reel' hanging on a fishing rod. It won't be so darn out-of-the-way like, then—*Lord!* How you made me jump, gripping my throat like you had violently done!"

"Just remember this, Tom Foolery. Speaking of your flint misadventure, I'm only a stone's throw away! Ha, ha, ha! Listen to me, and you'll be in like flint, ha, ha, ha! When I grabbed your neck, you got 'a feel' as to how I like to think! Ha, ha, ha!"

"I'm dashed, even though I haven't been running anywhere!" Tom Marvel acknowledged, trying to amusingly fit-in. "If this don't beat cock-fighting without using our limp penises! Most remarkable.

And there I can now see a rabbit runnin' clean through your 'hare', a full 5, 280 feet away, ha, ha, ha! Is your first name either Miles or Milo, Mr. Invisible Man? Not a bit of you is visible, ha, ha, ha! Only your black leather boots!" young Mr. Marvel pontificated.

Tom carefully and keenly scrutinized the apparently-empty space where the ethereal Voice had been originating. "You haven't been eatin' bread and cheese?" Mr. Marvel asked, holding the invisible arm with his grip. "If ya' like pumpernickel, then you must be 'well-bred', ha, ha, ha!"

"You're quite right, but its nutrition has not yet quite assimilated into my digestive system," the Invisible Man informed. "I do, however, need lots of 'dough', but I never get rolled by highway bandits or road crooks!"

"Ah! That's the spirit!" Mr. Marvel appreciatively attested. "Sort of ghostly divine intervention as far as your limited knowledge of the Universe goes."

"Of course, Thomas Marvel. All this magical invisible stuff isn't half so wonderful as you might think. For Christ's sake, Tom. Just remember this; the British cavalry was not crucified on Calvary, ha, ha, ha!"

"Why the fuck have you come to this quiet cow pasture and bugged the shit out of me?" Tom asked the Voice and wanted to learn.

"What I want to say to you at present is this: I need help. I have come to that necessary conclusion. This morning I came upon you suddenly. I was wandering, mad with rage, naked, impotent. I could have murdered anybody, or anyone. And then, in my disheveled wandering, I discovered you, a country hick possessing a fair amount of salient sagacity, along with an element of sophic perspicacious prescience, that is ostensibly based on the preponderance of my plethora of evidence. The vile question is, Tom boy; are you an efficaciously sapient Homo sapien?"

"*Lord!*" vernal Mr. Tom Marvel eloquently-but-inadvertently exclaimed. "Are you the Messiah who's come to this remote farm to initiate the Second Coming? Truthfully, it's been a while since I've had my 'Last Supper'!"

"I hope I haven't 'wounded' your frail and fragile ego," the Miraculous Voice empathized. "I trust that you're not a 'Doubting Thomas'? You do know the distinction between 'wound' and 'wound'? Don't you? Without you having neither 'a watch; nor 'a severe cut' on your body?"

"*Lord?*" Mr. Marvel again exclaimed. "But I'm all in a tizzy. May I ask—How is it so? And what you may be requiring of me in the way of you being and staying invisible!"

"I want and need your assistance as to somehow help me obtain much-needed clothes, food, and shelter. And then, some other essential items 'to boot', too. I've left most of those normal possessions long enough back in Iping. If you won't assist me, you *must*, or else I'll have no alternative other than eliminating your ass right out of England, and then, smack off the fuckin' planet."

"Look here," Mr. Marvel boldly insisted. "I'm too flabbergasted to even fart correctly. Don't knock me with your preposterous gibberish any more. And let me go free as a bird. I must get steady a bit, away from your obnoxious bullshit. You're contaminatin' my mind, and I really resent your putrid pollution!"

"Do you object to being questioned?" The Invisible Man innocently asked.

"And you've pretty near broken my big toe. It's all so unreasonable. I need to consider your judicious proposal in private. Empty downs; empty sky. Nothing visible for miles except the bosom of Nature, and those pesky peewit birds."

"Are you going to help me, Mr. Marvel, or do I have to exterminate you ass right here and now?"

"A Voice out of Heaven, or maybe from Hell, became apparent, because according to my minister," Mr. Marvel added, "Limbo and Purgatory are goin' extinct! And stones, too! And a solid fist to my throat and jaw to boot. Lord! And those hard flints to my big toe and head! I feel like I've already gotten 'stoned' without ever imbibing a second quart of rye whiskey!"

"Pull yourself together," the exotic Voice judiciously recommended. "For you must do the job I've chosen for you in order to avoid your imminent death without you having a proper burial or priest to send your pathetic ass to either Heaven or Hell!"

Mr. Marvel blew-out his cheeks, and his eyes were round and ambitious. "What should I do? I'm too damned young to visit St. Peter at the Pearly Gates, or ready to be working for all eternity for diabolical Satan, shoveling volcanic lava way down below?"

"Out of all humanity, Tom, I've especially chosen you for your allegiance to *my* sacred cause," the Voice admirably confessed. "You're the only eligible man available, except for some of those boneheaded fools over in Iping, who now know that there is such a living creature roamin' on this Earth as an Invisible Man."

"What the hell do you want me to do? Help you what?"

"You just have to be my helper, and you'll be amply rewarded for your loyal effort. Help me survive my dilemma, Tom, and I promise that I'll do great favors for you. An Invisible Man, as you are learning, is a Supernatural Man of tremendous power," the Inimitable Voice announced, before his invisible nostrils violently sneezed six consecutive times.

"And what if I don't help you?" Mr. Marvel protested.

"If you betray my confidence," the Voice strongly emphasized, "or if you fail to do as I direct, I'll castrate your dingle and feed it the nearest mangy mutt!"

"I don't want to betray you," Mr. Marvel whimpered and sobbed, edging away from the direction of the Voice's magic fingers and hand that had just appeared before the lad's eyes.

"Now that you can actually see me in three dimensions, well then, Mr. Thomas Marvel, you have now become a Man of Perfect Vision!"

Chapter 10

"MR. MARVEL'S VISIT TO IPING"

After the first gusty panic and major scuffle had spent itself, Iping's easy-going gentry had suddenly become largely argumentative pertaining to the disposition of the Invisible Man. Skepticism abounded and frequently reared its grotesque head, which regularly constituted unproductive nervous skepticism at *that* reality, but cynical skepticism nevertheless. It is so much easier not to believe in an Invisible Man than to place valid credence in his existence; and those villagers who had actually seen "the Male-Medusa Marvel" dissolve into the thinnest of air, or felt the strength of his virile arm, could easily be counted on the fingers of two hands.

And of those eyewitnesses to and participants of the bizarre Coach and Horses fracas, Mr. Sandy Wadgers was presently missing at the Whit Festival, having retired impregnably behind the bolts and bars of his own house. And Constable Bobby Jaffers was still-stunned from being injured and abused, was now drinking potent liquor inside the "Coach and Horses Bar". Great and strange ideas transcending experience often have less effect upon ordinary men and women than smaller, more tangible considerations.

On that particular Whit Monday, Iping was gay with bunting, with William and Jezebel Bunting admiring the wife's most reason banners, and everybody at the church festival was in gala dress, including the transvestite kids from the nearby Mohammed Elementary School.

Whit Monday had been looked forward to for a whole month or more, and every part of the graphic fight between the constable and his deputies against the incomparable Invisible Man was by then almost a minuscule 'whit' in the public's short memory.

By the afternoon, even those staunch citizens who had believed in the 'Unseen' were beginning to resume their trivial diversionary amusements in a tentative fashion, on the supposition that the 'Heinous Inn Tenant' had quite permanently gone away, and with the myriad Iping skeptics' vague recollection, the 'Invisible Man' had already been diminished to a mere jest. But on that special day, people attending the Whit Festival, skeptics and believers alike, were remarkably sociable and pleasant.

Haysman's Meadow was gay with a colorful brown decorated tent, in which Mrs. Jezebel Bunting, Miss Delilah Goodhead, Ms. Sheba Honeywell and other notable prominent church ladies were preparing tea, while, the obnoxious Sunday-School children ran races and played games under the nosey guidance of their religion teachers, Mrs. Connor Cuss and Mrs. Betty Sackbutt.

No doubt there was a slight uneasiness prevalent in the air, but attendees for the most part had the sense to conceal whatever imaginative qualms their brains were experiencing. On the village green, the S and M Unisex Coalition was assiduously distributing color-illustrated pamphlets, soliciting new members to join their ignoble organization.

There was also fine promenading being conducted, and the melodic steam organ played dissonant circus calliope music, the victrola being attached to a small roundabout, and its screeching sound filled the air with a pungent flavor of oil, and with equally annoying pungent music.

Members of the notorious Henry VIII Anglican Martyrs Club, who had attended church that same morning, were splendid while wearing badges of pink and green, and some of the gayer-fagots and lesbians had also adorned their bowler hats with brilliant-colored favors of multi-hued ribbons.

Old Fletcher, an intolerant and bigoted religious zealot, whose conceptions of holiday-making were severely biased and critical, was visible through the jasmine that had been hung about his insect-infested window, his skinny ass poised delicately upon a plank supported on two chairs, and the hoary curmudgeon was busy industriously whitewashing the grimy ceiling of his front display area.

About four o'clock, a stroller entered the village festival from the direction of the downs. The effervescent fellow was a short, stout individual costumed in an extraordinarily shabby top hat, and the ambling itinerant appeared to be very much out of breath, with his puffed cheeks being alternately limp and tightly swollen. The new arrival's mottled face seemed apprehensive in expression, and the exhausted trekker moved with a sort of reluctant alacrity.

The latest festival attendee turned the corner of the church, and soon directed his way to the popular "Coach and Horses Inn". Among others, Old Fletcher remembered seeing the straggler hiking the exhibits and inspecting each booth rather meticulously, and indeed, the wrinkled geezer was so struck by the man's peculiar agitation that the addictive snoop inadvertently allowed a quantity of whitewash to run down the brush into the sleeve of his coat, while disregarding *his* own activities.

The easily-identified out-of-town newcomer, to the perceptions of the proprietor of the Bashful Cocoanut Tent, appeared to be talking to himself, and Mr. Gilbert Huxter, proprietor of the village tobacco and illegal drug shop, remarked to Old Fletcher the exact same observation. The festival hiker stepped-away from the fairgrounds, and stopped at the foot of the "Coach and Horses" steps, and, according to reliable Mr. Gilbert Huxter, appeared to undergo a severe internal struggle before the prospective customer could induce himself to enter the house.

Finally, Iping's latest tourist marched up the stone steps, and was seen by Mr. Huxter turning to the left and opening the door to the parlor. Even from a distance, nosey Mr. Huxter heard voices from within the room and emanating from the bar, apprising the intruder of his detour error. "That room's private!" Charlie Hall lividly yelled, and then the reprimanded trespasser clumsily shut the door and rapidly entered into the inn's bar zone.

Within the course of a few minutes, the visitor reappeared, wiping his lips with the back of his hand, demonstrating an air of quiet satisfaction that somehow impressed Mr. Huxter as being awfully suspicious. Then, engaging in additional espionage, Mr. Huxter's curious surveillance observed the 'foreigner' walking in an oddly furtive manner towards the front yard gates.

The unaware walker, after some hesitation, leaned against one of the gate-posts, produced a short clay pipe, and prepared to fill it, but his fingers trembled while attempting to do so. The wanderer, not cognizant of Mr. Huxter's stealth reconnaissance, casually lit the smoking utensil, and folding his arms, began smoking with a languid attitude, an attitude which his occasional glances up the yard altogether belied.

All that departure from the ordinary spying Mr. Huxter noticed while stooping behind the canisters of the his 'snooping tobacco window', and the singularity of the new man's repetitive and fascinating behavior prompted the rubbernecking tobacconist to impatiently maintain *his* furtive observation.

Presently, the traveling pipe-puffer abruptly stood-up and placed his utensil inside his pocket. Then, the fellow vanished into the yard, preparing to depart the premises. Mr. Huxter, conceiving that he had been a witness to some petty larceny, leapt round his counter and ran out into the road to intercept 'the thief'.

As the crazed tobacco merchant did so, Mr. Marvel reappeared, his hat askew, and with him holding a big bundle inside a blue table-cloth in one hand, and three books tied together with Vicar William Bunting's braces in the other. The alleged crook spotted Mr. Huxter, gave the busybody a deep gasp, turned sharply to the left, and instantly initiated a quick escape.

"Stop, thief!" Mr. Gilbert Huxter's voice boomed, and the old fool set-off on foot after the apparent suspect. Huxter saw the rogue dash off, and observed the scoundrel sprinting briskly for the church corner, just before Hill Road.

"Stop Villain!" the nosey tobacco merchant again bawled. But much to his utter astonishment, Mr. Huxter's shin became caught in some mysterious fashion, and the old fart was no longer running, but instead, flying with inconceivable rapidity through the air. Being level with the Vicar's utility shed's roof, and approaching a cardiac arrest, the elderly codger was experiencing a severe panic attack.

Chapter 11

"INTHE COACH AND HORSES"

Now in order to clearly and fully understand what had actually happened inside the bawdy Horses and Coach Inn, it is necessary to go back to the moment when Mr. Marvel had first come into view of Mr. Gilbert Huxter's tobacco store window.

At that precise moment, Dr. Connor Cuss, the vulgar village surgeon, and Venerable Mr. William Bunting, the august Anglican Vicar, were discussing an important matter inside the inn's parlor. The conferees were seriously investigating the strange occurrences of that Whit Holiday weekend, and were, with Mr. Charlie Hall's permission, making a thorough examination of the Invisible Man's remaining abandoned belongings.

Constable Jaffers had partially recovered from his fall at the stone steps, had gone home to recuperate, and had been placed in the custody of his sympathetic friends. However, the Stranger's scattered garments had been removed by Mrs. Hall, and the room had been meticulously tidied-up. And upon the table under the window where the Stranger had been anxious to work and write notes, Dr. Cuss had almost at once discovered the sought-after three thick books and journal manuscripts, together labeled "Diary".

"Diary, Vicar Bill!" animated Dr. Cuss euphorically proclaimed, putting the three separate volumes upon the table. "Now, at any rate, I think we shall learn something pertinent."

The Vicar stood with his hands up on the table top, wholly speculating and contemplating Dr. Cuss's obscure commentary.

"Diary," repeated Cuss, sitting-down, putting two discovered volumes to support the third, and then opening the third. "H'm! No name on the fly-leaf. Bother! Plenty of cyphers and other fucked-up puzzled figures, though."

The Vicar came around to look over Cuss's shoulder. "Yes, Connor, but more fascinating than interesting, I would say!"

Dr. Cuss turned the first several pages over with a grim face, which soon appeared disappointed. "I'm; oh, dear me! It's all fucked-up cypher, Bunting."

"There aren't any diagrams?" Reverend Bunting asked. "No particular illustrations throwing light—"

"See for yourself," Dr. Cuss bluntly indicated. "Some of it is mathematical terminology, and some of it is Russian bullshit, or some such asshole Cyrillic language used by Ivan the Terrible or Peter the Great, and some of it is fuckin' scribbled in ancient Homeric Greek. Now the Greek references, I thought that *you*—"

"Of course," Mr. Bunting worriedly replied, taking-out and vigorously wiping his spectacles, and feeling suddenly very uncomfortable, for the Vicar had no ancient Greek vocabulary left inside his mind worth talking about. "Yes; the Greek alphabet, of course, that's where *you* may furnish a vital clue."

"I'll try and find you a dumb-ass place in this fucked-up text so that you can reference your extensive knowledge of Aristophanes, Thucydides, Sophocles, Euripides, Socrates, Plato, Aristotle, and Aeschylus."

"If you don't mind, Connor, I'd rather glance through and peruse the volumes first," Vicar Bunting answered, wiping and rubbing his brow, and being abnormally embarrassed for not knowing how to read and interpret ancient Greek nomenclature. "A general impression first, Cuss, and *then*, you know, we can go looking for larger and more substantial clues."

The slightly-mortified Vicar coughed, put on his dependable glasses, and fastidiously arranged the specs' arms over his ear lobes, coughed again, and wished that something more favorable would develop in order to avert the seemingly inevitable exposure of his deficiency in performing basic ancient Greek translation. Then, regaining his faltered composure, Reverend Bill took the volume that Dr. Cuss had handed him in a more relaxed, leisurely manner. And immediately, something out of the ordinary did happen.

The parlor door swung open and slammed against the side wall. Both searching gentlemen sitting at the table turned and reacted, and after looking around, were relieved to notice a sporadically rosy face showing beneath a furry silk hat. "Tap?" the intruder asked, and stood staring at the surprised pair.

"No," said both gentlemen together at once. "Over at the other side, my man," Reverend Bunting answered. "The inn's taproom is that way!"

"And don't be a retarded asshole and please shut that goddamned door," Dr. Cuss irritably added. "We need our damned privacy."

"All right," said the prospective bar customer, as his tone seemed spoken in a lower Voice, curiously different from the huskiness of his first inquiry. "Right you are," the intruder acknowledged in his former Voice. "Stand clear!" And in less than a wink, the inquirer vanished and abruptly closed the door.

"A lost sailor, I should judge," imagined and related Vicar Bunting. "Amusing fellows, they are. 'Stand clear'! indeed. A naughty nautical term, obviously referring to his getting back out of the room, I suppose."

"I dare say so," Dr. Cuss agreed. "My fucked-up nerves are all as loose as my bowels to-day. My anxiety quite made me jump, I mean, the stupid-shit unexpected door opening like that, and that thirsty asshole standing there with his thumb up his ass."

Vicar Bunting smiled as if he had not been jumpy or at all fazed. "I suspect that the Fiend who had been staying here was either an avowed agnostic or an unscrupulous atheist, but most definitely, a steadfast ally of Satan. And now, Connor", the Reverend stated with a deep sigh, "let's thoroughly examine and endeavor deciphering these cryptic notes."

"Didn't Jesus become invisible and had escaped Satan's worldly temptations of power and wealth?" Dr. Cuss remembered from his elementary school catechism class. "I'm still wondering which lucky apostles were porking Mary Magdalene. I had heard last week at the Sunday school that Peter needed to borrow a shit-load of silver from that pimp Paul in order to pay a high premium for Mary's notorious sexual favors! I think the bitch specialized in giving good head."

"One thing is indisputable," Vicar Bunting spoke-up, attempting to change to more delicate and acceptable subject. "There certainly have been some very strange events happening in Iping during the last few days, very unusual indeed. I cannot, of course, believe in this absurd invisibility story—"

"It's truly damned incredible," Dr. Cuss confirmed. "Fuckin' absolutely incredible without *you* even ever giving anyone fuckin' absolution. But Vicar Bill; the essential fact remains that I myself saw—yes, I certainly saw right down his sleeve—"

"But Connor, did you, well, are you sure? Suppose a mirror trick, for instance; its reflections often show hallucinations, misconceptions and illusions that are so commonplace and easily produced. I don't know if you've ever seen a really good conjuror—"

"I won't argue again, and unproductively debate what I can't fuckin' prove," Cuss replied in bitter anger. "I'm a man of science and medicine, and this magical Invisible Man bullshit is not my cup of tea. I've already thrashed that prospect out, Bunting. And just now, there's these shit-eating books. Ah! here's some of what I take to be Greek! Homeric letters, most certainly. Well Dr. Odysseus, are you ready to start interpreting?"

Dr. Cuss pointed his index finger to the middle of the page. Vicar Bunting flushed slightly, bringing his face nearer, apparently finding some difficulty with his dirty glasses. Suddenly, the paranoid Reverend became aware of a strange feeling being felt at the nape of his neck. Mr. Bunting tried to raise his head, but his effort encountered an immovable resistance.

The feeling was a curious hard pressure; the grip of a heavy, firm hand, and it bore and pushed the preacher's chin irresistibly to the table. "Don't move, little men," a creepy Voice whispered, "or I'll have to strangle you both!"

The petrified Vicar looked into Dr. Cuss's face, which was also lying against the parlor table parallel to Bunting's, and each encumbered victim's horrified expression was facing the other's visage.

"I'm sorry to handle you so roughly," the anonymous Voice apologized, "but such sadistic torture is unavoidable. You two genuine assholes should have more practice in dealing with this type of pain over at the popular S and M Sex Emporium."

"Since when did you learn to pry into an investigator's private memoranda," the Voice gruffly accused. And then, the two pinned-down chins were raised, next lowered, and soon wickedly and simultaneously slammed against the table, where two sets of teeth rattled in total disharmony.

"Since when did you two clowns learn to invade the private rooms of a man suffering chronic misfortune? And you, Vicar. You claim to be an honest, moral, God-fearing preacher. You're no better than Charity Knowgood, the biggest whore in town besides Millie, who sometimes practices her artistic skills in the back room here at the risqué Coach and Horses."

"Please tell us what you need to know?" Vicar Bunting begged, almost weeping.

"Okay, gentleman. I need to hear the naked truth. Where the hell have the Halls put my clothes?"

"Nothing but painful mumbles could be heard from the doctor and the minister's mouths, that were still being squashed and crushed against the parlor room table.

"Listen carefully," the Invisible Man's Voice imperatively commanded. "The windows in this room are fastened tight, and I've taken the key out of the door. I'm a fairly strong man; have taught boxing and jujitsu in the past, and I have the black iron poker handy, and best of all, I'm invisible, and am virtually impervious to any fruitless opposition you may try. There's not the slightest doubt that I could and would kill you both and get away quite easily if I wanted to go that route; do you two scumbag assholes understand? Very well. If I let you go, will you' two bozos solemnly promise not to try any foolish nonsense, and do what I tell you?"

The Invisible Man strongly lifted both heads from the table, and the thoroughly intimidated Vicar and the scared shitless doctor looked despairingly at one another, and the physician's weakened throat coughed-out, "Yes."

And then, under extreme duress, Mr. Bunting also endorsed the stated verbal contract. The intense squeezing pressure upon the dual necks was relaxed, and the doctor and the Vicar sat-up, both very red in the face, breathing deeply, and wriggling their heads left and right to gain better blood circulation into their much-abused brains.

"Please keep sitting where you are," the Invisible Man instructed. "Here's the iron poker, you see. You two buffoons must appreciate that I actually enjoy cracking skulls open!"

"What do you really want?" the Vicar asked.

"When I came into this room," continued the Invisible Man, after alternately presenting the poker to the tip of Dr. Cuss and the Vicar's noses, "I did not expect to find my former quarters being occupied, but instead, had expected to find, in addition to my books of memoranda, an outfit of clothing to wear in public. Where is it? No, men. Don't rise. I can see that my garments are gone. Now, just at present, though the days are quite warm enough for an accomplished Invisible Man such as myself to run about stark naked, the evenings are still quite chilly."

"You need clothes to wear in public!" Reverend Bunting repeated.

"I want and need clothing, and I also demand other vital accommodations; and I must also have those three books to safely continue my indispensable research." And with those special demands, the agitated Invisible Man proudly departed the parlor.

"That fellow means business," Dr. Cuss assessed and shared. "I don't want to mess around with his wrath. Just look at the major injuries he inflicted on poor Constable Jaffers. Next to Charlie Hall, and Mr. Fearenside, he's the toughest and strongest man in Iping."

"Let's get the fuck out of this hellhole before that shithead bastard returns and cuts our dicks and nuts right the fuck off our goddamned abdomens!" Vicar Bunting predicted. "That son-of-a-bitch Invisible Man, Dr. Cuss, is the Devil Incarnate, I say!"

Jay Dubya

Chapter 12

"THE INVISIBLE MAN'S TEMPER"

While those extraordinary activities were going on inside and outside the Coach and Horses' parlor, and while Mr. Gilbert Huxter was watching Mr. Marvel smoking his pipe against the establishment's gate, not a dozen-yards away were Mr. Charlie Hall and village tinker Teddy Henfrey discussing, in a state of cloudy puzzlement, one particular Iping, Sussex County topic.

Suddenly, there came a violent thud against the parlor door, followed by a sharp cry, and then silence.

"Hello!" Teddy Henfrey yelled. "'Who's in there?'"

"Hello!" came a more cordial response from the Tap, where Charlie Hall was serving bar.

Needless to say, Mr. Hall was a sluggish fellow who adjusted to and adapted new changes in problem-solving situations, rather slowly-but-surely. "That ain't right," Charlie grumbled, and the co-proprietor came around from behind the bar and paced towards the parlor door. "That damned room is off-limits at the moment."

Mr. Hall and Teddy approached the aforementioned door together, both men with intent faces. Their notion of deviation from the inn's rules was paramount in their narrow thinking.

"Something's wrong," Hall, said to Teddy, who had placed his bottle of cold brew on the counter and nodded in the affirmative. And to increase *their* dual interest, whiffs of an unpleasant chemical odor filtered all the way from the parlor to their nostrils, accompanied by a vague and low muffled sound; conversation had been distinguished, but the verbal exchanges inside the adjacent chamber were very rapid and quite subdued.

"You all right in there?" Hall shouted, rapping and then pounded his fists.

"'If you're havin' sex, ya' gotta' have it upstairs and be first payin' for your pleasure at the Tap. Millie, is that you in there gratifyin' a happy patron?"

The muttered conversation inside the parlor abruptly ceased, and a moment's silence ensued, but then the muffled conversation was resumed, gradually mutating into hissing whispers. Next, a sharp cry of "No! oh no, you don't!" was distinctly discerned. Finally, the sound of a sudden scraping upon the floor was audible, and the oversetting of a chair was occurring during a brief struggle, which soon ended again in silence.

"What the deuce?" a confused Teddy Henfrey yelled. 'I tell ya' Charlie, that's the queerest orgasm I've ever fuckin' heard."

"You all right in there?" Mr. Hall bellowed sharply again. "Open the latch on this door right this second, or I'll punch the sucker down and make you pay for the big damages twice."

The Vicar's high-pitched voice answered with a curious jerking intonation. "Quite right Mr. Hall. Please don't interrupt *our* communication."

"Odd!" Mr. Henfrey declared to Hall. "I saw the Vicar's wife only ten minutes ago, and I think the wacky minister might be in there pumpin' the poop out of someone else. Let's hear who owns the second voice and see if he's hittin' on whoring Charity Knowgood, Iping's only destitute prostitute!"

"Very odd!" Mr. Hall softly concluded. "I believe that the second voice is another male speaking. The Vicar might be heading for a rendezvous with Hell before the rest of us ever get there! I mean, Teddy, neither you nor me is certified or qualified to hear Reverend Bill's confession if he's beginnin' to die from a sex-related heart attack happenin' in my off-limits parlor."

"He's saying, 'Don't interrupt'," Henfrey confidently related, holding-up his left hand for additional silence.

"I just heard the commotion again," Charlie conveyed to the drunk-but-chatty tinker. "I think I'm gonna' stop drinkin' permanent. Too much weird shit's been goin' on ever since I began attendin' those boring temperance meetings in the church basement."

"And a sniff," Henfrey orally contributed in a whisper. "Strange sex goin' on with plenty of dumb-shit sneezin' sniffin' and snifflin'!"

The conscientious eavesdroppers remained listening for more peculiar sounds and noises. The conversation inside the inn's parlor was still rapid and subdued, and most of the exact words being communicated could not be easily identified. "I *can't*, Mr. Bunting," was one expression, with the current speaker's voice still not being positively recognized. "I tell you, sir, I *will* not."

"What was that?" Henfrey wondered and asked Hall. "Gay sex being allowed in your sacred parlor? I mean, Charlie, the Vicar having straight sex with a whore is much more acceptable in Iping than him getting' vigorously porked up the ass by some horny, big-dicked male stud!"

"Says he wasn't speaking to us out here, was he?" Hall asked and reminded Teddy. "If the Vicar is havin' sex in my parlor with either a vivacious whore or a fagot homo, I'll stop the bastard from ever becomin' bishop, that's what the fuck I'll do!"

"Do you think I want to go in there and have sex with two homos?" Teddy snapped back. "Listen Charlie; I might be a trifle soused, but I'm not that zonked to turn into a full-blown fagot. Now if Jezebel Bunting wants to have a threesome going inside the parlor, well, then that new scenario might be a different story."

"Disgraceful!" Mr. Bunting exclaimed from within. "Absolutely ungraceful and shameless."

"'Disgraceful and shameless," Mr. Theodore Henfrey mimicked the Vicar from the door leading to the bar. "I just heard it, Hall. Very distinctly this time. It's definitely the Vicar, or the Vicar's ventriloquist in there. Maybe Reverend Bill got his dingle caught in his fly! Who's that speaking now?" inquisitive Henfrey asked his chief confederate.

"Dr. Cuss, I suppose," Hall guessed and shared. "Teddy; can you hear anything else in there. To my ears, the ruckus sounds like they're throwing the table-cloth all about. Edith is really gonna' be pissed. She just washed and ironed that cover yesterday."

Mrs. Hall, tending to her myriad chores, then appeared behind the bar, wondering what all the commotion near the parlor room was about. Hall made gestures to his wife, symbolically suggesting her silence, accompanied with an invitation to join-in and listen. Those tacit signals aroused Mrs. Hall's wifely standard of verbal opposition. "What the hell you listenin' for, Charlie? Ain't you got nothin' better to do on a fucked-up busy day like this?"

Hall tried to convey everything by grimaces and dumb signaling, but Mrs. Hall was obdurate in her predictable admonition. The wife, feeling perturbed, raised her voice to a much-higher octave. So, Charlie Hall and Teddy Henfrey, with their obedient heads rather crestfallen, tiptoed back to the bar area, gesticulating and waving to no-nonsense Mrs. Hall, attempting to explain their justifiable motivation for stealthily eavesdropping.

At first, Edith refused to see anything especially valid or of merit in what the two drunkards had revealed and heard. Then, the inn's co-owner insisted on Hall to demonstrate admirable discipline by keeping silent, while Henfrey recited to her his story.

Moody Mrs. Hall was inclined to think the whole business to be unadulterated and unmitigated zoo material. "Perhaps the occupants were just moving and re-arranging the furniture," Teddy reported. "I heard someone say 'disgraceful'; *that* I did," the clock repairman insisted. "I'll swear to you Edith; I think it was Vicar Bunting talkin' in there."

"I heard the Vicar's voice, too," Charlie chimed-in. "Maybe Reverend Bunting can't speak right because he might've just gotten a deep throat blowjob administered to his Adam's apple, and he's chokin' on some other fagot guy's discharge! Who the hell would've ever thought this bullshit could ever happen? I mean, you just can't make this crap up!" Hall ejaculated.

"Hush!" Teddy softly uttered. "Didn't I just hear the window open. I'll bet the Vicar doesn't literally get caught with his pants down, and with massive amounts of sex juice spillin' out of his holier-than-thou mouth!"

"What window is Teddy talkin' about Charlie?" Mrs. Hall asked.

"Parlor window," Henfrey attested, much out of turn. "There's only one that's inside *that* haunted room. It must've been the Vicar's window of opportunity to escape public gossip, ridicule and condemnation. Vicar Bill has gotta' sneakily climb-outa' that single window to avoid gettin' caught, and then miraculously escape bein' tarred and feathered on a rail before bein' run outa' Iping for good."

The three speculators stood in place and continued listening intently. Mrs. Hall's eyes viewed through the latch crack the outside front lane, white and vivid, and Mr. Huxter's tobacco shop-front was still blistering in the June sun. Abruptly, the merchant's door opened, and Mr. Gilbert Huxter himself appeared, with his beady eyes staring with excitement, and the cantankerous old man's arms were wildly gesticulating, while rising and dangling about over and over again. "Yap!" Huxter cried his alarm. "Stop thief! Hey everybody! Listen! That slippery scoundrel just ran obliquely across the oblong towards the yard gates, and he's vanished down the lane."

Simultaneously came a tumult of male guzzlers evacuating from the 'haunted parlor room', and the sound of a window being forcefully closed, corresponded to the maddening rush. To Hall, to Mrs. Hall, and to Teddy, the general mystery being reviewed outside the parlor door was intensifying to a crescendo.

Charlie Hall and Teddy Henfrey, along with the other inebriated human imbibers inside the taproom, all at once rushed-out into the street to haphazardly organize a search party to be hastily initiated to capture "the sex-crazed trespasser". The drunken posse noticed someone whisk round the corner towards the distant crossroads, and Mr. Huxter was awkwardly executing a complicated leap over a low fence, and almost magically, floated and drifted into the air, which ended badly with the tobacco vendor landing solidly upon his face and right shoulder.

Mr. Gilbert Huxter had been stunned from being injured during his failed attempt at arresting the 'parlor room crook'. Feeling humanitarian, Teddy paused and stopped to discover the extent of the old gent's injuries, but Hall and two burly laborers from the Tap rushed at once to the street corner, the three nutcases shouting incoherent threats, nasty cliches, and derogatory slogans, and their astute pupils perceived recently-recruited Mr. Marvel vanishing by the corner of the church wall.

'I do believe *that* that's the Invisible Man fucker doin' his crazy shit again!" Teddy hollered to Hall as the out-of-breath pair pursued the suspected criminal.

But out-of-shape Charlie Hall had hardly run a dozen more yards before the obese landlord gave-out a loud shout of astonishment, and his body instantly went zooming headlong and sideways, with his right-hand clutching one of the laborers and bringing both him and himself plummeting to the concrete pavement.

The second laborer, who also had speedily exited the Tap, was reacting to an unknown force and came round in a circle, stared, and conceiving that Mr. Hall had tumbled over of his own accord, twisted in a semi-circle to resume the pursuit of the 'phantom inn trespasser', only to be tripped by the ankle just as wounded Mr. Huxter had been. Then, as the first laborer struggled to regain his equilibrium, the befuddled combatant was severely kicked sideways by a mighty blow that could have easily felled an ox.

As the contingent of shouters chased their assumed foe, the mad dash from the center of the village green came around the next corner. The first to appear was the proprietor of the Community Hardware Store, a burly man sporting a blue jersey. The nail, hammer, and saw salesman was more-than-astonished to see the lane empty and the three almost-unconscious workmen sprawling absurdly upon the damp ground.

And then something fairly peculiar happened to the hardware merchant's rear-most foot, and the poor retailer went headlong and rolled sideways, just in time to graze the feet of his younger brother and business partner, with both entrepreneurs plunging headlong onto the street. The volunteer defenders of Iping justice were then brutally kicked, knelt on, fallen over, and cursed by quite a number of over-hasty, bloodthirsty posse joiners, having no clue as to whom their dangerous enemy was supposed to be.

Now, when Mr. Hall and Mr. Henfrey and their laborer recruits had rushed out of the inn, Mrs. Hall, who had become self-disciplined from years of experience dealing with ruffians and hooligans, remained inside the bar, faithfully guarding the money till. And suddenly without notice, the parlor door swung open, and Mr. Conner Cuss appeared in the portal, and without glancing a second at Edith Hall, the brain surgeon frantically scurried down the front steps, and then scampered toward the corner. "Hold him!" the crazed physician cried. "Book thief he is! Don't let him drop that important parcel."

The doctor, of course, knew nothing about Thomas Marvel's existence, for the incomparable Invisible Man had cleverly handed-over the three essential notebooks, which were included in the bundle that had been transferred to Marvel by the Invisible Man, all happening in the inn's front yard.

Dr. Cuss's facial features expressed both anger and resolute determination, but the fanatic's costume was rather defective, a sort of limp white kilt or tunic that could have only passed acceptable muster in ancient Greece or Nero's Rome. "Hold him!" Dr. Connor bawled, while himself being almost nude. "He's got my fuckin' trousers! And the dirty bastard has pilfered every stitch of the Reverend Vicar's clothes, too!"

"'Tend to that fucked-up asshole in a minute!" Cuss cried to Henfrey as the two dodged pass the prostrate Mr. Huxter, and with their hurting legs coming around the corner to join the in-progress, ascending tumult. The good doctor, despite being half-nude, was promptly knocked off his feet and zipped right into a sprawling melee that truly resembled a raucous rugby scrum.

Somebody in full flight trod heavily upon Dr. Connor's middle right finger. The embattled surgeon, in need of medical attention himself, yelled a series of unsavory expletives like a livid Swiss yodeler, and the abused sawbones desperately struggled to regain his feet. But instantly, Dr. Cuss was sent zooming into the air, and his full anatomy was knocked against an apartment house wall. And that collision finally made Dr. Cuss aware that he had not been involved in a criminal capture, but instead, was a participant on the losing side of a lopsided rout.

Everyone in hot pursuit, including the village's tough and tumble college rugby team, became greatly intimidated, and the entire band of unsuccessful chasers began running back to the town square, and presumable, to the safe sanctuary of the Coach and Horses Tap bar.

Halfway up the inn's stone steps, defeated and bleeding Dr. Cuss recognized the inside parlor voice as that of the sinister Invisible Man, and the surgeon, needing minor knifework himself, decided that discretion indeed was the better part of valor, and wished to cease pursuing his principal adversary in the future in order for him to survive.

In another moment, the cantankerous village sawbones was breathing air fumes back inside the familiar parlor room. "He's fuckin' coming back, Bunting!" Dr. Cuss cussed, rushing inside the parlor all out of breath. "Save yourself from the mother-fucker if ya' ever want to be able to screw Jezebel again! That slippery invisible cocksucker is a threat to all fuckin' humanity! Fire and brimstone be fuckin' damned! When that mangy mother dies and goes down to Hell, Lucifer and his fallen angels will quickly evacuate *his* volcanic evil empire!"

Feeling a degree of modesty, Reverend Mr. Bunting was standing beside the parlor window, engaged in an attempt to clothe himself in the hearth-rug along with a wet morning copy of the *West Surrey Gazette*. "Who's coming?" the half-naked Vicar screamed, being so startled that the Reverend's sheer costume of protection narrowly escaped being disintegrated.

"It's the goddamned Invisible Man," recovering Dr. Cuss cursed, and the psycho surgeon quickly rushed onto the window sill. "We'd better clear-out from here if we don't want our balls and dingles turned inside-out and upside down! Holy shit, Reverend Bill! And our genitals will possibly be ripped and detached from our very tender abdomens! The Jerk-off's fighting mad, just like a corpulent bull elephant in heat! Fuckin' fighting mad, I say!"

"Good Heavens!" Vicar Bunting exclaimed, and then hesitating, the revered minister considered two horrible alternatives. The cowardly church administrator decided to escape humiliation by clambering out of the open window, and after successfully achieving his objective, Vicar William adjusted hastily his new-found flimsy and transparent costume, and managed to awkwardly flee up the village lane as fast as his short little legs would transport his tired frame.

From the moment when the Invisible Man had screamed with spine-tingling rage, and also precisely the same time when Vicar Bunting had made his memorable two-block flight up to the village church and vicarage, it became impossible to give a more accurate account of the evolving affairs in Iping on that Whit Monday evening.

Possibly the Invisible Man's original intention was simply to cover Tom Marvel's retreat with the purloined clothes and books. But his temper, at no time very good, seemed to have gone completely bonkers at receiving some chance blow or minor disappointment, and thereafter, the renegade rogue was eager to set to smiting and overthrowing his assumed enemies, simply for the mere satisfaction of hurting closed-minded, narrow-thinking Christian churchgoers and chronic, self-indulgent alcoholics.

The Invisible Man had developed an occupation of amusing himself by destructively breaking all the window panes inside the hallmark "Coach and Horses", and then the anonymous Impostor thrust a loose street lamp through the parlor window of Mrs. Gribble, the ladies' militant civil rights and suffrage libertarian.

I can't precisely or exactly remember, but the" Unseen Fanatic" must have maliciously sliced the telegraph wires, with some stolen cutlery obtained from the inn parlor, with the essential line going into Adderdean, just beyond Higgins' cottage on the unpaved Adderdean Road. And after that marvelous vandalism had been rather professionally enacted, as was his liberty to do so, the Invisible Man left Iping to the local historians' preposterous documentation. And as a result of *his* classic misadventures in pedestrian Iping, he absolutely and intentionally has vanished from *that* ass-backwards hellhole village forever.

Chapter 13

"MR. MARVEL AGAIN"

After the nocturnal dusk had been gathering and Iping was preparing for the next annual Community Bank Holiday, a short, thick-set man, sporting a shabby silk hat, was painfully marching through the twilight behind the picturesque beechwoods on the narrow road to Bramblehurst Station. The commonplace individual was carrying three books bound together by some sort of ornamental elastic ligature, accompanying a bundle, all the pilfered items wrapped inside a blue table-cloth obtained from the Coach and Horses parlor room.

The young fellow's rubicund face expressed certain characteristics of consternation and fatigue, and there, during his rapturous ramble, the *pedestrian* pedestrian appeared to be in a spasmodic sort of hurry. The mobile anatomy was accompanied by a Voice other than his own, and ever and again, the ambler winced under the touch of unseen, prodding hands.

"Lord, Mr. Marvel. If you give me the slip again," the Voice threatened the hiker, "if you ever attempt to give me the slip again, I'll crucify you twice without a fuckin' cross."

"Lord!" Mr. Marvel exclaimed. "You ain't no Lord Jesus, ya' know. That shoulder of mine consists of a mass of bruises as it is, but I didn't receive these nasty wounds nailed to a wooden cross in Jerusalem. I received these fucked-up wounds in Iping!"

"On my fraudulent honor," the Unseen Voice vowed and promised. "I'll kill you if necessary. My will in that regard is both omnipotent and omniscient."

"I didn't try to give you the 'slip'," Thomas Marvel stated, "because I believe that you ain't no damned fair-pussy female that needs one underneath your dress. I swear I didn't mean to offend you in any fucked-up way. I didn't know the blessed road turning on best how to leave the inn's property, that was all!" Mr. Marvel maintained. "How the devil was I to know the blessed proper route and how to get out of that hick town quick? As it is, thanks to your un-benign influence, I've been knocked about. How come you told me how to get into Iping, but not how the hell to get out of that pathetic dipshit hellhole?"

"You'll get knocked about a great deal less than you did back in Iping if you don't mind becoming an adult and strictly obey my important military instructions," the superior Voice corrected.

And with *that* wonderful chastisement being verbalized, Mr. Thomas Marvel abruptly became silent. The humiliated lad blew-out his cheeks, and his downtrodden eyes were reduced to advanced despair.

"It's bad enough to let these floundering yokels discover, explode and reveal my ultra-complex Invisible Man secret, without *your* cutting-off my books with conspiratorial intentions of selling *my* arcane knowledge to a greedy local publisher," the Invisible Man argued and accused. "It's lucky for some of those Iping bumpkins that the doltish imbeciles cut and ran from my superior powers when they did! Here am I, Mr. Marvel. No one there ever knew the dynamic potency of me being fabulously invisible! And now, Tom, what the hell am I to do? Only you, and you alone, are meritorious of comprehending *that* very remote fact."

"What am *I* to do about what?" Thomas Marvel innocently asked. "Should I be your traitor to England? You've already fucked-up my heart; contaminated my body, and corrupted my soul."

"Tom, I am both your mentor and your tormentor. In a nutshell, it's all about the Iping gossip mill. Soon, other hillbilly towns and villages in Sussex County will catch-on to my stellar activities, well actually, *our* stellar activities, and report our misadventure in Iping as important eyewitness news," the Invisible Man lectured to Mr. Marvel. "Our escape escapade will be in all the tabloid propaganda papers from London up to Manchester! Every fascinated asshole citizen, and every badged law enforcement shithead will be out looking for me, and also, for you; you got to understand that both you and me are now fugitives from societal slave justice; we're on the lam without the Iping Vicar being our shepherd, and we aren't part of the archbishop's asshole flock, either; everyone will be on their guard, even those bear hat sentinels standing at attention outsider Buckingham Palace." The frightening Voice then broke-off into vociferating vivid curses and after five-minutes of diatribe, ceased speaking.

The despair that had been welded upon Mr. Marvel's face was genuine melancholy, and the lad's energy level had seriously diminished, and his pace greatly slackened. Looking at the hopping peewit birds, at the crows and the scavenging flying buzzards circling overhead, Tom Marvel realized something significant. His small place in the vast Universe.

"Holy shit, Mr. Voice. I get it now. We're all part of a gigantic pecking order, and it all involves people and their connections, and you and me are perched on the lowest level of the fuckin' social food chain."

"Go on, Tom! Keep thinking and growing until you eventually reach and rival *my* elevated plateau!" the knowledgeable Voice urged. "What you've just said Mr. Marvel is only partially true. But your analysis has left-out one vital key truth. I have the power to be invisible, and none of those assholes out in society, including you, Tom, don't! And whatever you do, don't drop those highly cherished books. Just pretend that you're the sacred tabernacle inside the archbishop's cathedral, wholly responsible for keeping your host's Bible safe and sound inside your sanctuary. As God the Father had instructed Abraham, 'Never alter your altar'! Ha, ha, ha! What a fuckin' ham was that Biblical Abra*ham,* ha, ha, ha!"

Mr. Marvel's face soon assumed a greyish tint, showing between the ruddier patches. "Why the heck do I have to carry your damned heavy books all over creation, inside your damned even-heavier bundle?" Tom Marvel insisted. "They're *your* damned books and not mine. I wish this here first book I'm lugging was a Bible. If you, Mr. Voice, had the supreme power to turn the Old and New Testaments into liquid water, you would then make me sick in my stomach by having me imbibe the fuckin' liquid Bible."

"The fact is," the insulted Voice defensively retorted, "I shall have to make decent use of you and your services. We all have our liabilities and frail traits, Tom Marvel. Right now, you're but a poor tool, a common instrument like a comb or a screwdriver, but for my own protection and security, I must sagaciously manipulate and exploit your strengths and limit your mental weaknesses."

"I'm a *miserable* tool," Marvel complained. "If I start crying massive tears, would I then be a 'tool shed'?"

"Forget a tool shed, you' immature fool," the Voice lividly rankled. "If you listen to my indisputable brilliance and authority, you'll quickly develop into a majestic tool warehouse!"

'You should've been a common steer with all the bullshit you send in my direction," Marvel complained and grieved. "In fact, I do believe that I'd have a happier existence as a cow, a horse, or a sheep."

"The next village we visit, go into the hardware store and get a grip," the Voice lividly advised. "Yes, Tom. Your first lesson in escaping the bottom of the pecking order food chain is that you must learn how to first get a grip."

"I'm the worst possible tool you could ever have," Mr. Marvel articulated. "And I ain't 'toolin' around, either! And I ain't strong and invisible like you are. Only the odors from my arm pits, from my crotch, and from my toes are strong, and nothin' fuckin' else."

"My leadership will gradually make you strong and potent," the powerful Voice pledged. "Follow my fabulous example, Tom, and I'll make you an international sensation like Genghis Khan, like Alexander the Great, like Julius Caesar, like Aaron Burr, and just like Napoleon Bonaparte."

"And Mr. Voice, my damned heart is pathetically weak. That little business fiasco we had at the Coach and Horses Inn, well Mr. Voice, I was lucky I managed to pull through it all. Thanks to you, I nearly became decapitated by the insane mob, but if I had dropped your precious books, then *you* would've decapitated me, instead. I really don't know who or what is more dangerous; the fuckin' incensed mob, or fuckin' irate, vindictive you and your need for vengeance!"

"Have no fear, Tom Marvel. If you falter, I shall stimulate you! Remember always, dear Tom. Anger is only one letter short of danger."

"I don't need you to jerk me off. Quite frankly, I can work my stick all my myself!" Marvel rankled. "I've survived doing hardly anything before I have to toil like a slave being your stupid comrade."

"If indeed you are a jerk-off, you're merely a junior jerk-off at best!" the Voice asserted and then guffawed. "Keep listening to your own self and not to me, and the next thing you'll know, you'll be growing tits and breast-feeding future assholes juvenile delinquents over in backwoods Iping."

"I wish you wouldn't torment me so. I wouldn't like to mess up your plans, you know, even if you was a moron architect designing blue prints for my fucked-up future. But I might someday build an enormous house designed by you, and out of sheer funk and misery, find luckily fresh boots in my closet!"

"You'd better not try anything on your own without my personal consent and approval," the transcendent Voice communicated with quiet emphasis. "I think that you're already getting too big for your britches. Just remember one thing, Tom Marvel. Until you master how to become wonderfully invisible like me, your destiny is to *vanish* from ever becoming an important personage on this fucked-up planet. That fantastic propensity, Thomas Marvel, is the one tremendous advantage that I myself possess, which transcends all human civilization, and also transcends all major political and economic pursuits."

"I wish I was dead," Marvel intimated and lamented. "Maybe I could go to Palestine and commit suicide by drowning in the fuckin' Dead Sea; or perhaps journey to California, and successfully perish in Death Valley."

"Oh! *shut the fuck-up!*" the Voice angrily scolded the young apostate. "You, Tom Marvel, make more damned sense when you fart than when you speak. I'll see to building-up your social and mental development, all right. But until you improve your poor financial and social situations, you must do what you're told. You'll do it all right. You're a fool and all that, but you'll do it for two reasons: number one: you'll want to learn new things like how to become invisible like me, which over the years, I shall teach you. And number two: only I, your most spectacular Voice and sole companion, can instruct you on how to ascend, and then transcend, the lowbrow type of assholes that infect and populate Iping village and vicinity."

"I tell you, sir, I'm not the man for the job. I'm just not up to snuff. Respectfully—but it *is* so—"

"If you don't shut the fuck up, I'll severely twist your wrist again and again until your fingers fall off, and then I'll advance to tangling you bouncing balls into a double knot. It's all very elementary, Mr. Marvel. No pain, no gain!"

As the incompatible pair trekked onward, presently two oblongs of yellow light appeared through the oak trees, and the square tower of a distant church loomed through the celestial gloam. "I shall keep my hand upon your shoulder," the Voice sternly indicated. "All through the next village, I shall be your guiding light. Go straight through and try no deviant foolery, Tom. It will be the worse for you if you ever attempt any contempt."

"I know *that* consequence as basic fact from me being exposed to a day's bad experiences with you," Mr. Marvel disclosed and then deeply sighed. "I know all that lousy bullshit you're now describin' all-too-well."

The unhappy-looking figure in the obsolete silk hat passed up the street of the little village with his burdens crammed inside Mrs. Hall's lackluster tablecloth sack, and the pair of itinerant vagabonds soon vanished into the wilderness beyond the lights that were reflecting out of the local house's closed windows.

Chapter 14

"AT PORT STOWE"

Ten o'clock the next morning found Mr. Thomas Marvel, unshaven, dirty, and travel-stained, sitting with the three indecipherable notebooks beside him, with his grimy hands deep inside his pockets, looking very weary, nervous, and uncomfortable. The Invisible Man's singular assistant was inflating his cheeks at infrequent intervals, while the chosen apprentice aimlessly had been lazily sitting on a bench outside a little inn in downtown Port Stowe.

Lying beside the hobo-rascal were the three arcane books that had been authored in cryptic symbols and obscure math formulas by the resourceful Invisible Man, but now the three separate volumes had been tied together with taut string, which the savant Voice had taught Tom to deftly do. Outside Iping, the bundle had been abandoned and hidden in the pine-woods beyond Bramblehurst Station, in accordance with a change in plans of the Invisible Man, that is, before it had been retrieved to take to rural Port Stowe.

Lackadaisical Mr. Thomas Marvel sat comfortably on the rickety bench, and although no one took the slightest notice of his mediocre existence, the young rogue's agitation remained at fever heat. Tom's hands would go ever and again to his various pockets with a curious nervous fumbling that reflected his general insecurity.

When the Voice's apprentice had been sitting idle for the best part of an hour, however, an elderly mariner, carrying a morning newspaper, came-out of the Blue Boar Inn and sat-down beside the idle dreamer. "Pleasant day," the friendly mariner commenced. "You' new here in town?"

Mr. Marvel glanced about him with something akin to very culminating terror. "Very," the nervous assistant answered. "Yeah, I suppose I'm a newbie."

"Just seasonable weather for this time of year," the mariner remarked, taking no denial. "Can't wait until the next big blizzard to break this dumb-ass warm weather monotony."

"Quite maybe," Mr. Marvel tersely and succinctly declared. "That depends on whether weather is really weather, whether or not," Tom smartly replied with a cute play-on-words. "Yes, do I believe you ain't that ancient mariner I read about at school, aren't ya'? That fucked-up poem, if I recall, had no certain rhyme nor reason, but no special reason to its rhyme, either!"

"Oh yes," the old salt acknowledged. *"The Rime of the Ancient Mariner* was indeed a classic poem during American colonial times."

"That classic made the entire class sick!" jested Tom. "I remember vomiting on Susie Thompson's hair. The bitch was sitting in the desk in front of me in the row, so she stood-up and tossed a whole bottle of black ink flat smack into my face."

Ignoring Tom's propensity for frivolity, the mariner produced a huge toothpick, and soon became engrossed in cleaning his three remaining teeth, thereby saying nothing for several minutes.

Meanwhile, the alert sailor's eyes were at liberty to examine Mr. Marvel's scruffy-looking, dusty figure, and also began scrutinizing the odd books lying beside the Voice's principal helper. When the Old Salt had recently approached Mr. Marvel's bench location, the mariner had heard a sound analogous to the dropping of coins into a pants pocket. The greedy old bastard was struck by the contrast of Mr. Marvel's appearance with this new suggestion of his targeted mark being wealthy and possessing a fine degree of opulence and prosperity. Hence, the old fart's mind had wandered back again to a topic that had taken a curiously firm hold upon *his* frenzied imagination.

"Books?" the interested geezer asked, suddenly noisily finishing with adjusting his trademark toothpick, massaging the gaping cavities between his three teeth.

Mr. Marvel looked-down at the three wrapped texts still upon the bench. "Oh, yes," the Voice's sole aide confirmed. "Yes, they're books, alright, but not gotten from any damned public or school library. I owe no fines on any of the three."

"There's some extra-ordinary things mentioned in books," the knowledgeable mariner elucidated. "And my fifth cousin from Croydon is now a gambling sports bookie in Bristol, and he's doin' mighty well!"

"I believe you," Mr. Marvel replied. "But I'm quite gullible, especially when I see ocean birds flying. I even believe some incredible shit that's printed in the Koran."

"And people of all ilk obtain some extra-ordinary things out of reading quality literature, both fiction and non-fiction," the ancient mariner elaborated.

"True, likewise," Mr. Marvel nervously concurred. The Voice's new recruit closely eyed his interlocutor, and then glanced all about downtown Port Stowe. "Even folks and illiterate assholes livin' over in 'Reading' are 'reading' books all the friggin' time."

"There's some extra-ordinary things in newspapers, too, for example," the nosey sailor claimed, just to continue his flimsy get-acquainted narrative.

"Newspapers are propaganda instruments that keep the establishment in power," Mr. Marvel advocated, quoting the Voice's attitude, word for word. "Actually, the big city tabloids are extremely anti-intellectual, and are also of a mediocre nature in terms of providing literary quality. The city corporate press engenders and supports rudimentary language existing on a fourth-grade level. Their purpose is to dumb-down the public, thinking that the citizens can more easily be controlled and managed if they're all stupid."

"You're a pretty smart fellow," the sailor praised and commended.

"Thanks, Admiral. I have a very fond country teacher who has taught me all that I don't know!"

"Very interesting observation, my young man," the avid old fart favorably complimented. "You must have an excellent private 'tutor'. There's a story this morning in the local gazette," the mariner cited, fixing Mr. Marvel with an eye that was firm and deliberate. "Yes, there's a front-page story about an incredible Invisible Man."

Mr. Marvel pulled his mouth askew, scratched his cheek, and instantaneously felt his ears glowing. "I ain't got no tutor, but I learned in school that Henry the VIII was once a damned 'Tudor', and when the fat slob was a young boy, he had called his horn a 'tooter'. He also called his long hard farts 'tooters', too. What will the periodicals be writing about next?" the wise-ass Voice's apprentice asked quite faintly-but-defensively.

"When I say *here*," said the mariner, to Mr. Marvel's intense relief, "I don't of course mean here in this place. Instead, I mean hereabouts in this here area, right in the center of village Port Stowe."

"An Invisible Man!" Mr. Tom Marvel hooted, feigning excessive surprise and astonishment. "And what's *he* been up to? I presume around five-foot-eleven, I imagine."

"Everything," said the mariner, controlling Marvel with his open right eye, and then amplifying his stare. "Every blessed and unholy thing your' pea brain can ever reckon, well, that's the Invisible Man's prime bailiwick."

"I ain't seen a newspaper these last four days," Marvel admitted and convincingly fibbed. "Not even any written or recklessly printed by those barbarian Inka Indians down somewhere in South America."

"Nearby, over in Iping, is the exact place where the Invisible Man started implementin' his depravity like a poisonous gas vapor," the garrulous mariner informed Marvel. "The unpredictable Jerk amazingly disappeared several times amongst various reliable witnesses, and who the hell knows where the hell he happens to be right this minute. The crafty son-of-a-bitch might've strayed all the way here to Port Stowe. No one really ever knows, except for Satan, because the devil's always in the details."

"In-*deed!*" Mr. Thomas Marvel verified. "This elusive character you're describin' must be more slippery than an Arctic glacier. Without knowin' any special details about his activities, I'll bet that *your* Invisible Man sleeps under a blanket of snow, and often lies on a sheet of ice."

"He started there, as a novice in Iping," the arthritic sailor explained. "And where the menace came from, nobody in authority seems to know. Here is the headline in my hands: 'Peculiar Story from Iping'. And it says in this local-yokel rag that the evidence is extra-ordinary strong, yes, extra-ordinary strong horse manure."

"Lord!" Mr. Marvel marveled. "Simply outrageously marvelous! I hope that *that* formidable vanishing asshole never makes it here to Port Stowe."

"But then, it's quite an extraordinary story that's circulatin'," the mariner proceeded with his official analysis. "There is a clergyman and a medical gent over in Iping who are regarded as reliable witnesses, and who both saw the villain, or should I say 'criminal', all right and proper, performing his destructive misdeeds all over the fuckin' primitive village. This Invisible Fella' was staying there, it says, at a place called the 'Coach and Horses', and no one there had been 'aware of his string of terrible misfortunes. The article *says* that people over in Iping were generally aware of his various misfortunes, until during a violent altercation, both happening at and in the inn, his bandages on top of his hands, his face, and his head were torn off."

"Articles don't say anything," Marvel corrected. "Newspapers don't know how to speak fuckin' words. Who are ya' tryin' to bullshit? Newspapers don't talk!"

Unperturbed by Mr. Marvel's most excellent oral resistance, in defense of mediocre journalism, the adamant sailor resumed his annoying description and impertinent opposition. "It was then observed that his whole head was totally invisible. Attempts were at once made to secure his arrest, but casting off his garments, it says in the newspaper, the evasive phantom succeeded in escaping, but not until after a desperate struggle had ensued, in which the aggravated Invisible Man had inflicted many serious injuries, it says, especially on the village's worthy and able constable, Mr. B. A. Jaffers."

"Sounds like a perfectly credible story to me!" Tom Marvel blandly answered the naughty nautical speaker. "Almost as credible as Mother Goose!"

"Yeah; pretty straight story, eh? Names and everything. And the most fascinatin' detail is that several of the town brawlers pulled off the Invisible Man's nose, ears and pecker, and the wily wizard somehow picked those organs up off the ground and put them right back in their regular invisible places."

"Lord!" Mr. Marvel exclaimed, looking nervously all about his physical environment, trying to count the money in his pockets by his unaided sense of touch, and then grappling with his cerebrum that was full of strange and novel ideas. "Yes, your sensational story sounds most-astonishing, sir pirate."

"Don't it, though? Extra-ordinary; that's what *I* call it," the Old Salt continued. "Never heard tell of any indigenous Invisible Man before; perhaps a Martian or two. I haven't ever seen one in all my hundred-and-twenty-seven years, probably because it's hard to see an Invisible Man anywhere, except maybe in fucked-up Iping. But nowadays, Junior, one hears such a lot of exaggeratin', extra-ordinary chickenshit things—that—"

"That's all he did? This so-called Invisible Man; that's all he did over in Iping?" Marvel requested clarification, trying to seem more at ease about discussing the touchy and delicate subject.

"It's enough to contemplate and attempt to mentally process, ain't it?" the somewhat-superstitious mariner opined. "Imagine that. This Invisible Man culprit, or whatever the hell he is, probably drives his horse and buggy home each night, and then magically turns into his street. I vouch that this all-powerful fellow must have a couple of oracles inside his heart's auricles."

"He didn't have any pals to comfort him over in Iping, and the poor soul probably doesn't need any fucked-up Iping pals, either. It don't say anywhere in the false newspaper story that the human-ghost had any friends at all, does it?" Mr. Marvel rather apprehensively asked. "To tell you the unvarnished truth, I wouldn't dare even bein' remotely acquainted with the raunchy Bastard until I really got to know and trust him."

"Ain't one of a sort enough for you?" asked the doubtful mariner. "No, thank Heaven, as one might say, he didn't share his ideas with anybody over there in lousy Iping."

The obstinate storytelling/sailor was not significantly affected by Mr. Marvel's juvenile responses, and hence, carried-on with his illustrious narrative. "Makes me regular uncomfortable, the bare thought of that dangerous Chap running about the country on the lam! Presently, the toxic scamp supposedly is wanderin' the countryside at large, and from certain evidence and vague regional reports, it is conjectured that the heinous scoundrel might be headin' right here to Port Stowe."

"Well then, we don't have to worry about nothin'," Mr. Thomas Marvel lucidly commented, because neither you nor me are acquainted with this fucked-up, evil Invisible Man desperado. We can fully trust each other now, because actually, we don't know the nefarious Bastard's whereabouts."

"Just think of all the destructive things the Psycho Felon might do!" the concerned sailor suggested. "Where'd you be, if he ripped your neck off your shoulders, or had a sudden fancy to go for your testicles? Suppose he wants to rob your wallet, I mean, who the hell can prevent him? That nasty fugitive can trespass; he can burgle; he could walk through a cordon of policemen as easy as me or you could give the slip to a blind man! Yes, much easier as a matter of fact! For those here fifty-seven blind chaps stayin' here in Port Stowe at the downtown eyesight clinic, for example, each one could be an easy victim for that lunatic Invisible Man to swindle and molest."

"He's got a tremendous advantage, most certainly," Mr. Marvel declared. "And this magical mage could even furtively steal all the tennis balls from the gangster Mafia racketeers over in Wimbledon!"

"You're right," echoed the amenable mariner. "I'll bet he'll eventually get around to performin' *that* illegal fraudulent mischief by the end of summer."

All that particular time, Mr. Marvel had been glancing about his area rather intently, listening for faint footfalls, and keenly trying to detect any and all imperceptible and unusual movements. The increasingly perturbed lad seemed to be arriving at the point of some great resolution. Tom coughed behind his hand to awkwardly disguise his imagined guilt pertaining to his recent direct association with the amazing Invisible Man, along with *his* inexplicable influential Unseen Voice.

Tom was now widely convinced that the Old Salt, still seated next to him, would be a reliable friend and ally. So, the young yokel looked about his area again, listened, bent towards the mariner's ear, and lowered his voice: "The fact of it is, old man, that I happen to know just a thing or two about this elusive Invisible Man."

"Oh!" exclaimed the mariner, very interested. *"You' say you do know?"*

"Yes," said Mr. Marvel. "Me. I know his methods."

"Indeed!" the stunned mariner answered. "And may I ask that you should remarkably tell me your incredible fiction. I know a publisher in London who might be interested in organizing your tale into a terrific novel. It could be a best seller on the children's fable list."

"The fact is," Mr. Marvel declared, eagerly shifting into a contrived confidential undertone. Suddenly, the speaker's expression and his rising excitement marvelously changed. "Ow!" Tom yelped. The lad rose stiffly from his bench seat. Mr. Marvel's face was showing high amounts of physical and emotional duress. "Wow!" Mr. Marvel again whooped.

"What's up?" asked the startled mariner, apparently very concerned. "You havin' a wicked hemorrhoid attack? I hope ya' don't fart those nasty suckers right-out of your swollen ass and then bleed to death! I mean, swollen hemorrhoids are not too swell!"

"Toothache," Mr. Marvel prevaricated, pointing to his mouth, and next putting his hand up to his ear to demonstrate the sensation of heightened pain. Feeling too interrogated by the old sailor's oral probing, Tom caught hold of his entrusted books. "I must be getting along now, I think," the Voice's Apprentice conveyed to his audience of one, attempting to politely excuse himself. Finally, young Marvel edged in a curious way along the wooden seat, slowly moving-away from his bothersome interlocutor.

"But you *was* just a-going to tell me all about this here ridiculous fella', that itinerant Invisible Man!" the disappointed mariner protested. But Mr. Marvel seemed to consult with his inner self and heard a familiar Voice verbalize, "Hoax! It's a hoax," Mr. Marvel repeated his prompt received from the Invisible Man's current near-ear telepathy.

"But it's in the morning paper," the mariner yelled, refusing to terminate the Port Stowe bench conversation. "It's all just gotta' be true as the Bible! Just like the reverse headline news that sells papers over in London with the valid headline, 'Man bites dog'."

"Hoax, all the same," Marvel adamantly insisted. "I personally know the deceiving chap that started the abominable lie. Fact is, there ain't no Invisible Man whatsoever. Callow bullshit, that local malarkey is!"

"But how about this newspaper story? Do you mean to say—?"

"Not a word of it is accurate," Mr. Tom Marvel stoutly hollered in anger. "Total monkey crap, and not even amounting to gorilla turds invented by a conniving reporter!"

The perplexed mariner stared, newspaper in hand, his affected mind questioning the authenticity of both big city and small-town tabloid news. Mr. Thomas Marvel jerkily faced about, and then casually munched on a mouthful of beef jerky.

"Wait a bit," the ancient mariner pleaded. "Then why the hell did you let me go on for ten-minutes and tell you all this blasted Invisible Man stuff? What do ya' mean by letting a good, loyal former seaman make a fool of himself like that? Eh?"

"Well now, Mr. Seaman. I do believe that at your ripe old age, you fuckin' need more 'semen' in your shriveled-up testicles in order that you can think better," Tom, inspired by lectures and lessons taught by the omniscient Voice, orally related. "It seems, Captain Ahab, that you need to have some sort of 'seminal' moment! I mean, you oughta' sail your rowboat across the Atlantic to Florida and confer with the damned 'Seminoles' about the disingenuous aspects of lying big city newspapers!"

Mr. Marvel again blew-out his blue cheeks. Contrary to *that* act of blatant defiance occurring, the hoary mariner was suddenly very red-faced indeed; then the Old Salt clenched his hands. "I been talking here like an idiot these last ten-minutes," the ocean-voyaging veteran blustered. "And you, you little pot-bellied, leathery-faced son of an old boot, couldn't have the elementary manners—"

"Nice try there, Mr. Ancient Mariner," Tom Marvel wonderfully chided. "I think ya' gotta' change your formal name to Al Batross! Ha, ha, ha!"

"What's ya' mean Sonny? Where did you learn all of this preposterous shit? Who's your fuckin' master?"

"I'm not sayin' or revealin'," Tom hollered back. "One thing's for damned sure. It's not that fucked-up Invisible Man who's instructin' me. Instead, it's a queer Voice that puts all of this academic bullshit into my receptive skull. I've learned all this heavy pedagogue balderdash without even ever setting a blessed foot into either Oxford or Cambridge."

"Come up," commanded a Voice, and Mr. Marvel was suddenly whirled about into the air like a miniature human cyclone, and the lad started marching in the thin space parallel to the Port Stowe business stores, in a most curious and spasmodic manner. "You'd better move on," the aged mariner encouraged and yelled. "I hope you don't 'fall', at least not until autumn!"

"Watch out for the Invisible Man!" Tom Marvel screamed to the raunchy Old Salt from his apparent six-foot-high, high-flying elevation.

"What the fuck's happenin'?" the old barnacle shouted-up to the soaring anti-gravity youth. "I gotta' get the hell off the booze wagon before I can get the spirit's puzzle straightened-out in my shrinkin' brain."

"See ya' later, Agitator!" Thomas Marvel shouted-down to the now-traumatized old mariner, with the flying apprentice having both hands cupped over his mouth, as if the erratic imbecile were screaming into, and through, a regular college cheerleader's megaphone.

Jay Dubya

Chapter 15

"THE MAN WHO WAS RUNNING"

In the early evening, Dr. Kemp was calmly sitting in his study in the upstairs belvedere window room facing the inclined hill overlooking Port Burdock. It was a pleasant little room, with three windows: north, west, and south, and shelves were covered with textbooks and advanced scientific publications. A broad expensive writing-table was situated below the westside window, and under the north window, a microscope, several glass slips, minute specialized instruments, some recently-obtained skin and blood cultures, along with scattered bottles of reagents, were strewn about.

Dr. Kemp's solar lamp was brightly lit, albeit the sky was still bright, with the sunset's remaining illumination evident on the lower horizon. And the respectable Professor's blinds were, as regular, raised-up because there were never any snooping Peeping Toms peering inside his cozy residence, spying upon the reputable chemist/researcher's valued privacy.

Dr. Kemp was a tall and slender young man, with flaxen hair, and his countenance featured a curved moustache, almost entirely white, and the essence of his noble labor was financed by a fine endowment from the local university. Indeed, the ambitious drug and blood experimenter hoped that the greatly-desired fellowship to the Royal Society would be granted soon, so highly did the renowned young scientist pursue *that* rather lofty, academic recognition.

Presently wandering from his designated important work, the researcher stopped and momentarily perceived the majestic sunset blazing at the back of the Sussex County hill. For a minute perhaps, the preoccupied chemist sat, with pen in mouth, admiring the rich golden color shining above the ridge's crest, and then his attention had been attracted to a rapidly approaching running figure.

A portly little man, with inky-black hair, had been futilely zipping over the hill-brow in the direction of Dr. Kemp's secluded residence. The beleaguered sprinter was a rather shortish Englishman, and the odd fellow was wearing a high hat, and was scampering so fast up the incline that his legs verily twinkled.

'Another of those damned drunken fools,' Dr. Kemp thought and evaluated. 'Morons of *his* ilk never contribute anything valuable towards the betterment of society. They're mostly pathetic drunks and detrimental parasites living off the government dole,' Dr. Kemp further assessed. 'Like that dumb-ass who ran into me this morning around the downtown corner, screaming like a goddamned psycho maniac the sensational phraseology 'Watch out! Be safe! Invisible Man a-coming, sir!' I can't imagine what possesses people to fly off the handle and behave like primitive cavemen. One might think we're still ignorant medieval alchemists and surfs living in the damned ninth century.'

Dr. Kemp quickly rose from his cherished red leather chair, hastily stepped to the belvedere room's best window, stared-out at the dusky hillside, and closely scrutinized the 'amusing dark little figure' tearing his escape route down the steep slope. 'The fool seems to be in a confounded hurry,' the scientist imagined as he lit his favorite pipe. 'But the absurd ignoramus doesn't seem to be making good progress towards the town. If his pockets were full of lead, he couldn't run heavier.'

In another moment, the higher country villas that had been constructed upon the rolling hills, just outside Burdock, had temporarily occulted the running figure from Dr. Kemp's elevated window view. The curious sprinter soon was visible again, but only for a moment, and again, and then again, appearing three times between the three detached houses that had been built next to each other in a straight line upon the ridge, and then, the remaining hillside terrace shadows again hid the runners forward progress.

'Asses! Dumb cretin asshole!' Dr. Kemp judged and laughed, swinging around on his heels and walking back to his treasured writing-table.

But those others in the neighborhood who had noticed the frantic fugitive at a much nearer vantage point, and who had perceived the abject terror evident upon the desperate fleer's perspiring face, being themselves in the open roadway, felt a great sympathy for the frenzied sprinter, and did not share either the doctor's instinctive contempt, nor his excessive criticism.

As the intimidated fellow frenetically ran ahead, a sack of heavy coins chinked at his side like a well-filled purse that was being tossed repeatedly and rhythmically impacting against a solid wall. The vastly-frightened runner looked neither to the right nor to the left, but his dilated eyes stared only straight downhill to where the town's night lamps were being lit, and the residents were crowded, casually strolling in the busy street.

'If properly educated, that nutjob jerk running on the hill might think he's a contemporary Phidippides doing a classic marathon from Thermopylae to ancient Athens,' the eminent scientist thought and smiled. 'And I'll bet that saliva is dripping from his nose in a similar manner to my Port Stowe cousin's hundred-and-fifty-pound mastiff's mouth always does. I'll wager that there's a good amount of mucus leaking from *his* nostrils, too!'

All those bystanders that the petrified runner had passed, stopped in wonder at his approach, and the trekkers began staring-up the road and down, and neighbors commenced interrogating one another with an inkling of discomfort for the specific reason of *his* haste and fright.

And then presently, far up the hill, a mongrel dog playing in the road yelped and ran under a protective gate, and as the appalled spectators still wondered about the weird circumstances that were responsible for the fellow's heightened apprehension, something like a gusty wind blowing, and a constant pad, pad, pad sound, analogous to desperate deep panting and labored breathing, were speedily rushing by the many horrified bystanders.

People screamed and many of them yelled vulgar rhetoric directed at the scared-shitless running stranger. Other concerned folks found it necessary to spring off the pavement in order to avoid being knocked-down in a hard collision.

Petrified Tom Marvel was now halfway to the town center. The shocked Burdock residents, failing to comprehend the exact reason for the short man's excessive horror, hastily entered their own homes, and others also dashed into the safety of friends' houses, but everyone immediately bolted all exit doors, and next securely double-locked each and every one.

"The Invisible Man is coming! The Invisible Man is coming this way!" the terrified courier shouted. "No one will be safe! I repeat! Absolutely no one!"

"What the hell is going on out there?" Dr. Kemp asked the window frame. "It's a veritable Sodom and Gomorrah out there without the blazing fire and raining brimstone!"

Chapter 16

"IN THE JOLLY CRICKETS"

The "Jolly Crickets" is situated just at the bottom of the hill in Port Burdock, right where the tram-lines begin loading their daily passengers. The barman leant his fat red arms upon the counter and talked of horse breeds with an anemic cabman, while a black-bearded man, dressed in grey, snapped-up a biscuit and cheese snack, drank a double bourbon, and conversed in American English with an affable off-duty village policeman.

"What's all that obnoxious shouting about out there!" the anemic cabman shrieked, going off at a tangent, trying to see up the hill over the dirty yellow blind inside the low window of the popular Jolly Crickets Inn.

"Some crazy fuck just sped by outside in sheer haste. Fire, perhaps," the barman surmised and related. "It's big news around here whenever some drunken asshole runs down the street for no friggin' reason at all. I mean, thank goodness we don't work in London, or else we'd have to get off our dumpy asses at least once a day, and do something like breaking-up a minor fight."

Footsteps were heard approaching, and then the sound of a person fleeing or running heavily was again discerned. The Jolly Crickets' front door was violently pushed-open, and inside rushed Mr. Thomas Marvel, weeping, flustered, disheveled, and heavily perspiring. The sprinter's signature hat was missing from atop his cranium, and the neck of his coat torn wide open. The young fellow made a convulsive right turn detour, and strenuously attempted shutting the front door, but it was being kept half-open by a thick leather strap.

"Coming!" Marvel frantically bawled, with his childish high-pitched voice shrieking with great terror. "He's coming. The Invisible Man! Coming like a dozen insane maniacs after me! For God's sake! Somebody! Anybody! Help me! Help! Help!"

"Shut the fuckin' doors!" the hefty off-duty policeman sternly commanded. "Who the hell is coming? What's the row?" The off-duty constable approached and grabbed the door, released the strap, and then it slammed shut. The burly American, grasping the situation, simultaneously closed the other entrance door.

"Let me stay safe inside," Mr. Marvel begged, staggering and weeping, but still clutching the three secret knowledge books. "Please let me stay safely inside. Lock me in somewhere so that I can remain protected with my ass, throat and nuts still attached. I tell you he's after me with a vengeance. I gave him the slip, and then the crazy Bastard promised he'd kill me as if I'm a fuckin' dirty cockroach, and I do believe that the fanatical Son-of-a-Bitch will keep his promise."

"*You're* perfectly safe from harm now," the burly American with the black beard, a former professional wrestling star, confidently declared. "The door's been shut. What's it all about? Is your gay lover wanting to kill you for deciding to go fuckin' straight, or what?"

"Please let's go deeper inside the building," Marvel begged, and the junior jerk-off then shrieked aloud in horror when a blow from a strong invisible fist suddenly made the fastened door shiver. The powerful thud was soon followed by a hurried rapping and a loud shouting originating from outside.

"Hello!" the rattled policeman yelled. "Who the hell's out there?" Unfamiliar with the layout of the Jolly Crickets Bar, Mr. Thomas Marvel, feeling exceptionally terrorized, began making frantic dives at walnut wall panels that looked like available escape hatches. "He'll kill me; he's got a knife or something else sharp. For God's sake! The Bastard is more dangerous than Guy Fawkes and Jack the Ripper together on a really bad day!"

"Here you are," the bartender greeted Marvel as the Jolly Crickets employee began opening the bar flap. "Come on in back here." And grateful Mr. Marvel ducked-down under the held-up flap, which admitted the terrorized idiot behind the serving counter.

"Don't any of you dare open the damned door," the antagonized moron screamed. "*Please* don't open the damned door. *Where* shall I hide from *his* horrible revenge?"

"Is this the Invisible Man, from Iping then?" the grizzle-bearded tough American inquired, holding one hand behind him, indicating that he was doubting Tom Marvel's 'childish false testimony'. "I guess it's about time we saw this phantom murderer face to face."

The Jolly Crickets front window was suddenly smashed-in, and there was plenty of chaotic screaming and running into the street as multiple patrons evacuated and stampeded from the premises. The constable had been standing on a settee staring-out the now-shattered glass, craning his neck to observe who or what had been causing such great havoc at the door. The off-duty cop got down low with raised eyebrows. "It's that invisible ogre I've read about in the papers."

The barman stood in front of the bar-parlor door, which was now locked. Meanwhile, scared-shitless Mr. Thomas Marvel stared in shock at the smashed window, and nervously came around to join the two other addled-and-concerned men.

Everything inside the bawdy establishment was suddenly quiet. "I wish I had my utilitarian truncheon," the policeman regretfully stated, going irresolutely to the door. "Once we open the portal, and the belligerent fuck comes inside, who the hell knows what will happen in regard to that Invisible Maniac. From what I've read, there's no stopping the Ornery Dolt, I suppose."

"Don't you be in too much of a damned hurry about opening that door," the anemic cabman anxiously insisted. "If I ever get murdered, it better not be by some dumb-ass Invisible Man. I'd want to see who the fuck was killing me!"

"Draw the lock bolts," the impatient American customer with the black beard ordered. "And if he does come inside, I'll have to administer my kind of swift New York justice," the tough patron announced, proudly showing everyone his trusty revolver.

"That won't do," the lily-hearted liberal off-duty policeman challenged. "That's murder that you're suggesting, and it's fuckin' illegal to commit *that* sort of felony in this fine outstanding community."

"I know what country I'm drinking whiskey in," the bearded American argued. "I'm going to blast off at his legs if the hostile Asshole dares to attack me. Draw the bolts, I say. I'm not scared of nothin'. I often use *this* fine weapon to take target practice every afternoon in my Brooklyn neighbor's back yard."

"Not with that blinking thing going off behind me," the apprehensive barman contested, craning over the front blind to peer outside. "If you shoot-off that son-of-a-bitch gun inside this bar, you'll shatter glass from the back mirror, and also from the whiskey bottles arranged on the rear shelf, all over the fuckin' place. It'll look like one of those American Wild, Wild West saloon shootings we read about in the London tabloids."

"Very well," consented the black bearded U.S. ring wrestler, who then shouted expletives outside the front door, inviting and challenging the Invisible Man to enter the Jolly Crickets to "fight like a man".

"Come in," loudly bellowed the bearded man, standing back and facing the unbolted doors.

No one came in through the then-accessible portal, and the front door still remained closed. Five minutes afterwards, a second cabman cautiously pushed his head inside the Jolly Crickets, and an anxious face peered-out of the bar-parlor and supplied the wary and neurotic patrons with insightful and pertinent information.

"Are all the doors of the house shut?" Tom Marvel worriedly asked. "I know his nefarious methods pretty good. The Formidable Fiend's now going around, prowling the property like a bloodhound, just waiting to make his daring move. He's as artful as, and maybe even more tricky than, the devil himself, and I know exactly how the clever fuck thinks and acts. I know for a fact that the Invisible Man reads both homicide and horror books all the fuckin' time!"

"Good Lord!" the burly surly barman exclaimed. "There's also the back entrance to worry about! Just watch them damned doors, too!"

The fearful beer and whiskey tender looked about his full working area rather helplessly. The bar-parlor door again mysteriously slammed, and the petrified Jolly Crickets' regular clientele, along with its almost-paralyzed employees, heard the key turn. "There's also the yard door and the private door," the bartender hollered. "The yard door—"

The three-hundred-pound bartender rushed out of the bar area into the back poker room, and ten seconds later, reappeared, holding a lengthy carving-knife in his right hand. "The yard door was open!" bartender Clarence Figg announced, and then his fat underlip suddenly dropped and trembled.

"The Invisible Man from Iping may be scoping-out the Jolly Crickets right this minute!" the chatty first cabman yelled. "Killers always stalk for days before doing their murder thing!"

"He's not in the kitchen," the barman reported. "There're two old bag whores playing blackjack for money inside there, and I've carefully stabbed every inch of the cook-room with this convenient beef slicer of mine. And the retired bitches don't think he's come in through that rear entrance. They haven't noticed—"

"Have you fastened it?" first cabman asked.

"I'm out of frocks," the barman regretted and answered. 'But I'm sure that my cutlery tool here in my hand will do proper injury to the assailant should he try attacking my ass!"

The bearded American relaxed and placed his revolver inside his shoulder holster. And even as the muscular chap did so, the flap of the bar was swiftly and mystically shut-down, the bolt clicked, and then with a tremendous thud, the door catch snapped, and the Jolly Crickets' bar-parlor door instantly burst wide open.

The traumatized patrons heard Tom Marvel squeal like a caught leveret, and patrons and servers alike were clambering and scrambling all over the bar in order to rescue stalked Tom from being heinously killed by his on-a-mission invisible foe.

The bearded man's revolver cracked a bullet, and the looking-glass at the back of the parlor shelf, along with five bottles of expensive whiskey, splattered and shattered into shards, and then the entire mess came smashing and tinkling-down.

As the barman frightfully entered the tumultuous room, the official bouncer immediately noticed Mr. Marvel, curiously crumpled-up, and struggling against the door that led to the yard and kitchen.

The door flew open while the barman hesitated, and Marvel was roughly dragged into a brawl by an Invisible Force, and his frame was callously shoved into the kitchen. There was a scream and a resultant dissonant clatter of pots and pans. Marvel, with his head pinned down, was lifted and catapulted directly into the open kitchen door, and next the iron bolts were drawn.

Then, the astonished off-duty policeman, who had been trying to get past the barman to achieve a safer zone, rushed-into the former battle area, followed by one of the cabmen, and the intrepid pair courageously gripped the wrist of an invisible hand that had just collared Tom Marvel, who was then wickedly smashed in the face, and as a direct result, Tom's entire body reeled-up almost to the low ceiling.

After plummeting to the floor with a loud boom, Mr. Marvel slowly rose in a daze, and with great difficulty, the lad initiated a frantic effort to obtain a more-secure area in which to shelter.

Then, the brave cabman, a happily retired champion weightlifter and renown British ruffian, luckily collared something tangible-but-invisible. "I got him good," the Olympic contender screamed. The barman's red hands came clawing like a berserk lobster at the Unseen Aggressor. "I have him by the balls! Here in my grip is where the invisible fuck is!"

Mr. Marvel, being released from the Invisible Man's grasp, suddenly dropped to the floor, and made a desperate attempt to crawl behind the legs of the still-fighting pugilists trying to assist the champion weightlifter in subduing the lunatic Invisible Man. The intense monumental struggle next blundered around to the edge of the Jolly Crickets Inn entrance door.

During that particular interval of the truly raucous melee, the Invisible Man's Voice was heard for the first time, yelling-out curses rather sharply, as the valiant off-duty policeman stomped repeatedly upon the frenetic Voice's invisible left foot. Then, the Unseen Perpetrator, obviously needing serious anger management, cried-out passionately, and his fists flew around his adversaries' heads like wild rotating boat propellers.

The cabman suddenly whooped and doubled-up in excruciating pain, after being severely kicked under his diaphragm, rupturing his entire scrotum sac. The kitchen door into the bar-parlor slammed, and the distraction actually beneficially covered Mr. Marvel's hasty retreat. The traumatized Jolly Crickets patrons, still wildly brawling thin air inside the kitchen, punching and thrashing at their Invisible Opponent, now found themselves clutching at and struggling with empty atmosphere.

"Where's he gone?" the astounded bearded American bellowed. "Out where?"

"This way," the off-duty policeman indicated with his swollen left hand, while stepping into the yard and then stopping. "I think he's now this way!"

A piece of counter tile was next thrown, and the sharp projectile whizzed-by the off-duty constable's head, then smashing among the crockery pieces that had been lying upon the kitchen table.

"I'll show the ornery prick no mercy," the black bearded American bully boomed. And suddenly, a steel barrel was produced over the demoralized policeman's shoulder, and five bullets had followed one another, discharged into the direction that the sharp tile missile had been thrown.

Much to his credit, the experienced bearded marksman had adroitly moved his hand in a horizontal curve, so that his accurate shots radiated-out into the narrow yard like separate spokes orbiting-out from a spinning wheel.

A welcomed silence followed the wild Jolly Crickets marathon scuffle. "Five cartridges," the American with the black beard announced to his remaining shocked barroom audience. "I thought that weird shit like this only happens out west in my country. That's the best feature about all of this barroom battle. Four aces and a joker solved the riddle. Get a lantern, someone, and come and feel about the floor for *his* limp body.

"I believe that you've just committed murder," the off-duty constable stated. "You'll have to stand trial."

"Here's my defense. I believe I've just shot the dirty Bastard and prevented the lousy Son-of-a-Bitch from killing everyone in here, and if he's still invisible and has no physical, visible dead body to give as evidence of murder, then I'm sure that an honest jury of Brits will most certainly acquit me of committin' first degree murder at your fine bar, this here Jolly Crickets."

Chapter 17

"DR. KEMP'S VISITOR"

D r. Darrell Kemp had continued writing his academic journal research thesis inside his study until his preoccupied ears heard the revolver shots occurring down in the village at the bawdy Jolly Crickets. 'What idiot is firing a handgun downtown? Peaceful England is becoming more-and-more like the American Wild, Wild West each and every day! Intoxicated asses! Somnolent, serene Burdock sounds like it's now the O.K. Corral!'

Dr. Kemp rose from his desk and paced to his southern belvedere window, opened it, and leaning-out, stared-down and noticed the ordinary beaded gas-lamps and familiar shops in the distance, with the usual network of black roofs and yard intricacies that made-up the regularly placid town at night. 'Looks like there's a rowdy crowd down the hill gathered outside the infamous Jolly Crickets Inn,' the eminent Professor logically interpreted.

The scholar's eyes wandered away from Port Burdock's Main Street to where the harbor ships' lights shone, and the old pier glowed in a contrasted lighter-yellow illumination. The moon was in its first quarter, hanging over the westward hill, and the twinkling stars were cloudlessly clear and almost-tropically bright.

After five minutes of pleasurable observation and intent listening, Dr. Darrell Kemp temporarily lost his concentration, principally focused upon his important research project, with his mind fancifully speculating on the cause of the irregular downtown Burdock disturbance. Getting back to his primary concern that was nearing completion, the serious author pulled-down the office's window again, and returned to his very important research project.

An hour after the bizarre shooting incident, the front-door bell rang. Being distracted by the remembrance of downtown gun shots, Dr. Darrell Kemp had been writing distracted, and with intervals of interrupted abstraction, his serious mind had been temporarily diverted from his main endeavor. Listening astutely, the Professor heard his servant answering the downstairs door, and he waited for her feet arriving upon the staircase, but Maria Torano never appeared to announce what the loud downstairs rapping was all about. 'Wonder what that was? And where's Maria?'

Kemp tried resuming his challenging work, but failed in his noteworthy pursuit. The prudent scientist again rose from his labor, stepped to the landing, and called over the balustrade to his loyal housemaid as Maria appeared in the hallway below. "Was that a letter being delivered?" Kemp curiously asked.

"Only a runaway ring, sir," the servant politely answered. "I ignored the bell and the door! I know Dr. Kemp that you don't want contact with strangers while you're working at night."

"I'm fairly restless and agitated tonight," the good physician honestly confessed. "I believe I should retire early and continue my paper promptly in the morning when I'm more rested. Good night, Maria."

After returning to his private study, Dr. Darrell Kemp attempted resolutely resuming his meritorious work. The only familiar sounds in the room were the ticking of the clock and the subdued shrillness of his pen's quill, hurrying its scribble upon a writing tablet in the very center of the well-lit, rectangular desk.

It was two o'clock in the early morning before exhausted Dr. Kemp had finished his dedicated work for the night. After rising and wiping his weary eyes, the fatigued man rose, yawned, and again stepped downstairs to prepare for bed. After already-removing his coat and vest, the fully-spent author realized that he had become quite thirsty, so with a parched tongue, took a candle and entered the dining-room in search of a syphon and whiskey.

Darrell Kemp's various scientific pursuits had made him a very observant and pragmatic observer, and as his feet recrossed the hall, the fine gentleman noticed a dark spot on the linoleum at the foot of the stairs, right next to the entrance mat.

'What could that spot on the linoleum possibly be?' Dr. Kemp speculated. 'It's unlike Maria to not have noticed and cleaned-it up! Oh well; at least I can enjoy my post-midnight drink and finally celebrate completing my rough draft. But first, I think I'll bend-down and examine this rather peculiar blemish. Why, it seems to be the color of drying blood!'

And after completing his cursory investigation, the Doctor climbed upstairs and was both astonished and intrigued to discover a similar bloodstain visibly evident on the doorknob of his private study.

Looking at his own hand, Darrell Kemp realized that his palm and fingers were still quite clean, and then he remembered that the door of his room had been open when he had come down from his study, and that consequently, he had not touched nor seen the handle.

Being fascinated by the apparent compelling mystery, the medical man walked straight into his room, his face quite calm, perhaps a trifle more resolute than usual. His glance, wandering inquisitively, suddenly scrutinized the bed. On the counterpane was another messy bloodstain, and the top sheet had unexpectedly been torn. 'What the hell is going on here? Am I hallucinating? I think I must've worked too long and too hard on my paper that's due next Tuesday for administrative review. And my bedclothes are depressed as if someone has been randomly inspecting them? Goldie Locks perhaps?'

Then, the befuddled resident, a skeptic in regard to primitive superstition and community gossip, had an odd impression that he had heard a low voice that definitely was not Maria's feminine tone.

Kemp began staring wonderingly at the tumbled, disheveled and wrinkled sheets. 'Was that really a human voice that I had heard? What the hell's really going on here?'

Upon evaluating his puzzling observations, Dr. Kemp then distinctly heard a movement occurring across the room, near the hand-wash stand. All men, no matter how highly educated, retain some atavistic, superstitious inklings. The feeling that is often-described as "eerie" immediately descended upon the practical and objective man's thinking.

After closing the door to the room, and with his mind still in a quandary, the perplexed Professor paced forward to the dressing-table, and put-down his whiskey glass along with its designated drinking container. Suddenly, with a start, the Doctor's astute eyes perceived a coiled and blood-stained bandage showing upon a tawdry linen rag, which was incredibly hanging in mid-air, amazingly suspended between himself and the wash-stand.

Dr. Kemp stared incredulously at *that* phenomenon in sheer amazement. It was indeed an empty bandage, a bandage properly tied, but most certainly, quite empty without any head or arm inside. While reaching to touch and further examine the arcane mystery, a Weird Voice began speaking behind Kemp's head.

"Kemp!" the squealy Voice greeted. "I know that you're the renowned Dr. Kemp! You're just the fellow I need to see!"

"Eh? Where are you?" Darrell Kemp exclaimed in a surprised and startled tone, accentuated with his mouth then agape.

"Keep your nerve," the Voice commanded. "I'm an Invisible Man. In fact, I am *the* Invisible Man!"

Dr. Kemp, being quite stunned and shocked, contrary to his normal calm disposition, made no answer for a brief space, but simply stared at the wavering bandage. "Invisible Man? That's pure London tabloid newspaper propaganda bullshit!"

"I *am* an Invisible Man; *the* Invisible Man!" the 'occult Voice' imperatively reiterated.

"Don't be silly, Intruder. You're a wounded trespasser breaking into my home seeking medical attention. And for the record, I place little credence in sensational newspaper headlines, and I think that you're an absolute impostor. I'm inclined to notify the constable about your uninvited entrance into my home."

"Then, you don't believe my claim," the sinister-sounding Voice challenged. "I recommend that you be very careful in what you now say and do. A faulty misstep with my patience may cause you your life."

"Have you a bandage on?" Kemp curiously asked. "I'm a trained medical physician and can treat and rewrap your injury."

"Yes," said the Invisible Man. "I can definitely use your indispensable services."

"Oh!" said Kemp, and then roused himself. "I say that this entire extraordinary encounter inside my home is pure theatrical nonsense. It's some quack-like trickery. Here now. Are you a traveling magician? Perhaps a circus soothsayer? Let me closely look at your wound. I'll treat your cuts without any expense on your part, and then you can be on your merry way."

Feeling where he had suspected the bleeding might be, Dr. Kemp's hand immediately recoiled at the initial touch, and his facial color changed from florid to pallid.

"Keep steady, Kemp, for God's sake, I say, keep steady! I want and need your professional help badly. Stop, I say!"

Then, the Invisible Man's other hand tightly gripped Kemp's left arm. "Kemp!" the Voice cried-out loudly. "Kemp! Keep steady!" And the foreign grip tightened and pressed-down even harder.

A frantic desire to free himself took possession of Dr. Kemp's self-preservation needs. The hand of the bandaged arm next tightly gripped *his* available shoulder, and the benign victim was suddenly tripped and flung backwards upon the bed.

Dr. Kemp opened his mouth to shout for Maria, but the corner of the bedsheet was quickly and forcefully thrust between his teeth. The Invisible Man had savagely pinned the young physician down upon the bed, but Kemp's arms were still free, and the victim struck and flailed-away frantically, desperately trying to kick his escape from being maliciously assaulted and injured.

"Listen to reason, will you?" the insane Invisible Man yelled. "Stop punching my sensitive ribs. By Heaven and Hell! You'll certainly madden me in a minute! If you anger me any further, I'll be inclined to brutally kill your ass!"

"What do you want from me besides professional medical attention?"

"Lie still, you dumb-fuck fool!" the crazed Invisible Man bawled into Kemp's ear. "I might need a doctor, but if you don't cooperate, soon you'll need a mortician!"

Kemp struggled for another moment, and then realizing the futility of his predicament, finally rested and lay still.

"If you shout once more, I promise that I'll smash your face into pulp and break your skull into fragments," the Invisible Man threatened, relieving his grip around the doctor's aching throat.

"What do you really want with me?" Dr. Kemp gasped, holding his injured neck.

"Listen to me. I am an Invisible Man. In fact, I am *the* Invisible Man. It's no foolishness I'm describing as you may think, and most certainly, it's no ridiculous magic, either. I really *am* an Invisible Man, who like yourself, practices science objectivity. Yes, sir, Dr. Kemp. Proven scientific principles and not superstitious black magic or elementary witchcraft," the queer Voice stressed and emphasized. "And now, I want and require your expert help. I don't want to hurt you, but if you behave like a frantic rustic bumpkin and resist my demands, then I have no other plausible alternative but to dispense of you. Don't you remember me, Kemp? I'm Griffin, of your University College?"

"Please let me get up," Kemp pleaded. "I'll stop resisting you and stay where I am. And please let me sit quiet for a minute to regain my sensibilities and composure. My neck has been severely twisted. For a moment, I felt like a pretzel."

"Yes, Dr. Kemp. I am Griffin, of University College, and I've successfully accomplished how to make myself invisible. I'm just an ordinary man, a man from your past that you had once known, made invisible, partially from mastering *your* magnificent academic teaching theories."

"Griffin?" Kemp wondered and recalled. "A former student at the university?"

"Yes, Griffin," the Voice answered, slighted at possibly not being immediately remembered. "I had been a younger student than you were; almost, but not quite an albino; six-feet-tall, and broad, with a pink and white face along with red eyes, and I was the candidate who had won the distinguished medal for chemistry. The department head had chosen me over you. I believe that you had envied my achievement!"

"I am confused," Kemp replied. "My brain is rioting inside my head. What has this medical assistance intrusion of yours have to do with Griffin?"

"I *am* Griffin. That's all the hell you need to know!"

Kemp thought for a moment. "It's horrible. If I recall from an undergraduate mythology class, 'a griffin' was a creature having a lion's' body and a bird's head, usually an eagle. But what deviltry must happen to a college educated man to want to become invisible and cause immense chaos all over Sussex County?"

"Listen, Dr. Kemp. I'm here to tell you what you have to do for me, and I'm not here to value your academic rhetoric. It's no deviltry. And this Griffin is not a griffin. Plain and simple. Quite succinctly, I am Griffin, a remote acquaintance of yours at the college, active in the school's chemistry program. This invisibility matter is a sophisticated scientific process that I've perfected, quite sane and intelligible enough—"

"It's horrible and anti-Christian. You're playing God and evilly tinkering with natural laws. How on earth—?"

"It's horrible enough, Doctor. But I'm now wounded and in intolerable pain, and abnormally tired, too. Great God Kemp! You're an honorable man devoted to science. Take it steady. Think it over. Kindly give me some food and drink, and let me sit-down here to recover from my many injuries. I beg that you be discreet and rational about my identity. If you ever report me to the police, I shall kill both you and them as easily as you may want to drink a glass of water."

Darrell Kemp stared at the dancing bandage as it floated and moved across the room, and then noticed a basket chair being swiftly dragged on its own accord across the floor, coming to rest near the bed. The resident observer rubbed his eyes and felt his throbbing neck again. "This beats the notion of ghosts and specters," the

Professor acknowledged, and began laughing in a totally silly manner.

"That's much better. Thank Heavens man; you're becoming fairly manageable. You're finally getting to be more sensible! At least that's what I think now. Congratulations, Dr. Kemp. I do believe that now, we can develop a meaningful relationship. Now give me some whiskey. I'm nearly dead and require sustenance."

"If I get up from this bed, shall I run into you? *There!* all right. Whiskey you say? Here. Where shall I give it to you?"

The chair creaked and Kemp felt the whiskey drawn away from his grasp, instinctively and reactively letting go. The raised glass came to rest, being poised twenty inches above the front edge of the chair.

Dr. Kemp stared at the supernatural enigma in infinite perplexity. "This is—this must be—, well magical, yes, some sort of illusionary hypnotism. You've suggested that you are invisible."

"Stuff and nonsense," the Voice lividly objected. "Merely limited stuff and nonsense, totally assumed by your orthodox academic perception."

"I had demonstrated conclusively this morning," began Kemp, "that invisibility—"

"Never mind what you've demonstrated, you dunderhead! Can't you fuckin' see that I'm starving," the perturbed Voice ranted. "And the nights are chilly to a naked man without clothes. And when I'm suffering from not having my biological needs satisfied, all you want to discuss is dumb-ass magic and hypnotism!"

"Yes, basic needs. You want and need food, clothing and shelter from the elements?" Kemp answered, not knowing what else to say.

The tumbler of whiskey tilted itself. "Yes," the Invisible Man answered, before quaffing-down the delicious liquor. "Have you a dressing-gown?"

Kemp made some indiscernible exclamation in an undertone. The reluctant host walked to a wardrobe closet and produced a dull robe of dingy scarlet. "Will this do?"

"Yes, it's a fuckin' start, anyway. But right now, I'll also need a shirt, drawers, socks, and comfortable slippers," the Unseen Invisible Man curtly demanded. "And don't forget the food. I might be invisible as you now well-know, but just like yourself, I need food to live and survive."

"Anything, you so desire that I'm able to readily provide. But I must confess, Invisible Guest, this entire scenario is the most insane thing I've ever experienced in my entire life!"

Kemp left his Invisible Guest inside the upstairs study, went downstairs, and returned with a tray of bread, a fresh ripe banana, and a hot cup of tea, and then the Doctor pulled-up a light table, and placed the items before his unexpected Visitor.

"Never mind knives," the Invisible Man austerely articulated. Kemp then noticed that a cutlet was hanging above *his* own head in mid-air, and his auditory perception detected a queer gnawing.

"Invisible!" Kemp said and realized, and slowly sat down upon the bedroom chair. 'Quite miraculous and inexplicable!' his bewildered mind assessed.

"I always like to get a clean vest wrapped about my neck before I eat and swallow," the Invisible Man related, with a full mouth of banana and bread, eating greedily. "Queer fancy!"

"I suppose that your bleeding wrist is all right now," Kemp commented. 'I wrapped it firmly."

"Trust me," the Invisible Man replied. "I'll only tell you what I need, and little about how I had developed my unique capabilities."

"Of all the strange and wonderful—"

"Exactly, Dr. Kemp. You're beginning to understand my true motivation. But it's rather odd that I should blunder into *your* house just to simply get my new bandaging. Yes, perhaps *that* fortunate enterprise was my first stroke of good luck! Anyhow, I had meant to sleep in this house tonight; of course, not being aware at first that this residence was yours. It's a filthy nuisance, my blood showing on your floor and door knob, isn't it? Quite a clot over there. Gets fairly visible as it coagulates, I see. It's only the living tissue that I've learned how to change, and only for as long as I'm alive and breathing. You might not know, but I've been hiding inside your cozy house for three hours."

"But how's it done?" Kemp wondered and asked, demonstrating a tone of exasperation. "Confound it, Griffin! The whole preposterous business you're selling is completely illogical; fraudulent I maintain; it's unreasonable and sheer fantasy, from its alpha all the way to its omega. You're selling jungle voodoo, and I'm not buying it!"

"Quite unreasonable, you retarded fool," the Invisible Man argued and protested. "Perfectly reasonable from your limited perspective, but total garbage and rubbish in regard to my superior acumen, as a matter of fact."

Recalling the gun shots that had occurred in Burdock, Dr. Kemp asked his intruder, "Tell me', now. What were the shots I had heard down in the village? How did the shooting begin? Did they happen at the Jolly Crickets?"

"There was a real fool, a naïve and gullible young man, a sort of confederate of mine, curse the stupid bastard! That disloyal lunatic then tried to steal my money. *Has* in fact done so. The insolent twerp is Thomas Marvel, a pathetic cross who's something between an imp and a twit."

"Is *he* invisible too?"

"No. The stupid greedy shit doesn't have the mental ability to even enter phase one; my former assistant lacks the intestinal fortitude to enter phase two, and is deficient the necessary phase three ambition. Mr. Marvel does not possess the essential wherewithal to ever master the wonderful practice that I've successfully achieved. Can't I have some more to eat before I elaborate about my totally aberrant apprentice? I'm insufferably hungry and in deep pain. I realize, Dr. Kemp, that it's hard for you to believe that an Invisible Man can hurt, sacrifice, and bleed when injured. And now, you want me to tell irrelevant stories about my traitorous former apprentice!"

Kemp got-up from his study's chair. "*You* didn't do any shooting? Who the hell did?"

"Not me," the Invincible Man's Voice admitted. "Some fool I'd never before seen fired at random. A lot of the patrons got scared when I started to pummel and beat the shit out of their puny asses. The drunken crowd all got intimidated at me and began assaulting my prowess. Curse the cretin bastards and bitches! I say fuck them all! I want more to eat than this, Dr. Kemp. You must accommodate my demands if you wish to stay breathing upon this Earth."

"I'll see what there is to eat downstairs," Kemp consented. "Not much, I'm afraid."

"Are there any others now living in this house?"

"Only my maid Maria. My two male servants, one of them being my gardener, have the weekend off!"

* * * * * * * * * * * *

After the Invisible Man had finished eating Kemp's provisions, and had consumed a decent meal provided by his new-found host, the Voice demanded a cigar. He bit the end savagely like a famished cannibal before Kemp could even find a knife, and the belligerent and Impatient Guest cursed when the outer leaf loosened. It was strange to see an Invisible Man incessantly smoking; his mouth, throat, and pharynx became visible as a sort of whirling and swirling smoke spiral exiting from his invisible neck.

"This blessed gift of smoking is a fabulous pleasure!" the Voice stated as the Invisible Man puffed vigorously. "I'm lucky to have fallen upon you, Kemp. You must help me endure my frustrating circumstances. Fancy tumbling on you just now! I'm really in a devilish scrape. I've been going mad, Bedlam-mad, I think. The things I've been through! But *we* will do magnificent things yet. Let me tell you—"

The ghostly intruder helped himself to more whiskey. Kemp got-up, looked about the room, and fetched a clean glass from his spare cabinet. "It's wild, but I suppose I may drink some more."

"Are you an alcoholic?" Dr. Kemp asked. "You appear to savor your liquor!"

The Mercurial Invisible Man ignored Dr. Kemp's innocent inquiry. "You haven't changed much, Kemp, these last dozen years, but conversely, I most certainly have. You fair academic men on the faculty don't deviate from your lowlife professions. I must tell you. We will work and accomplish greatness together! I recall that you had been jealous and envious of me beating you out for the chemistry merit award, and hopefully, *that* negative animosity has all been erased by the past."

"For God's sake, how was it all done?" Kemp insisted on learning. "And how did you ever get like this ungodly attainment I'm now witnessing?"

"Forget God's sake. I'm now a loyal ally of Satan. Let me smoke in peace for a little while! And then I'll begin telling you the whole chronology, I promise."

But the promised story was not told that night. The Invisible Man's wrist was growing painful and required additional treatment; he was feverish, exhausted, and his vacillating mind came around to relentlessly brooding upon his recent chase of Tom Marvel down the hill to Burdock, and about the struggle and major altercation that had transpired inside the infamous Jolly Crickets Inn. The wily "Prestidigitator" spoke in informative fragments of a certain Thomas Marvel, and erratically smoked much faster, with his fluctuating voice growing angry to the point of being hostile. Kemp tried to methodically gather what new background he could.

"From the start, Mr. Marvel was afraid of me, and I could see on his face that the disloyal prick was scared-shitless of me," the Invisible Man repeated many times over. "The little fuck meant to give me the slip. What a fucked-up fool I was. The despicable cur! I should've killed him twice over!"

"Where did you get the money for your research?" Kemp abruptly inquired. "I mean, the gold coins alluded to in the recent newspaper story."

The Invisible Man was silent for a space. "I can't tell you *that* specific detail tonight. I need to trust you more than I do now. Listen, Kemp. I've had no sleep for nearly three days, except a couple of meager dozes of an hour or so. I must sleep soon, or else I might die from sheer exhaustion and malnutrition."

"Well, you may have my room downstairs; or you may have *this* room."

"But how can I sleep? If I sleep, this dangerous villain Thomas Marvel will most certainly get away from my pursuit. Ugh! What the hell does it matter now?"

The Invisible Man appeared to be regarding Kemp's dubious nature suspiciously. "Because I've a particular objection to being caught by my fellow-men," the Strange Guest slowly said. "Only the diabolical Devil should retrieve my soul upon my death, fool that I am!" yelled the Invisible Man, striking and then pounding the table in accelerated frustration. "Yes Kemp; everyone on Earth is a self-centered fool, including you and me. Oh no! I think I've just successfully transferred and placed my impeccable secret ideas, and accidentally deposited them, into your vulnerable head."

Jay Dubya

Chapter 18

"THE INVISIBLE MAN SLEEPS"

Fatigued and wounded as the incomparable Invisible Man had become, "the Diabolical Rogue" refused to accept Kemp's word that *his* freedom and independence should be respected by society. The paranoid "Sorcerer" next examined the two windows of the downstairs bedroom, fretfully drew-up the blinds, and opened the sashes, endeavoring to confirm Kemp's statement that *their* 'impending planned retreat' into the wilderness would be both possible and successful.

Outside, the night was very cloudless, quiet and still, and the moon was setting over the down. Then, the distrustful Invisible Man examined the keys connected with the bedroom suite several times, and thoroughly inspected the two dressing-room doors, in order to satisfy himself that those portals could also be made assurances of attaining wonderful freedom from the bothersome law. Finally, the "Surreptitious Salacious Savant" mentally expressed himself as being satisfied and confident. The Intruder stood impatiently upon the hearth rug, and Kemp heard the sound of a vigorous yawn being emitted from his guest's invisible throat.

"I'm sorry," the Invisible Man awkwardly apologized. "I cannot tell you all that I've recently done tonight. But believe me when I say that I'm totally worn-out. It's a grotesque matter, no doubt. In fact, it's reprehensibly horrible! But dear Dr. Kemp, in spite of your mediocre arguments advanced this morning, it is quite a possible thing, and *my* truth is evidenced with the fact that you just hear my Voice, but cannot see my whole nakedness right this minute. I've made a fantastic discovery that shall be *our* confidential secret, and our secret alone. Originally, I meant to keep it all to myself. But for some remote reason, I can't. I must share my vital discovery with a reliable partner such as yourself. And I believe that ally is you,

Doctor. We can do such unbelievable things that transcend everyday expectations. But it'll all have to wait until sometime tomorrow when I am stronger. Now, Kemp. I feel as though I must either sleep or perish."

Dr. Kemp stood in the middle of the downstairs bedroom, staring in wonder at the headless speaking garment. "I suppose I must leave you drowning in your colossal misery. It's truly incredible, I must admit. I'm actually now adjusting to your totally bizarre dilemma, and I'm gaining an amount of sympathy for your dire situation," Kemp admitted. "Three things in my lackluster life happening like this, would be overturning all of my preconceptions; yes, would definitely make me extremely insane beyond the point of no return. But it's plainly real! You're plainly real! There really isn't anything more to say. Can I get you anything else before you slumber?"

"Only bid me good-night," Griffin commented. "Even speaking a short sentence is rapidly depleting the remainder of my energy."

"Good-night, then," Kemp declared, and next awkwardly shook an invisible hand. The Doctor then walked sideways to the door. Suddenly, the dressing-gown leaped into the air and maneuvered quickly and erratically towards him. "Understand me!" warned the dressing-gown. "No attempts to either hamper me, or capture me! Or else—"

Kemp's face changed a little in both expression and color. "I thought I gave you' my solemn word. My word is my bond."

Dr. Kemp closed and locked the door to ensure the Invisible Man's safety and privacy. Then, as the host stood with an expression of passive amazement upon his shaven face, the Invisible Man's rapid feet came to the door of the dressing-room, and that too was quickly locked from inside.

Dr. Kemp slapped his brow with his hand. "Am I dreaming? Has all the world gone mad? Or just have I deteriorated? Ha, ha, ha. I'm barred out of my own bedroom, by a flagrant absurdity pretending to be an Invisible-but-dangerous-Man! It all has to be either a blasted hoax or a terribly fake canard!"

Dr. Kemp walked to the head of the staircase, turned, and for a while simply stared at the locked doors. 'It's fact,' he decided. 'Common logic has been defeated! Yes; sorcery has triumphed over science! Undeniable, and indisputable fact!'

The eminent researcher lit the dining-room lamp, got out a cigar, and began pacing the room like a famished tiger in a cage. Now and then, the good Doctor would argue with himself about his *former* fake scientific beliefs. 'Invisible! Materially functioning in a non-material world! How totally absurd! Still needing basic food, shelter and clothing!'

Then, the fully-beleaguered and befuddled scientist evaluated some other alien ideas. 'Is there such a thing as an invisible animal existing in the sea? All the millions of tiny larvae; all the little nauplii and microorganisms; all the infinite varieties of jelly-fish, too. In the oceans, there are more things invisible than visible! I never before thought of *that* radical concept. And in the ponds and swamps, too! All those little pond-life things—specks of colorless translucent jelly! And that's just here on Earth. What about the billions of planets that abound in the Universe circling billions and billions of stars in other galaxies?'

Dr. Kemp reflected some more on the proposition of he himself learning how to become invisible, and perhaps creating an intense rivalry between himself and the fantastic Invisible Man. 'Even if I was made of transparent crystal glass, I think I would still be visible.'

The Thinker's uninterrupted meditation became even more profound. The bulk of three cigars had filtered and passed into the invisible or diffused realm as the last white ash flaked over the carpet before the Conceiver imagined an "invisible fantasy world" again.

Then, before Kemp realized it, the morning's paper lay carelessly opened and thrown aside upon the front steps. The resident picked-up the gazette and his eyes scanned the unusual sensationalized headline, and then comprehensively read the supporting front-page article. "Strange Story from Iping", as organized from an interview with a retired mariner at Port Stowe, who had disclosed to a certain

Mr. Thomas Marvel, the essential main idea of an incredible Invisible Man being described. Dr. Kemp voraciously read the intriguing piece very swiftly.

'Wrapped up!' the Doctor concluded. 'Disguised! Hiding his identity! No one seems to have been aware or even care about *his* tremendous pain and misfortune. What the devil *is* his game? All of the other nimrods around here want to do is hunt him down and eagerly destroy what the numerous dumb shits don't know and absolutely fear; anyone who is different than them!'

The reader dropped the newspaper upon the front step, and his eye went seeking reinforcement and news from another source. 'Ah! It's the *St. James' Gazette*,' Kemp thought, discovering upon the lawn the more-prestigious periodical lying folded-up, just as it had earlier arrived. 'Now we shall get at the truth by employing the scientific method of verification,' Dr. Kemp reckoned. The reader was positively stunned to comprehend the confirmation headline. "An Entire Village in Sussex goes Mad".

'Good Heavens!' the Doctor considered and mentally exclaimed to himself while rapidly reading a positively incredulous account of the extraordinary events in Iping, which seemed to parallel what had more-recently occurred in Burdock at the notorious Jolly Crickets Inn.

'The suspected culprit ran through the streets striking everyone in his path, both right and left. The Invisible Man had knocked Constable Bobby Jaffers insensible and unconscious. Mr. Gilbert Huxter is in great pain, and still is so traumatized that the tobacco merchant is unable to even begin describing precisely what extraordinary violence he had seen. Painful humiliation prevails, because the Iping Vicar's former authority and good reputable in the community are now being traduced and publicly scorned. Woman are ill with terror! Windows have been smashed and demolished.'

"This 'fictional' story must certainly be a weird fabrication," Dr. Darrell Kemp's ratiocination-like, scientific training suggested, as the respected university Physician whispered his personal evaluation to himself.

The newspaper subscriber dropped the second paper and stared blankly at the front lawn. 'Probably an erroneous fabrication, no doubt! Fiction seems to sell better these days than does non-fiction. But when and where does the conniving tramp Thomas Marvel come into the evolving plot? Why the deuce was my complicated Guest vigorously chasing a lowlife common tramp?'

Feeling woozy, Dr. Kemp, sat-down abruptly on the surgical bench. 'He's not only invisible,' Kemp concluded. 'He's mad! Either homicidal or suicidal, or perhaps both! Griffin needs immediate psychiatric care, and I must provide it.'

Thinking about the convoluted headlines in the two early morning newspapers, Dr. Kemp was too excited to sleep. He gave Maria quite explicit instructions to lay breakfast for two in the belvedere study, and then to later confine her cleaning activities to the basement and to the ground-floor.

Then, the bemused Researcher continued pacing the dining-room until the third morning's newspaper arrived. That edition had much immaterial news to convey, and little else to tell or describe about the activities of the oddball Invisible Man; that is, beyond the confirmation of the evening before, and a very badly written account of another remarkable tale of violence coming from nearby Port Burdock.

That third news article gave Dr. Kemp the essence of the exact happenings that had occurred at the risqué "Jolly Crickets", and the name of mischievous Mr. Thomas Marvel had been mentioned several times.

"He had made me keep guard over him for twenty-four hours while he still sleeps," Thomas Marvel had testified to the pompous Burdock town authorities.

Certain minor facts were collaborated with the Iping news story, notably the cutting of the village telegraph-wires connected to several neighboring communities. But there was nothing additional in the third paper to throw *light* on the association between the Invisible Man and the indigent tramp Thomas Marvel; and as for Mr. Marvel, the untrustworthy prevaricator had supplied no useful information about the cryptic three books in his personal custody, or the undependable imp could not truthfully account for the abundant money with which his pockets were lined.

Kemp read every scrap of the additional report three times, and sent his housemaid out to purchase every one of the morning regional papers that she could find. Maria returned with three more rather-sensationalized gazettes from surrounding villages, and Dr. Kemp read each one several times, rather voraciously.

"He is indeed invisible. And it reads like exploding rage growing and evolving into mass mania! The things he may do, either good or evil; either selfish or humanitarian are too staggering to even consider. Yes, the things he may do! And he's free as the air itself. What on Earth ought I to do?'

Dr. Kemp then had a massive inspiration. The Researcher anxiously approached his untidy downstairs corner desk, and immediately began jotting-down an imperative note. Finally, the Invisible Man's newest apprentice quickly grabbed an envelope and addressed it to "Colonel Adye, Port Burdock."

The Invisible Man coincidentally awoke, even as Kemp was engaged in doing *that* clandestine correspondence. The "Magnificent Mage" had awoken in an evil temper, and Kemp, alert for every unusual or peculiar sound, heard *his* pattering feet rush suddenly across the upstairs bedroom. Then, a chair had been turbulently flung over, glasses and bottles shattered, and the standing wash-hand tumbler smashed to the floor. Kemp hurried upstairs and his fist repeatedly rapped on the office door.

Chapter 19

"CERTAIN FIRST PRINCIPLES"

"What's the matter?" Dr. Kemp asked the Invisible Man, when the concerned Physician admitted Griffin into the upstairs office. "What wrong that induces you to commit loud violence?"

"Nothing," was the instant answer. "Everything's copesetic. Sometimes things go awry. I just can't explain it. But I'm alright now."

"But, confound it! The smash? I heard the wild racket downstairs. Were you having a panic attack?"

"An occasional fit of temper," the Invisible Man confessed. "It's an inadvertent reaction my body gets when I experience excruciating pain. I forgot to rub the salve on this arm; and it's become sore."

"You're rather liable to cause additional pain if you forget to treat that sort of thing as I had advised. You really are a unique specimen," Dr. Kemp declared. "You'll either be celebrated in a health museum, or you'll make medical history at being featured in all the international medical journals."

Dr. Kemp walked across the room and picked-up the numerous fragments of broken glass off the floor. "All the facts are out about you," Kemp shared, standing-up with a dozen shards of glass in his hands. "All that had happened over in Iping, and also the turmoil you had caused down the hill in Burdock at the Jolly Crickets. The world has become aware of its Invisible Citizen. But fortunately for us, no one knows you are here."

The Invisible Man felt compelled to incessantly swear when he learned of the bad news. "We have to get the hell out of here. Someone's liable to trace us down, and Tom Marvel will most-certainly squeal on me, because the dumb-fuck wants to be me, but doesn't have a clue as to how to ever complete his aspiration."

Jay Dubya

"The secret's out," Dr. Kemp reaffirmed. "I gather it was still a secret until your old sidekick Thomas Marvel talked to that old salt on the Port Stowe store-front bench. I don't know what your current plans are, but of course, I'm anxious to help you in any way I can."

The Invisible Man sat-down on the desk chair and complained. "Sometimes I wish I were normal again, leading a regular life. But other times, I would easily become abnormal, becoming bored with daily humdrum, doldrum-type, everyday piss activities. It's a devil-be-damned conundrum, that's for damned sure."

"There's breakfast to be served in the belvedere," Kemp announced. "And I'll perform the serving upstairs where we could eat our food in complete privacy. But before we can do anything else and together cooperate on a plan," Kemp asserted, "I must understand a little more about this invisibility ability of yours."

After retrieving the food from the downstairs pantry, Kemp caried a tray upstairs and conducted a strategy session with the "Invisible Magic Man", who was headless, footless, and handless in his contrived dressing-gown, and was busily wiping his unseen lips upon a miraculously-held physical serviette.

"It's simple and plain enough, and also credible enough," Griffin vaguely explained, putting the serviette aside, and leaning his invisible head upon an equally invisible hand. At first my special talent seemed rather wonderful and thrilling, no doubt. But now, great God! I often turn negative without warning, and feel that I have to fight, steal, cause trouble, and even kill. But I predict, Doctor, that together we shall attempt and achieve great things! I first came on the basic stuff I practice at Chesilstowe."

"Chesilstowe?"

"I went there after I left London. You know; I dropped medicine and took-up physics in the big city. Oh well, I did. At the time, the unique properties of *Light* especially fascinated me."

"Ah! How illuminating!" Kemp joked. "Good old Roy G. Biv being formed from white light after it is refracted through a triangular prism. Yes, I do remember now: Red, Orange, Yellow,

168

Green, Blue, Indigo and Violet, in that exact order. I recall memorizing *that* cute little ditty from my fifth-grade science class."

"Optical density!" the Invisible Man testily replied, not at all appreciating Dr. Kemp's elementary-level science humor one iota. "The whole subject is composed of a complex network of interconnected riddles; yes, a network with solutions glimmering elusively through each element. And me being but two-and-twenty, and full of enthusiasm, I excitedly thought, 'I'll devote my life to this singular purpose. A revolutionary project that is truly worthwhile.' Well, Dr. Kemp, you know what frivolous fools we generally are at age two-and-twenty?"

"Fools then, and fools now," Kemp agreed and added. "Even rich men are accomplished fools, but their wealth is what keeps them out of the mental institutions, because most people believe that if you're rich, you're also smart, and that you still have your scruples."

"Sounds like you also got an A in Sociology," the Invisible Man critically countered and mocked. "But I went to work feverishly, like a scientific slave. And I had hardly worked and thought about the matter six months before of imaginatively employing *light.*"

"Sounds like you were 'light years' in front of everyone else," Kemp jested, much to the Invisible Man's utter chagrin.

"In my trial-and-error experiments, I found a general principle of pigments and refraction, which I then organized into a viable formula; you might say a geometrical expression involving four dimensions," the semi-naked Visitor attempted to fully quantify. "Fools, common men, and even common mathematicians, do not know anything of what some general expression may mean to the dedicated academic student of molecular physics."

"Well, now, you're sounding just like God in the beginning of the Book of Genesis where it is quoted, 'Let there be light'! Do you want to be God! That's what the hell I think!"

"No, Dr. Kemp. According to my pessimistic and negative emotional moods, and my wild pendulum anger swings, I think I really admire and want to be Satan!"

"Have you memorized all of your efficacious formulas and vile mathematical equations? I presume that they would be extremely difficult to duplicate."

"That's my basic dilemma, Dr. Kemp. They're all documented in the three volumes that *that* tramp Thomas Marvel had absconded with, and more than likely has hidden, perhaps in an isolated cave somewhere in the hills."

"Very interesting indeed, that is, your current debacle involving this asshole instigator, this Marvel character. But please continue your narrative. Exactly how did the *thought* become the *thing?*"

The Invisible Man paused for a moment to better organize his extemporaneous recitation. "But this was not a *method* I had developed; it was an *idea,* Dr. Kemp; a very powerful *idea* that might lead to a *method* by which the *thing* would be possible, without changing any other major property of matter except, in some instances, colors, which is your simplified Roy G. Biv scenario. I had theorized that in order to lower the refractive index of a particular substance," the strange Guest resumed, "either solid or liquid, to that weight of common air, namely the combination of essentially oxygen, hydrogen and nitrogen, and then balance the equation with the composition of matter, including my own flesh and bones, so far, Dr. Kemp, *so far* as all practical physics laws and applicational purposes are concerned."

"Phew!" Kemp interjected. "Heavy-duty stuff you're divulging. But now I think I'm actually getting the gravity of your dissertation."

"This is no time for comedy hour at the Jolly Crickets, Dr. Kemp," Griffin angrily scolded. "But please consider this; visibility depends on the action of the visible bodies upon their interaction or actions with *light.* Either a body absorbs light, or it reflects it, or it refracts it, or it does all those things simultaneously. According to the laws of *light,* if the body neither reflects nor refracts, nor absorbs light, the foreign object all by itself, cannot of itself, become visible. Light must therefore interact with other properties to change their appearances."

"Well, as a Scientist, I must admit *that* notion which you've described about the interaction of light particles changing the appearance of different materials, well then, I find *that* theory rather intriguing. Could you provide me with one or two suitable examples?"

"When you see an opaque red box, Dr. Kemp, the color absorbs some of the light, and it reflects the rest, which is all the red part of the light seen by you. If it did not absorb any particular part of the light, but instead reflected it all, then it would be simply a shining white box. Yes, it would only appear as Silver!" the Invisible Man stressed. "A diamond box would neither absorb much of the light, nor reflect much from the general surface, but just here and there, where the surfaces were favorable and compatible, the light would be reflected and refracted, so that you would get a brilliant appearance of flashing reflections and translucencies; actually, sort of a graphic skeleton of light."

"Rather intricate and complicated indeed, I must say. Proceed with presenting your fascinating hypothesis."

"An ordinary glass box would not be so brilliant, nor so clearly visible, as let's say, a diamond box, because there would be less refraction and reflection. See that? From certain points of view, you would see quite clearly through it. Some kinds of glass would be more visible than others; for example, a box of flint glass would be brighter than a box of ordinary window glass. A box of very thin common glass would be hard to see in a bad light, because it would absorb hardly any light, and refract and reflect very little."

"I think I understand your fundamental theory now," Dr. Kemp commended. "Even though I specialize in medicine and blood analysis, I do have an adequate background in mathematics and physics."

"And Doctor, if you put a sheet of common 'white' glass in water, still more, if you put it in some denser liquid other than water, the glass would vanish almost altogether, because light passing from water to glass is only slightly refracted or reflected, or indeed hardly affected in any dynamic way from medium-to-medium. It is almost as invisible as a jet of coal gas, or hydrogen molecules invisible in the air. And for precisely the same reason!"

"Yes," Kemp concurred. "Those fabulous analogies are plain and simple, and smooth sailing, too."

"And here is another fact you'll know to be true. If a sheet of glass is smashed, Dr. Kemp, and then beaten into a thin powder, it becomes much more visible while it is in the air; it becomes at last, an opaque white powder. This is because the powdering multiplies the surfaces of the glass at which refraction and reflection occur. In the sheet of glass, there are only two surfaces; in the powder, the light is reflected or refracted by each grain it passes through, and very little gets right into and through the powder."

"What if the crushed powder in the white glass is submerged in water?"

"I was getting to that special point, Dr. Kemp. Please be more patient and don't constantly interrupt me and demolish my chain-of-thought," the Critical Invisible Man rebuked. "If the white powdered glass is put into water, it forthwith vanishes. The powdered glass and water have much the same refractive index; that is, the light undergoes very little refraction or reflection in passing from one medium to the other."

"Yes, yes," Kemp realized and agreed. "A very novel approach you've just identified. But there's one basic problem; a man's not powdered glass!"

"No," Griffin ascertained and replied. "He's actually more transparent!"

"Nonsense!"

"That falsehood you're endorsing, and coming from a famous Medical Doctor! How one soon forgets! Have you already forgotten your college physics, in ten short years? Just think of all the things that are transparent and seem not to be so. Paper, for instance, is made-up of transparent fibers, and it is white and opaque, but only for the same reason that a powder composed of glass is white and opaque. If you oil a sheet of white paper, and fill-up the interstices between the particles with more oil so that there is no longer refraction or reflection, except at the surfaces, and soon it becomes as transparent as glass. And not only paper, but cotton fiber, linen fiber, wool fiber, woody fiber, and *bone fiber*, Kemp, yes; even Kemp *flesh*, Kemp, *hair*, Kemp, *nails* and Kemp *nerves*, Dr. Kemp," the very crazed Invisible Man maintained. "In fact, the whole fabric of a man, except the red of his blood and the black pigment of his hair, are all made-up of transparent, colorless tissue. So, it suffices that to make us visible, one to the other, *light* must be radically altered. For the most part, the fibers of a living creature are no more-opaque than water itself."

"Great Heavens!" Kemp euphorically exclaimed. "Of course, of course! I was thinking only last night of the sea larvae, and all the transparent jelly-fish in the sea!"

"I've given you a general synopsis of my theory, Dr. Kemp, but I've deliberately left five basic key parts out so that you won't be able to easily replicate my research. But after three years of secrecy and emotional exasperation, I finally found that to fully complete my *creative* work would be futilely impossible."

"How?" Kemp asked. "You are invisible, aren't you? What more needs to be fulfilled? You've already accomplished your original objective, haven't you?"

"Two major difficulties, Dr. Kemp: Money and my soul," the Invisible Man replied. And then the transparent figure stepped to the window again to keenly stare and gaze outside. The mostly Unseen Personage abruptly turned around to face Dr. Kemp.

"I had robbed the old man at the Iping vicarage; I also stole money from *my* father. I later discovered that the money was not his; my father had borrowed the huge sum from a close friend. Sadly enough, my father felt guilty because he did not have the resources to repay the large debt, so then, he shot and killed himself because of my powerful and overwhelming greed."

Jay Dubya

Chapter 20

"THE HOUSE IN GT. PORTLAND STREET"

For a brief moment, Dr. Darrell Kemp sat in sheer silence, staring at the back of the wondrous headless figure standing at the upstairs belvedere windows. Then, struck by an inspiration, the Doctor rose, took the Invisible Man's Unseen Left Arm, and turned Griffin away from the outlook.

"You're tired, my friend. And while I sit, you walk about like you're an angry, trapped jungle animal. You've already had your exercise session for the day. Let's trade places. Please take my chair. And I'll do the walking-around the room."

But Griffin refused to cooperate with sound reason, and amply resented obeying taking any suggestion or logical command from Dr. Kemp. The Invisible Man then resumed his autobiographical account. "By that time, I had left the Chesilstowe cottage already, when my 'light property' theory was set into motion last December. I had taken a room in London, a large unfurnished room in a big, ill-managed lodging-house inside a ramshackle slum near Great Portland Street."

"Everyone's story has a beginning, a middle, and an end," Dr. Kemp interrupted the nervous pacer. "For example, in my younger days, I had lived in Liverpool; in my college years in London, and now I've finally wound-up here in suburban Burdock. Please continue with your illustrious story."

"Anyway, Dr. Kemp. The shabby room I had rented on Great Portland Street was soon full of the appliances, which I had bought with my deceased father's borrowed money. My initial work was going fairly well and steadily, actually quite successfully, and finally drawing near an end. I was like a man emerging from a thicket, and suddenly coming upon some unmeaning tragedy. I traveled back to London to properly bury my father."

"I think you're still journeying on a serious guilt trip," Dr. Kemp concluded and mentioned. "Anyone with any conscience or sense of morality would also feel culpable if he or she had done to their father exactly what the hell you had done to yours."

"Well then, Doctor, although I'm a suicide candidate, please allow me to proceed. My mind was still-focused on my advanced research on light properties, and I did not lift a finger to save *his* character or his financial situation prior to *his* death. I remember the church funeral; the cheap hearse; the scant ceremony; the windy frost-bitten hillside, and the old college friend of his, who read the service prayer over his corpse—a shitty, black, bent, old asshole with a sniveling cold, who coughed like he had both tuberculosis and emphysema, sneezing all over the fuckin' church's altar."

"I see now what you're saying. You were upset inside the dilapidated church because this old geezer, your deceased father's hoary friend since childhood, was coughin' over his coffin in the squalid edifice!"

"Doctor, if you can't say anything respectful or constructive, then I believe that you should just shut the fuck up! Now then. I remember walking back to the empty shabby house, through the place that had once been an alley landmark, and the decayed building was now patched and tinkered by the jerry builders into the ugly likeness of a sleazy town bordello. Every which way, the roads ran-out at last into the desecrated fields, and their routes ended in rubble heaps, and also in rank wet weed fields. I remember myself as a gaunt figure who despised pedestrian people who were also trekking along the slippery, shiny pavement, and the strange sense of detachment I had felt from the seedy respectability, yes Kemp, that same grotesque, gloomy environment around depressing Great Portland Street, and the inadequate feeling which I had received from the sordid, destitute commercialism of the very miserable, drab, and dreary place."

"You should've entered into a monastery and became a monk, or you could've become an unconventional transvestite transgender and entered a convent as a horny-kinky nun," Dr. Kemp quipped. "Sounds like you're still down in the damned dumps!"

"I did not feel a bit sorry and had little remorse for my father's passing. The old goat seemed to me to be the victim of his own foolish sentimentality. The current 'affair' required my attendance at his funeral, but it was really not my affair to savor."

"People usually don't have affairs at funeral services inside the church. They're usually done before or after the church ceremony, when attendees ordinarily switch marital partners, and then merrily shack-up."

"Very unfunny, Dr. Kemp. But hiking along lackluster High Street, my old life came back to me for a space, for I coincidentally met a girl I had known ten years before. Soon our eyes met."

"You didn't meet the rest of her face or body?"

"Don't be so fuckin' silly. It was all like a dream, actually more like a friggin' terrible nightmare. I did not feel right then that I was horribly lonely; and that I had come-out from a religious church fantasy world into a forbidden, desolate city hellscape."

"I see. You found your old dream girl as you were strolling down the pavement on High Street, while not being melancholy or sentimental about burying your father, whom you had robbed and stolen his borrowed money, simply to advance your dumb-ass post-college light invisibility project."

"Well Dr. Kemp, that's one fuckin' way to bluntly put it. Re-entering my dingy room on Great Portland Street seemed like it being my much-needed drastic recovery from brutal reality. There were the paraphernalia and items I knew and loved all around me. There stood the apparatus, the experiments, the illegal drugs, all arranged and waiting for my personal and private secret usage. And now, there was scarcely a difficulty or major obstacle left in my light experiment preparation; that is, beyond the planning of last-minute details."

"I understand quite fully. You just buried your father, and now you decided to gravely get deeply buried in your work to forget about burying your father."

"I will tell you, Dr. Kemp, sooner or later, all the complicated processes I had endured after burying my father. We need not go into *that* irrelevant bullshit right now. For the most part, saving certain gaps, *we* together must hunt-down that impish rogue Tom Marvel and kill the dirty shithead," obsessed Mr. Griffin declared. "Those three secret books of mine that are still in *his* avaricious possession contain the missing knowledge that I've laboriously obtained to further investigate how precisely light makes me invisible, but I never got to the point as to how light can make me more mentally, emotionally, and physically stable. I desperately need light to reverse the flow of itself in order to basically uncrazy myself. Does my dilemma make sense to you?"

"You've mentioned the word 'stable'. Did your father own a stable with horses and donkeys in it? Is that why you hate this Thomas Marvel asshole, because the irascible punk was always horsing around?"

"I strongly and highly recommend, Dr. Kemp, that *we* must immediately intercept and possess *my* three pilfered books, so that I can figure-out a viable cure for my mental, emotional, and physical health disabilities. Do you now fathom the magnitude of my debacle?"

"If you can't cure your mental, emotional, and physical maladies, then I suggest that you learn how to cure hams in a smokehouse. But I do 'fathom' one thing; your father had been buried six-feet-deep."

"Dr. Kemp. Stop your annoying zaniness! I insist that we must get those three fuckin' books back from Thomas Marvel. Yes sir; we must get those books again. But the essential phase at *that* Great Portland Street time, in my deteriorating mind, was to place the transparent object, whose refractive index was to be lowered between two radiating centers of a sort of ethereal vibration, of which I will tell you more fully later. No, not those Wilhelm Röntgen Radiology vibrations. I basically mean, Dr. Kemp, good, good, good vibrations. I don't know that those other principles I've employed have been adequately described."

"You had mentioned that you must get those fuckin' books back. Quite confidentially, I've never seen books fuck other books!"

"Yet Dr. Kemp; I had needed two little dynamos, and these I worked with a small, cheap utilitarian gas engine. My first experiment was with a bit of white wool fabric. It was the strangest thing in the world to see it perform in the flicker of the flashes; soft and white, and then to watch the experimental wool fade like a wreath of smoke, and soon quickly vanish."

"Holy smokes, Invisible Man. I think that you're a real gas because you're trying to again pull the damned wool over my eyes, just like marvelous Thomas Marvel had been successful at pulling the wool over *your'* damned eyes."

"I'm warning you; stop interrupting me with your nonsensical drivel! And then, Dr. Kemp, came a terribly curious experience I'll never forget. I heard a meow behind me, and turning, my eyes, saw a lean white cat, very dirty, and it had been sitting and meowing on the cistern cover outside the window."

"I suspected that you were the cat's meow, and now I really know you are!"

"This cat came-in, purring, and the poor beast was starving too, so I gave her some curdled milk to drink. All my rancid food was in a cupboard in the corner of the raunchy room. After that act of domestic kindness, the dirty white cat went smelling all around the room, evidently with the idea of making herself at home. The invisible rag I was wearing around my wrist upset her a bit; you should've seen her spit and hiss at it! But I made her comfortable on the pillow of my truckle-bed. And I gave her butter to get her to wash her paws."

"Most pussies don't like rags when their having their monthly periods," Dr. Kemp joked. "Even unhappy female orchestra players, who dislike other minstrels, hate their menstruals even more. And next you successfully processed the cat?"

"Yes, Dr. Kemp; I processed her. But giving drugs to a cat is no joke, Kemp! And the complicated process failed."

"Holy shit! You had failed! What a catastrophe to catalog in your' fucked-up mind. Did the poor animal enter into a catatonic state, or find a quality grooming device in a nearby catacomb?"

"Then thereafter, my dear Dr. Kemp. It was night outside, and nothing was to be seen but the animal's dim eyes and the cat's sharp claws. I stopped the gas engine, and felt for and stroked the cat's fur."

"Midnight is the worst time to have a stroke, even for a cat, but not for Santa Claus! It's hard to get an ambulance at that time of night to transport a white dirty cat to a certified veterinarian. You don't mean to say that there's an invisible cat prowling around at large!" Kemp demanded knowing.

"If it hasn't been killed, why not? It certainly is quite possible! It's very probably been killed," the Invisible Man confidently remarked. "It was alive four days after, I know for a fact, Dr. Kemp, because I later saw the creature scavenging for rabid mice down a road grating on Great Titchfield Street. I must've gone up Great Portland without ever realizing my mental mistake. I remember the barracks on Albany Street, and the horse-soldiers coming-out, and at last I found the summit of Primrose Hill. It was a sunny day in January; yes, one of those sunny, frosty days that come before the annual snows this year. My weary brain tried to formulate the exact position of how I should plot-out a strategic plan of action."

"Ah yes. 'Primrose Hill. Life's a holiday on Primrose Hill. Life's not a holiday on Primrose Hill, with you.' Catchy melody, wouldn't you agree?"

"At the time, Dr. Kemp, I had disregarded the cat that I had administered the potent drug to, and to tell you the truth, I was quite apathetic about the entire fucked-up matter."

"Besides being 'apathetic', you sound right now that you're still *a pathetic* wreck. Say, did you ever attend Fairly Ridiculous University over in New Jersey?"

"That night my snoopy landlord came to my door, holding a lit candle with an eviction notice. Upon serving me with the bad-luck paper, the old coot looked at my pallid face with half of it missing, dropped the eviction letter and the candle to the ground, shit his pants twice, and smelling like a stenchy cesspool, scurried away from my apartment faster than greased lightning."

"Your mediocre story only proves that your nasty, grumpy curmudgeon of a landlord couldn't hold a candle to your overwhelming genius!"

"My grumpy, grouchy stubborn, old fart landlord, an hour later, returned to my door with another condemning eviction notion. At the fear of the possibility of my work being exposed or rudely interrupted at its very climax, I became very angry and pro-active. I hurried-outside with my cheque-book to finally pay my landlord the debt I had owed him in the dark. The old fogey, smoking a stogie, spoke to me in Cockney English."

"I think that you would've been happier and more satisfied if you had reached a climax with the girl you had met from your childhood on or near Great Portland at the beginning of your story, rather than trying to have abnormal, up the ass sex in the middle of a slum with a ninety-seven-year-old daft codger like your' goddamned ancient landlord, who apparently, according to your perverted description, was so old that he didn't know the exact difference between his cock and his knee."

"This is no time for your perverted comedy, Dr. Kemp. Then finally, feeling exceptionally hungry, I left my apartment to trek to a late dinner at a cheap restaurant, but on the way, I had slipped on a box of matches while skirting around a high pile of street rubbish. My body landed squarely upon a bicycle tire made of rubber."

"If you slipped on a rubber, then I think that, just like your old geezer landlord, you don't know the difference between your cock and your knee."

"Dr. Kemp. I do truthfully believe that I would prefer to have that conniving imbecile Thomas Marvel as my personal assistant and an apprentice, rather than have to listen to your caustic, acerbic, ball-busting whims, while futilely exploring and searching in the vast rural Sussex County wilderness in vital quest of my three missing volumes of indispensable notes."

Chapter 21

"IN OXFORD STREET"

"Now in my going downstairs, Dr. Kemp, the first time I had done so after my initial preliminary experiments, I found an unexpected difficulty because I could not see my feet; indeed, I had stumbled twice, and there was an unaccustomed clumsiness in my gripping the door bolt. By not looking down, however, for a brief duration, I managed to walk on the level, passably well."

"Instead of unbolting the damned door, I think you should've bolted the hell away from there as soon as possible," Dr. Kemp jokingly replied.

"I must say that my mood, Dr. Kemp, was one of extreme exaltation. I felt as a seeing man might do, with padded feet and with noiseless clothes, existing independently in a repulsive city of the ambulating blind. I experienced a wild impulse to engage in jest; I had the urge to startle and shock unsuspecting people; I strongly desired to clap and pound men on the back, and violently knock-out their false teeth; I wanted to fling people's hats astray, and generally, to revel in my extraordinary advantage over their inferior and doomed asses. Do I communicate precisely how I felt?"

"I see. You were an asinine jester merrily practicing your entire nine gestures."

"But hardly had I emerged upon Great Portland Street, however, when I heard a clashing concussion, and was severely impacted from behind, and turning my eyes, I saw a man carrying a basket of soda-water syphons, and I strained my pupils, looking in amazement at his heavy burden. Now allow me to tell you, Dr. Kemp. Although the incidental blow had really badly hurt me, I found something so irresistible in the aggressor's astonishment that I began laughing aloud. 'As is often said, the devil is in the basket,' I mentally considered, and suddenly, my invisible hand had twisted the damned basket out of his powerful grasp. The bloke let go incontinently, and I managed to then swing the whole weight into the air."

"Well now, Invisible Man. I once choked an obnoxious pupil in my freshman chemistry class, but in comparison to what you had done to the syphon carrier on the London Street, I must congratulate you on making the clumsy fool a complete basket case."

"But Dr. Kemp; then a fool of a cabman, standing outside a public unisex whorehouse, made a sudden rush for that same basket, and his extended fingernails punctured me with excruciating pain, under my left ear. I then cleverly let the whole weight of the basket down with a smash on the cabman's noggin, and then, with shouts and the clatter of feet maneuvering about me, with curious people coming out of shops to view the great commotion, and with a myriad of vehicles pulling-up, I quickly realized what a menace I had initiated for myself. And cursing my folly, I backed against a shop window and adequately prepared to dodge-out of the massive confusion when that fortuitous opportunity should arise."

"Wow! You could've been the Artful Dodger in Charles Dickens' classic novel 'Oliver Twist', or better yet, you could've played second base for the Brooklyn Trolley Dodgers across the pond over in politically corrupt New York City."

"In a moment, Dr. Kemp, I came to realize that I would be futilely wedged into a hostile crowd, and my invisible hand would inevitably be discovered. I pushed by a crippled butcher boy, who luckily did not turn to see the nothingness that had shoved him aside and onto the pavement, and my legs quickly dodged behind the cabman's four-wheeler. I hurried straight across the road, which to my joy, was happily clear, and hardly heeding which way to run and turn, in the fright of detection that the harrowing incident had given me, I incidentally had plunged into the afternoon throng of promenading amblers down Oxford Street."

"Of course, you were wearing your oxfords and not your damned leather bathroom slippers," Dr. Kemp jested. "And if you were escaping your harrowing London encounters out into the suburban countryside, you could've been doing a farmer a favor by 'harrowing' his field."

"Stop being so damned facetious and frivolous, Dr. Kemp. You've broken my balls into smithereens all this inglorious morning," the Paranoid Psycho Case accused. "Now then; I tried to get into the regular stream of people, but in a moment, my heels were being trodden upon. I took to the gutter, the roughness of which I found painful to my feet, and forthwith, the shaft of a crawling hansom dug me forcibly under the shoulder blade, reminding me that I was already-bruised rather severely. I clumsily staggered-out of the errant cab's way; my wobbly legs avoided a perambulator by enacting a convulsive movement, and I soon found myself standing directly behind the hansom."

"I hope your bruised heel had healed over time. Was it a handsome hansom driver who had viciously plowed into your ass?"

"Next now, Dr. Kemp; a happy inspiration saved me, and I followed in its immediate wake, trembling and astonished at the various turns of my stressful, ongoing misadventure. And not only shaking and trembling, but also shivering as well. It was a bright day in January, and I was stark naked, and the thin slime of mud that covered the road was absolutely freezing. Foolish as it seems to me now, I had not reckoned that, transparent or not, I was still amenable to the whims of winter weather, and to all its diabolical consequences."

"You would still have to 'worry', even if your first name was Jan, and your middle name initial was 'the letter U' for Ulysses!"

"Then suddenly, Dr. Kemp, a bright idea came flashing into my hard head. I ran around the side of the hansom and anxiously clambered-around the cab. And so, shivering, scared, and sniffing with the first intimations of a cold, and with the bruises in the small of my back growing greater upon my attention, I intrepidly hopped aboard and commandeered the vacant hansom, and driving the cab slowly along Oxford Street, speeding right past Tottenham Court Road, with the hansom's driver standing on the rear sidewalk, shouting a litany of expletives. My mood was as different from that in which I had sallied-forth ten minutes before, as it is ever possible to imagine. 'This tremendous invisibility factor indeed!' I reckoned to myself. The one thought that possessed me most was, Dr. Kemp, how the hell was I going to get out of the ongoing scrape I was in?"

"You had already told me that you had scraped your heel, and now you're telling me that you've also scraped your entire body on Tottendam Court Road? My God, Man! You had scraped your heel twice! You were indeed becoming a 'roads scholar'!"

"Well Dr. Kemp, on my bruised knees I crawled past Mudie's Library Printing, and there a tall woman with five or six yellow-labeled books hailed my former cab, and I sprang out just in time to escape her confrontation, shaving a railway van narrowly in my flight. I made-off up the roadway to Bloomsbury Square, intending to strike north past the Museum, and so flee into the more-quiet and safe district. I was now cruelly chilled, and the strangeness of my situation so unnerved me that I perpetually whimpered as I desperately ran. At the northward corner of the popular Square, a little white dog ran-out of the Pharmaceutical Society's offices, and incontinently made for me, nose down."

"You're saying that the dog was incontinent and had shit all over you?"

"Well, Dr. Kemp. I had never realized it before, but the nose is to the mind of a dog what the eye is to the mind of a seeing human being. Dogs perceive the scent of a man or a woman moving, just as men and women perceive their own vision. This persistent brute began barking and leaping all the fuck over me, showing, as it seemed, only too plainly that the hideous mongrel was keenly aware of my presence. I crossed Great Russell Street, worriedly glancing over my shoulder as I did so, and next painfully sauntered some way along Montague Street, before I realized what I was running towards."

"There appears to be lots of cats and doggerel in your myriad experiences," I must confess. "Was it raining cats and dogs at the time?"

"Then, Dr. Kemp; I became aware of an annoying blare of music, and looking along the street, my eyes saw a number of people advancing out of Russell Square, wearing red shirts, and the procession participants were wildly waving the banner of the *Salvation Army*. Such a crowd, chanting in the roadway, and scoffing on the pavement, that I could not hope to penetrate their' density, and dreading to go back further away from my dingy apartment again, and deciding on the spur of the moment, I ran up the white steps of a house facing the museum railings, and stood there until the raucous crowd should pass. Happily, the persistent and dogged canine simultaneously had stopped at the noise of the band, too; the carnivorous mutt hesitated, and luckily turned tail, running again back to the cur's familiarity with Bloomsbury Square."

"Thank goodness the ferocious dog had been easily distracted. Quite obviously," Dr. Kemp elaborated, "you had gained your salvation from the dog's bite by the inadvertent mercy of the charity army's hysterical members waving their soliciting red banners. Luckily for you, the fierce cur had reacted to the big rustle going on in Russell Square."

"On came the bothersome band, Dr. Kemp, bawling with unconscious irony, some fucked-up hymn about 'When shall we see His face?' And it seemed an interminable time to me before the tide of the crowd washed along the pavement, passing straight by me. Thud, thud, thud, came the band's annoying bass drum with a vibrating resonance, and for the moment, I did not notice two punk urchins stopping at the railings by me. 'See 'em,' noticed and reported the first little asshole. 'See what?' asked the other diminutive asshole. 'Why them footmarks; they're as bare as a fat nudist's ass. The weird marks look like what you make playin' and walkin' in mud'."

"As you had so graphically described, I'm glad to learn that you didn't get ripped in the tide of people that were washing along the damned sidewalk!"

"I looked down and saw that the punk youngsters had stopped and were then gaping at the muddy footmarks I had left behind me, while ascending the newly-whitened steps. Next thing I knew, Dr. Kemp. My ears heard an alert jerk-off yelling, 'Thud, thud, thud, thud. There's a barefoot man gone up them white steps, or I don't know nothing else. And he ain't never come down again. And his foot was a-bleeding, but the fucker had no damned foot, nor no damned leg, either'."

"The bloke was only speaking the bloody truth. What's so fuckin' wrong about that type of pure and sincere honesty? Tell me, Invisible Man. How long have you been a bloody atheist?"

"The thick of the crowd had already passed. 'Looky there, Ted,' hollered the younger of the two bobbies standing on the corner, doing nothing as usual. And the second curious cop pointed straight to my feet to his don't give-a-shit bobby partner. I looked-down and saw at once the dim suggestion of my feet outlined, sketched in splashes of soft wet mud. For a moment, I was mentally and physically paralyzed."

"I hate to tell you, but must people who become paralyzed stay paralyzed. You definitely are, and were, the exception."

"Why, that's rum," said the elder patrolman. 'Dashed rum! It's just like the ghost of a foot, ain't it, Billy Boy?' The two patrolmen hesitated and advanced with their outstretched hands and raised night clubs. A man pulled-up short to see what the bobbies were catching, and then a teenaged girl's attention had been attracted, also. Now back to the two idiotic kids, in another moment, the first little punk's hand would've touched me. Then, Dr. Kemp, I saw exactly what I should do. I made a hasty step, and the inquisitive scamp started back with a loud exclamation, and with a rapid movement, I swung myself over into the portico of the next house. But the smaller obnoxious punk was sharp-eyed enough to follow my invisible acrobatic movement, and before I was well-down the steps and upon the sidewalk's pavement, the curious and retarded imp had recovered from his momentary astonishment, and the junior jerk-off was shouting-out that only my feet had gone over the wall."

"You should've stayed in bed under the covers *that* morning," Dr. Kemp constructively suggested. "Even London 'undercover agents' would've never caught or detected you being invisible and stark naked in bed! And please tell me, Griffin. How could two weak bobbies ever raise a single night club. I'll wager that the pair couldn't even raise a small restaurant, either!"

"The other pedestrians immediately rushed-over and crowded all around the scene of confusion, and the multitude of enamored eyewitnesses saw my fresh footmarks flash into existence, seemingly penetrating into the lower stone step, and also being absorbed upon the dense sidewalk pavement. 'What's up?' asked an anonymous someone. 'Feet! Look! Invisible feet running, without any fuckin' knees or legs'!"

"More people would've been interested in your adventurous escapade if you had been penetrating a surprised bimbo up the ass in Bloomsbury Square with your stark-naked, erect pecker."

"Everybody in the road, Dr. Kemp, except my three amazed pursuers, was pouring along after the seemingly magnetic, very lackluster, Salvation Army Band. There was an eddy of surprise along with random interrogations being loudly yelled. At the cost of bowling-over one young fellow chasing me down a narrow lane, I got through the belligerent throng, and in another moment, I was rushing headlong around the full circuit of Russell Square, with six or seven terribly antagonistic people speedily trailing my newly-established footmarks. There was no time for glib explanation, Dr. Kemp, or else the whole host of assholes would've been after my ass."

'First of all, I'm now your host, and I have no fuckin' desire to have ever been there in Russell Square watching you trying to flee and escape a bunch of raving maniacs, you completely paranoid and neurotic Asshole! Second of all, Mr. Invisible Man, you had failed to bowl-over any of your spectators when running down the narrow lane, so your mind was probably already in the gutter, and I can accurately presume that on that oddball day, bowling was not up your alley."

"Twice I had doubled my route in circles around the Square's four corners, Dr. Kemp, and my legs thrice crossed the road and came back upon my original tracks. And then, as my feet grew hot and dry, the damp mud impressions began to fade. At last, I had a relatively good breathing space, and I conscientiously rubbed my feet clean with my hands, and so got away from their imminent danger altogether. The last I saw of the chase was a little group of at least a dozen or so people perhaps, studying with infinite perplexity a slowly drying footprint that had resulted from a puddle in Tavistock Square, a footprint as isolated and as incomprehensible to them as Robinson Crusoe's solitary discovery on the isolated island had been to him."

"I believe, sir, that Robinson Crusoe had discovered that mind-boggling footprint on Friday, if I correctly remember from Daniel Defoe's classic novel, which I had read eight times in kindergarten. Holy shit, Invisible Man. I think you need a shrink, just like my inflamed hemorrhoids!"

"This exhaustive running, which I had just done, warmed me to a certain extent, and I went on with a better courage through the maze of less frequented roads that runs thereabouts. Yes, dear Dr. Kemp. My back had then become very stiff and sore; my tonsils were painful from the cabman's lengthy fingernails, and the skin of my neck had been scratched by his long sharp nails; my feet hurt exceedingly, and I had become lame from a little cut upon one foot. I saw in time a blind man approaching me, and fled his encroaching encounter, limping like a wounded cripple, for I feared his subtle intuitions, despite the fact that the idiot could never see me. Once or twice, accidental street collisions had occurred with unwary pedestrians, and I had left other innocent people amazed, screaming my delirious unaccountable curses into their disbelieving ears."

"Well Griffin, what the hell boring bullshit happened next? Did you ever get laid?"

"Then came something silent and quiet against my face, and across the Square, my invisible skin felt a thin veil of slowly falling flakes of snow. I had caught a cold, and do as I would, I could not avoid an occasional sneeze. And every dog that came in sight of me,

Chapter 22

"IN THE EMPORIUM"

"So, erudite Dr. Kemp, last January, with the beginning of a massive recorded snowstorm in the air. and weary, cold, painful, inexpressibly wretched and weak, and still but only half-convinced of my invisible capabilities, I began this new life to which I'm now fully committed. I had no refuge, no appliances, no human being in the world in whom I could confide."

"You might be committed to your project, but I think you oughta' be committed to St. Mary's of Bethlehem for intense observation, analysis, and rehabilitation. I'll personally author the script."

"Nevertheless, Dr. Kemp, most surely you are jesting and trying to amuse me. I was half-minded to accost some passer-by and throw myself upon his or her mercy. But I knew too clearly the terror and brutal cruelty my unexpected advances would evoke. I made no plans to involve the streets and major thoroughfares. My sole objective was to get shelter from the snow; yes, to get myself covered and warm; then I might hope to plan without discomfort. But even to me, a lonely and independent Invisible Man, the rows of London houses stood latched, and barred, as I moved about the city."

"You were definitely right about the 'half-minded' comment," Kemp agreed. "Not everyone has worms for brains like you do."

"And then, Doctor, I conceived a most brilliant strategy. I turned down one of the roads leading from Gower Street to Tottenham Court Road, and found myself outside Omniums, the big establishment where everything imaginable is to be bought; you know the place: meat, grocery, linen, furniture, clothing, kids sex toys, penis prosthetics, oil paintings, cross-dressing clothes, dildos, even—a huge meandering collection of shops rather than just *a shop.*"

"That kind of place is called a Mall, you stupid twit! One stop shopping! A Mall; you fuckin' got it!"

"Anyway Dr. Kemp, I had thought I should find the doors open, but the entrances were closed, and as I stood in the wide portico, a carriage stopped outside, and a man in uniform, you know the kind of personage with the designated logo 'Omnium' upon his cap, arrived and flung-open the door. I contrived to enter, and walking down the first aisle, it was a department where the salespersons were selling ribbons, gloves and stockings, and that kind of junk merchandise, and soon I came to a more spacious region devoted to simple picnic baskets and wicker furniture."

"My goodness gracious, Griffin! Have you been living your whole life inside a dark cave or under a damned rock. I've been shopping in that horrendous rip-off place for decadent decades."

"I did not feel safe being there; customers, as was their custom, were coming and going like swarming bees inside a busy hive, and I prowled restlessly about until I came upon a huge section in an upper floor containing multitudes of bedsteads, and over these I clambered and leaped, and found a resting-place at last among a huge pile of folded flock mattresses."

"You should've demonstrated better discipline and 'behived' in an organized fashion like your role model bees behaved inside their buzzing hive colony."

"Anyway, Dr. Kemp. The place was already lit-up and agreeably warm, and I decided to remain where I was, keeping a cautious eye on the two or three sets of shopmen and early customers who were meandering through that section, I presumed, until closing time would come. Then, I should be able to rob the place for needed food and clothing, and wearing a pilfered disguise, prowl through the store and examine its resources, perhaps even sleeping on some of the bedding, which seemed an acceptable plan. My idea was to procure clothing to make myself a muffled-but-acceptable figure; to obtain money, and then to recover my books and parcels wherever the three volumes awaited me. Hereafter, I schemed to take a lodging somewhere in the countryside, and form elaborate plans for the complete realization of the advantages that my invisibility would give me over my fellow-humans."

"Have you ever contemplated committing suicide? If not, I'll gladly volunteer performing a homicide for you! I think you need death right now!"

"Closing time arrived quickly enough Dr. Kemp. It could not have been more than ten hours after I took-up my position on the mattresses before I noticed the blinds of the windows being drawn, and customers being marched to the revolving exit doors. And then a number of brisk young men began with remarkable alacrity to tidy-up the goods that had remained disturbed. I left my lair as the crowds diminished, and prowled cautiously out into the less desolate parts of the huge department store. I was really surprised to observe how rapidly the young men and women whipped-away the goods displayed for sale during the day."

"Is there a main idea to this fucked-up department store story? I couldn't be more bored if I were a recently drilled water well!"

"All the boxes of essential clothing products; including shirts, blouses and shoes; all of the hanging fabrics; the festoons of lace; the boxes of sweets inside the grocery section; the displays of this and that, were being whipped-down, folded-up, slapped into tidy receptacles, and everything that could not be taken-down and put away had sheets of some coarse material like sacking flung over them."

"Of course, the sheets were coarse, but from your amazement at the variety of articles that were for sale, you must've spent the majority of your life crawling around in your playpen and inside your sandbox."

"Finally, Dr. Kemp. All the chairs were turned-up onto the counters, leaving the floor clear. Then came a lot of dumb-shit youngsters scattering sawdust and carrying pails and brooms. I had to dodge to get out of their insolent way, and as it was, my ankle got stung with the sawdust. For some time, wandering through the swathed and darkened departments, I could hear the brooms at work. And at last, a good hour or more after the shop had been closed, came a noise of locking doors. Silence came upon the entire place, and I found myself wandering through the vast and intricate shops, and galleries, all alone. It was very still; in one place I remember passing near one of the Tottenham Court Road entrances, and listening to the tapping of boot-heels of the passers-by outside."

"You mean to tell me that you never in all your life saw dust like that sawdust on the floor? Did those common brooms come alive, and swept your ass off your invisible feet?"

"My first visit was to the place where I had seen stockings and gloves for sale. Now Dr. Kemp, it was dark, and I had the devil of a hunt to find matches, which I found at last in the drawer of a little cash desk. Then, I had to find and get a candle. I had to tear down wrappings and ransack a number of boxes and drawers, but at last, I managed to turn-out and discover what I had sought; the box label called them' lambswool pants', and 'lambswool vests. Then, I located woolen socks, a thick comforter, and next I arrived at the clothing place and got trousers, a lounge jacket, an overcoat, and a slouch hat, a clerical sort of hat with the brim turned-down. After that cost-free shopping spree, I began to feel like a hungry human being again, and my next thought was 'food'."

"I think I'm going to telegraph the London authorities and see how much of a cash reward I'll get for turning your crazy illegal ass in. I have but one single question to ask you. Have you ever taken a shit?"

"Upstairs, Dr. Kemp, was a refreshment department, and there I acquired some cold meat. There was coffee still in the urn, and I lit the gas and warmed it up again, and altogether, I did not do too badly. Afterwards, prowling through the place in search of blankets, I had to put up at last with a heap of downy quilts. Next, I came upon a grocery section with a lot of chocolate and candied fruits, more than would be good for me, and much to my satisfaction, I found some white burgundy to imbibe. And near that wonderful area was a toy department, and soon I had a brilliant idea. I located some artificial noses, actually dummy noses, you know, and I thought of grabbing several dark glasses. Finally, I dozed-off to sleep in a heap of down quilts, very warm and comfortable."

"Well, not to sound too redundant, but I'm glad you didn't make a fucked-up spectacle out of yourself in the glasses department, even though the huge department store was devoid of workers, and only you had been locked inside."

"My last thoughts before sleeping were the most agreeable ones I had had since my dramatic invisibility change. I was in a state of physical serenity, and that peace was reflected throughout my mind. I thought that I should be able to slip-out unobserved in the morning, with my new clothes upon me, muffling my face with a white wrapper I had purloined. I also had stolen spectacles and so forth, and so I had completed my disguise."

"Damned it! If you were a cesspool, I'd know exactly what the fuck to do with you!"

"The pale London dawn had finally arrived; and the place was full of a chilly grey light that filtered round the edges of the window blinds. I sat-up, and for a time, I could not think where this ample apartment, with its counters, its piles of rolled stuff, its heap of quilts and cushions, and its iron pillars, might be. Then, as recollection came back, and I heard distant voices in conversation."

"It stands to reason that if you heard different voices speaking, fuckin' conversation was going on somewhere in your vicinity!"

"Then, far down the aisle, in the brighter light of some department which had already raised its blinds, I noticed two men approaching. I scrambled to my feet, looking about me for some way of escape, and even as I did so, the sound of my movement made them aware of my illicit presence. I suppose they saw merely a figure moving quietly and quickly away. 'Who's that?' cried one, and 'Stop there!' shouted the other. I dashed around a corner and came full tilt, a faceless figure, mind you, upon a lanky lad of fifteen. He yelled and I bowled him over, rushed past his ass, turned another corner, and by a happy inspiration, threw myself behind a counter. In another moment, feet went running past my location, and I heard voices shouting, 'All hands immediately to the doors!' and the employees were giving one another advice on how to catch me."

"You must've impressed the more-horny women employees that you were a dashing young man!"

"Lying on the floor, I felt scared out of my wits. But really Dr. Kemp, odd as it may seem, it did not occur to me at that moment to take off my clothes as I should have done. I had made up my mind, I suppose, to get away wearing them, and *that* dominant thought ruled me. And then down the vista of the myriad counters came a bawling of "There he is!""

"You could've played a game of strip poker with the guards and told them you were the president of the Leatherhead Nudist Colony Association if you had lost the decisive hand."

"I instantly sprang to my feet, Dr. Kemp. I whipped a chair near the counter, and sent the seat whirling at the fool who had been shouting commands in my direction. My head turned, and my blow sent the bellicose bloke spinning onto the floor. I then decided to scamper up the stairs to continue my in-progress escape. My determined pursuer kept his footing, and the bastard came up the staircase hot after me."

"If your pursuer was dragging a stubborn donkey behind him, you could've kicked his ass good!"

"That's it! Splendid art pots were hanging from the ceiling," I instantly recognized. "Well, Dr. Kemp; I turned at the top step and swung around, plucked one out of a pile and smashed it onto his silly head as the dumb-shit came at me. The whole pile of pots went headlong, and I heard shouting and footsteps running from all parts. My feet made a mad rush for the refreshment place, and there was a fat slob dressed in white, looking like a cook, who voluntarily deputized himself, and the obese asshole took-up the chase. I made one last desperate turn, and found myself among lamps and ironmongery. My body went behind the counter of that sales area, and I waited for the cook to come by, and as he bolted in at the head of the chase, I doubled him up with a metallic lamp. Down the chef went, and I crouched-over behind the counter and began whipping-off my clothes as fast as I could. Coat, jacket, trousers, shoes, and everything else. I heard more motivated men sprinting towards me, and the hostile corpulent cook was lying quiet on the other side of the counter, either stunned or scared speechless, and I had to make another dash for it, like a rabbit hunted out of a wood-pile."

"I suppose the chef never found-out what was cooking with you. He probably was really pissed-off because you were stirring the pot in the colossal department store, without ever obtaining his expressed permission."

"'I heard voices screaming, 'This way, policeman'! Next, I heard someone shouting 'What the fuck'? I found myself in my bedstead storeroom again, and hiding at the end of a wilderness of wardrobes. Then Dr. Kemp, I rushed among them, went flat, got rid of my vest after gyrating and exercising infinite wriggling, and finally, I stood a free man, naked again, and invisible to their detection, panting and scared, as the policeman and three of the shopmen came hustling around the corner. The chasers made a blitz for the acquired vest and pants, and managed to collar the trousers. 'He's dropping his plunder,' yelled one of the young bouncers. 'He *must* be somewhere in here'."

"Did you ever go into the detergent department. Your fucked-up story is sounding more and more like a stupid-assed soap opera!"

"I stood watching the incompetent fools hunt my ass for a long time, and I skillfully hid from their amateur scrutiny, all-the-while cursing my ill-luck in losing the essential clothes that I truly needed. Then, I noticed that the coast was clear. I wandered again into the refreshment-chamber, and I drank a little milk that I had found there. Lastly, Dr. Kemp, I sat-down by the Omnium Department Store's kiddie sex toy and dildo department to consider my next move."

"You really were fucked-up inside, "Dr. Kemp concluded and declared. "I suspect that you were actually geographically disoriented. When you thought that 'the coast was clear', you were probably thinking that you were being chased on a Japanese beach just outside downtown Tokyo!"

Jay Dubya

Chapter 23

"IN DRURY LANE"

"But you should begin now to realize and appreciate my full horrendous dilemma, Dr. Kemp," the Invisible Man stated, resuming his garrulous monologue. "I had almost-completed the first phase of my research when I encountered no shelter, no clothing, and no food, and I had to make myself into a strange and terrible desperate thief in order to acquire *those* three basic needs. I was fasting to conserve energy and weight in order to attempt becoming more permanently invisible. If I ate too much and consumed food too often, I would then egregiously fill myself with unassimilated matter, and obviously, I would soon become grotesquely visible again with the additional volume and weight added to my body. I quickly realized that I had to have a minimal diet in order to be able to stay invisible."

"I never thought of *that* aspect to your deplorable plight," Dr. Kemp objectively comprehended. "Now I know why Martin Luther had a Diet of Worms!"

"And Dr. Kemp; the falling snow had warned me of other prospective dangers. I could not go abroad in snow; it would settle on me, flake by flake, and transpose me into someone like Frosty the Snowman. Rain, too, would make me a watery outline, a glistening surface of a semi-man, basically a miserable human bubble. And in regard to fog, I should be like a fainter bubble in a denser fog, a mere surface, a greasy glimmer of a fading humanity that doesn't know shit about shit. Moreover, Doctor, as I ventured further into the city, foul London air gathered dirt about my ankles; floating bugs, smuts, and dust landed and encrusted upon my exposed skin. I did not know how long it would be before I should become visible from that formidable external bombardment. But I saw clearly that it could not be for too long."

"I understand your predicament perfectly," Dr. Kemp affirmed, nodding his head. "You couldn't 'get the fog' out of London soon enough, because the fog got you the fuck out of London in a fast fart's propulsion!"

"I went into the sleazy slums over towards Great Portland Street, and found myself at the end of the alley in which I had lodged. I did not go my usual direct route, because of the crowd of gawkers that had assembled halfway down the lane, standing opposite to the still smoking ruins of the burning house in which I had lived."

"Your apartment on fire must have really burned you up!" Dr. Kemp assessed and spoke. "You should've invited your lame-brain neighbors and non-friends over for a housewarming."

"Pity me greatly, Dr. Kemp, for I have suffered tremendous emotional anguish and physical agony, with too little exhilaration and ecstasy with which to balance-out the unlevel equation. My most immediate problem, besides the raging conflagration, was how to acquire and retain clothing. What to do with my face also puzzled me. Then, leaving my flaming apartment address, I saw in one of those little miscellaneous shops that sells news, sweets, toys, stationery, big rubber sex dolls, and belated Christmas tomfoolery, an array of masks and noses. I realized that my physical appearance problem could be ingeniously solved. In a flash, my course of action materialized inside my shallow brain. I automatically headed towards the back streets north of the Strand; for I remembered, though not very distinctly from where, that some theatrical costumers had been operating trade shops in that thespian district."

"Yes, there seems to be a strand of hope for you around Piccadilly. Did you wind-up buying a fake nose from a thespian lesbian?" Dr. Kemp rather sagaciously inquired. "I Mean, Mr. Invisible, that you just had to revolt against *light,* and act-out your frustrations in order to stage some sort of illuminating personal rebellion against your devastating debilitating condition."

"The day was cold, Dr. Kemp, with a nipping wind down the northward running through all the parallel streets. I hadn't eaten, so naturally, I walked fast to mentally negate my fast. I stubbornly refused to be overtaken or arrested. Every intersection crossing was a potential danger, and every exiting cab passenger, or pavement walker, another potential hazard to alertly watch and avoid. One man, a shabby-looking mendicant, I believe, I had encountered at the top of Bedford Street. The lousy scumbag turned upon me abruptly and smashed his fist into my abdomen rather abominably, sending me into the road, and me almost again being crushed under the wheel of a passing hansom. I was so unnerved by that near-death-experience that I hustled into Covent Garden Market and sat-down nude for some time in a quiet corner by a stall of violets, my lungs panting and trembling. I found that I had caught a fresh cold, and had to turn-out after a time, lest my louder sneezes should unwantedly attract attention."

"I see," Dr. Kemp eloquently fathomed and stated. "Your deep inhalation, along with your heavy exhalation, was indeed your very inspiration."

"Quit with the extraneous bullshit, Dr. Kemp. At last, I reached the object of my quest, a dirty, fly-blown, shabby, little retail shop near non-magnificent Drury Lane. The disgusting shithole featured a window full of tinsel robes, sham artificial jewelry, wigs, slippers, dominoes, and faded theatrical photographs. The shop was old-fashioned, had a low ceiling, and was dark and dismal. I peered through the storefront window, and seeing no one within, I furtively entered. My bare-feet hurriedly walked around a costume stand, and then my legs swayed into a corner behind a vertical cheval glass. For a minute or so, employees came into the sales area. Then, I heard heavy feet striding across the room, and a dark-skinned Arab behemoth appeared down in the rear of the shop."

"Did the gigantic Arab first try to sell you a flying magic carpet, and then ask you if you were Ali Baba looking for your fucked-up seven thieves?"

"My plans were now perfectly definite, Dr. Kemp. I proposed to myself to make my way further into the building, secrete myself upstairs, watch my every opportunity, and when everything was quiet, rummage-out a wig, a mask, spectacles, and a suitable costume, and then go into the outside world, perhaps as a grotesque transvestite, but still presenting myself as a very credible pedophile member of Parliament. And incidentally, of course, Dr. Kemp. I could then easily rob any house of any available money I might require at my own discretion and leisure."

"How the hell could you propose to yourself, let alone secrete yourself?" Kemp wanted to know. "Did you think that your body was a damned testicle, and that you were semen?"

"Apparently, Dr. Kemp, I had rudely interrupted the Arab's main meal of the day. The gargantuan bloke stared about the lackluster shop with an expression suggestive of beating the living shit out of me. This fear I felt gave way to surprise, and then evolved and ascended to anger, as the humongous brute saw the shop being empty of customers. Thank nature that the beast left me to my lonesome, presumably stepping outside to beat the shit out of somebody else."

"Was that intimidating colossal Arab fellow facing Mecca?" Dr. Kemp wanted to know. "In his pea-brain mind, he probably sphinx he had planned to a-nil-a-lite your ass!"

"I stood hesitating, with my vulnerable body frozen like an Eskimo igloo. Suddenly, Dr. Kemp, I heard *his* quick footsteps returning, and as the front store door pushed open, the impressive Goliath, even though the fucker was an Arab and not a Philistine, stood looking about the shop like a confused idiot who was still not satisfied. Then, murmuring to himself, the disenchanted ogre examined the back of the counter, and peered at some cheap display fixtures. Next, the colossus became excessively doubtful and skeptically suspicious. I then shrewdly and surreptitiously escaped to the rear stairs, and clambering up the steep steps, entered *his* small residence in the rear of the store."

"What the hell's especially wrong with your fucked-up cerebrum?" Dr. Kemp challenged the Invisible Man. "Haven't you ever been to an Arab bordello or brothel before? What kind of limited dumb-shit childhood and thwarted life experiences did you have in your fucked-up youth? No fuckin' wonder that you stole from your father's already-borrowed money! The so-called small store you were in was a front for an Arab whorehouse!"

"It was a queer little room, poorly furnished, and with a number of big masks displayed in the far-right corner. On the table was *his* belated breakfast, and it was a confoundedly exasperating thing for me, Dr. Kemp, to have to sniff his coffee and stand watching while the frightening brute came in and resumed his nauseous meal. And his table manners were terribly irritating, too. Two separate doors opened into the little room, one going upstairs and one down, but the two portals were both shut tight. I was trapped like a captured bear and could not get out of the kitchen zone while the brawny maniac was still around inside there. In fact, Dr. Kemp; I could scarcely move because of his general alertness, and there was a slight draft flowing down my back. Twice I strangled a sneeze just in time, before accidentally blowing a nostril off my freezing face."

"Look here, Mr. Invisible Man," eminent Dr. Kemp imperatively lectured. "Rooms cannot and are not queer as you had stated. You had meant to say that this giant Arab jerk-off might be the 'Q" in the LBGTQRSTUVW unisex community!"

"The spectacular quality of my sensations was both curious and novel, but Dr. Kemp, for all that expenditure of valuable energy, I was heavily tired and angry, long before the demented Sultan had finished his extensive eating. But at last, the behemoth made an end to his consumption, and putting his beggarly crockery back onto the black tin tray upon which he had had his dinky teapot, and after gathering all the crumbs up onto the mustard-stained cloth, the Arab Titan carried the whole lot of things he had collected back into the tiny store."

"I suppose that the giant Arab had enough energy to finally catch-up to his task and muster-up the myriad bread crumbs with his grimy mustard-stained rag!" Dr. Kemp imagined and orally conveyed. "Did the fearsome brute have a menagerie of camels grazing in his backyard? Did he desert his dessert while contemplating a relaxing return to the Arabian desert!"

"Now please allow me to adroitly finish my many misadventures experienced in downtown London, Dr. Darrell Kemp. I had the displeasure of seeing this Sultan-wannbe' begin-washing-up, and then, finding no good in me keeping shelter in the small kitchen, and the brick floor being cold on my feet, I sat in *his* chair by the fire. It was burning low, and scarcely thinking, I put on a little coal from the scuttle. The noise of that activity brought him at once into my area, and the dumb-fuck stood directly below my position on the stairs. I quickly and instinctively grabbed a funeral urn from a landing curio display, and cracked his skull open with a mighty force, and much to my horror, cremated ashes flew all around the giant Arab's head, as his massive frame crashed with a thud onto the red brick floor. As the Arab Brobdingnagian was falling from the metal urn's impact, I noticed that the formidable monster was even taller than I had supposed he had been, because the shithead had more-than-likely been plagued with a terribly bad case of advanced scoliosis."

"Knocked him on the head, you say?" Dr. Kemp asked. "You're now telling me that you had earned advanced survival skills by creatively using the curio urn loaded with cremated funeral ashes. The Arab leviathan, who later was found lying on the floor in an unconscious state, possibly wound-up in a London hospital because of you, Invisible Man; you were not too hospitable to the pugnacious pugilist while you were standing and hiding upon the stairsteps."

"The more I thought the entire scenario over, Dr. Kemp, the more I began realizing what a helpless absurdity it would be for an Invisible Man to be living in a cold and dirty city climate, populated by narrow-minded urban barbarians."

"But how and why did you eventually get to Iping?" Kemp asked the Invisible Man. "I presume that your principal intention was to compare educated London city barbarians to an aggregate of illiterate rural country- bumpkin barbarians. You had to make a rational choice," Dr. Kemp explained to the Invisible Man. "You had to compare and contrast civilized and educated city barbarians with ignorant, illiterate country barbarians, plain and simple. But tell me,

Griffin. What was your honest motivation to stay in primitive Iping?"

"I had traveled to Iping to work peacefully and alone on secretly developing the remainder of my clandestine *light property thesis.* And as you well-know, Dr. Kemp, according to *your* published newspaper accounts, *that* particular bombastic enterprise didn't work-out too satisfactorily, either. I have one question to ask you that might soothe and steady my mercurial conscience. Did I kill either the Iping constable or the tobacco store lout to whom I also had a conflict?"

"No," Dr. Kemp candidly and negatively emphasized. "According to the morning newspapers, they're both expected to fully recover."

"I don't know about that tramp acquaintance of mine, namely irresponsible and covetous Thomas Marvel. If I have to deal with much more of his insufferable insolence and nefarious deportment, I shall go insanely bonkers."

"No doubt, my friend; your entire scenario in regard to your learning the physics of invisibility is indubitably both exasperating and exacerbating, that is, when it's not collaborative and corroborative," Dr. Kemp dryly and coyly finished.

Jay Dubya

Chapter 24

"THE PLAN THAT FAILED"

"**B**ut now, my Illustrious Visitor," Dr. Darrell Kemp commenced his remarks, with a side glance given to the upstairs belvedere window. "I want to get serious for a minute. What are *we* to do Mr. Griffin? You're here as an uninvited Guest inside my Burdock home. And from my point of view, I'm illegally harboring you as a fugitive from justice if the law decides that a warrant has to be issued for your arrest. I could potentially go to jail, and then have my highly-valued teaching and research certificates revoked."

"I didn't mean to cause you grief," the Invisible Man replied. "I came here to obtain medical assistance, and then I planned to leave and track-down that thief and untrustworthy con-artist, Mr. Tom Marvel, who had deceitfully absconded with my vital records."

"Now Griffin; I need to know the truth about you. What were you planning to do when you were heading for Port Burdock? *Had* you any plan in mind?"

"Let me be frank, even though my name is Griffin," the Invisible Man stated in imitation of Dr. Kemp's zany humor. "For you see, Professor. I'm aware of the silly mind games you've been playing with your ridiculous puns. You, sir, have been playing me for a fool, but now it's time to bite the damned bullet."

"Well, Griffin; from the start, I didn't place too much credence in your inferiority complex. You want and need power under the pretext of making an obscure contribution to the improvement of civilization. And that's no joking around, either."

"Okay, Doctor Kemp. If you want the truth, I'm about to reveal it to you. I was going to escape and take my project clear out of the country and start anew, perhaps in Mexico, or maybe even Canada. But recently, because of events over in Iping, in Port Stowe, and in

Burdock, I've altered that initial plan rather drastically since seeing you. I thought it would be wise and prudent, now that the weather is hot and my invisibility possible, to make a run for the American South, maybe Alabama, or perhaps Mississippi, where there are less people to snoop around my business than there are around Sussex County. Especially since my secret is at least partially known around Burdock, and everyone would be on the general lookout for a masked and muffled Man, with some missing appendage, face, penis, or other regular body feature."

"You do have your significant limitations," Kemp reminder Griffin. "Most sensible people learn to cope with their own boundaries and borders."

"Let me proceed," Griffin bluntly interrupted Kemp. "You have a line of steamers from here that sail to France. My latest scheme was to get aboard one of those transports and run the risk of being captured in the *Atlantic* or the *British Channel* during the passage. From France, I could easily travel by train into Spain, or else have as my destination Algiers. It would not be too difficult a task, and my only major obstacle would be language translation. In northern Africa, a man might always be invisible, and yet live and thrive at his work in private, and do things independent of village gossip and scrutiny. I was using that undependable tramp Thomas Marvel as a money box and also as an expedient luggage carrier, until I decided how to get my books and things sent overseas to catch-up with me."

"That's plainly clear," Dr. Kemp opined. "I must admit that your plan had been adequately organized. Forgive me, Griffin. Before *this* candid conversation, I was going to joke, saying that you need not change your citizenship to European because *you're a peon* right here in Sussex County, and you don't give a shit about *youth-in-Asia,* or about killings anywhere else in England or in the rest of the world. I want you to know that I jest with you because I think that you're a worse menace to society than your petty thief assistant, Tom Marvel."

"And then, the filthy pond-scum must need to rob me! He *has* maliciously hidden my books, Dr. Kemp. Hidden my three precious books, I say! If I can lay my hands on him, without any hesitation, I'd strangle the bastard right into the next world in a freakin' microsecond! That little bastard even stole my black boots!"

"Best plan is that you should get the books out of *his* possession first thing, without killing Marvel," the Doctor wisely recommended.

"But where is he? Do you know?" the Invisible Man asked.

"Yes, Griffin. You're being a little too rambunctious. Mr. Thomas Marvel is currently incarcerated in the town police station, locked-up by *his* own request, and in the strongest cell in the Burdock Jail. My housemaid Maria has told me that!"

"Cur!" Griffin responded. "The jerk's a damned mongrel dog who needs a veterinarian to do brain surgery on his frontal lobes."

"But that hangs up your plans a little if Marvel's idly sitting in a jail cell. He's in one place and can be interrogated about where your cherished books are right now, without you having to kill him."

"We must get those books; those books are vital."

"Maybe he wants a ransom."

"No, Darrell. The asshole is too damned stupid to even know what the hell a ransom is. He's just a lowlife petty thief, and nothing more."

"Certainly, a value judgment on your part," Kemp begrudgingly agreed, a little nervously. "Most certainly Griffin; yes, most certainly. We must get those books to abate your growing hostility. I'll help you in *that* endeavor. But that assignment won't be difficult, if Marvel doesn't know I'm buying the volumes for you."

Dr. Kemp thought that he heard low murmuring voices coming from outside, but being unsure, the honorable physician did not reveal his present suspicion to Griffin. But the doctor really wanted to keep the conversation going with the Invisible Man, because he himself could also be involved in a difficult and complicated legal felony.

"Blundering into your house, Kemp," Griffin regretted, "has changed all my plans. You're educated, Darrell, just like me. You see, Dr. Kemp, you *are* a man that can understand my multi-faceted, three-dimensional predicament. In spite of all that has happened in three villages; in spite of this negative press publicity; in spite of the loss of my three books; in spite of what I have greatly suffered, there still remain great possibilities, huge possibilities to explore. But you must first level with me. It's either shit or get off the pot time. Have you told anyone I am here?"

Kemp hesitated before answering, realizing that the letter to Colonel Adye had been *written* communication and not speech. "That was always implied in all *our* dialogues."

"No one?" Griffin probed further. "Fuck the word 'implied'. I want either a yes or a no, or else I might feel compelled to slit your throat and pull-out your lying larynx. If we fight, Dr. Kemp, then I, being wholly invisible, will hold the distinct advantage."

"I said not one word to a living or dead soul. That is my promise and my pledge!"

The Invisible Man stood-up, and sticking his arms akimbo, began to pace around the upstairs study in widening concentric circles.

"I had made a vast mistake, Darrell, if I can call you on a first name basis. Yes, my thinking was a bit too erroneous. My misjudgment was the simple fact which, in time, encompassed a huge mistake in carrying this entire agenda through. By working alone, I've wasted both strength and time, not to mention progress and opportunities. Yes, working alone, my friend. It is quite wonderful how little a Man can do while working alone! To rob a little, to injure an enemy, but you and me working together, Darrell, we can achieve virtually any set goal to which we aspire. We can be invincible, and in total control of our destinies."

"Even though you're stark-raving mad, you are correct in everything you've just cited," Dr. Kemp stated. "But *that* type of arrangement you're suggesting is only satisfactory when the two parties can one-hundred-percent trust one another. Just look at how Mr. Marvel had easily betrayed *your* trust?"

"What I want, Kemp, is a good *goal-keeper,* a good helper, and a good hiding-place, and most of all, a good arrangement whereby I can sleep, eat, and *rest in peace,* without dying of course. Ha, ha, ha, Dr. Kemp. Your levity is definitely influencing me, ha, ha, ha."

"I'll help you get your books, but I'll not participate in murdering Mr. Marvel; do you understand?"

"You're sabotaging my plan!" Griffin argued. "I must have a confederate, and that confederate will be you. With a reliable confederate, providing me with substantial food and rest, thousands of fantastic things are possible, and the whole world will soon become *our* big, delicious oyster."

Dr. Kemp seemed to clam-up at hearing Griffin's partnership proposal. "Having a minor in English nomenclature, I know you were speaking figuratively and not literally, Griffin, but to tell you the truth, I hate soccer and I resent being your blasted goalkeeper."

"Before now, Doctor, I had conducted my studies of *light* on vague, two-dimensional lines. We have to consider all the supreme possibilities that invisibility means, and then balance those *goals* with all that it does *not* mean. It means little advantage for common practices such as eavesdropping, gossiping, trite talk, and so forth, where one makes *sounds*. For example, invisibility would be of little help in housebreaking, because of the usage of sound. Once you've caught me engaged in a criminal act, you could easily imprison me. But on the other hand, I am hard to catch. This invisibility, in fact, is only good in two cases: it's useful in getting away from a pursuit, and it's useful in approaching the unaware target. It's particularly useful, therefore, in the art of killing, Dr. Kemp. I can walk around a man, despite whatever weapon he has, choose my point, and strike decisively as I like. I can dodge as I like, without my confused opponent ever seeing my Unseen Maneuvers. That's what the hell happened over there in Iping at the notorious Coach and Horses, as well as down the hill here in Burdock at the Jolly Crickets. Escape will be *our* forte, Dr. Kemp, while *we* expertly employ invisibility."

Kemp's hand went to his moustache to contemplate what Griffin had been describing. Then, the Doctor again believed that his ears had discerned a muffled conversation emanating from near the front door as being a distinct movement downstairs.

"I still say that you're insane, and might even need two straightjackets to control!" Dr. Kemp strongly said.

"And it is killing we must do, Kemp. Who the hell is ever going to catch us for prosecution. Think it over before you lose your career; your reputation, and your future. Just think of that asshole Vicar over in Iping. He's going to lose everything since the whole village is condemning his actions with *me*. The townspeople even believe that he stole money from his own parish, when I had done the misdeed. But then, that dirty son-of-a-bitch Tom Marvel stole the Vicar's gold coins from me, the Vindictive-and Invincible Invisible Man."

"If it is killing that we must do," Kemp began replying, before hesitating, "I shall *not* be available. I have no wife or kids to worry about; only my career and my good name, which, thanks to your' being in this house, are all now obviously in jeopardy. On the other hand, I don't wish for either my career or my reputation to be sentenced to prison by a jury panel of uneducated, gossiping village buffoons! I'm listening to your plan, Griffin, but I'm not agreeing about one particular aspect of it. *Why* the killing?"

"Not wanton killing, Darrell, but a judicious slaying when it's necessary and warranted," Griffin declared. "The main point is, Doctor, that the public and the law now know that there is indeed an Invisible Man, as well as *we* know that there is indeed an Invisible Man. And that Invisible Man, Kemp, must now establish, just like Robespierre had done in France, a second Reign of Terror. Yes; imagine that! A second Reign of Terror. We can take a town such as Burdock and terrify and dominate it. The lame-brain public must obey and honor our strict orders. Yes Darrell, the idiots must obey our orders or face execution. As long as everyone values *our* code of conduct, everything will be copesetic. And all who disobey *our* orders must be strictly killed, and we'll slay all the gossiping imbeciles who would defend those defiant assholes. Think of it in a different *light,* Doctor Kemp? *You* will be telling the college administration what you want to have taught at the university. In fact, Doctor, the absolute power will be in *your* hands, because you'll be the new administration!"

"Humph!" Professor Kemp reacted in the form of an interjection, no longer intently listening to Griffin's bizarre and insane sales pitch, but instead, to the sound of his front door opening and closing.

"It seems to me, Griffin," Kemp said, stalling to organize the right words upon his tongue, "that your confederate would be in a difficult position if he is being pursued by the county sheriff, and being sentenced by the county judge, Justice Clark Shuffleboard."

"No one in Burdock would know that you were my confidential confederate," the Invisible Man eagerly related. And then suddenly, "Kemp! Hush! What's that noise downstairs?"

"Nothing," Kemp answered. "It's possibly that new invention, that electric generator I'm having installed."

And suddenly, the low, muffled downstairs sound began to speak in voice tones, louder and faster.

"I don't agree with your impractical strategy, Griffin. Understand me, I don't agree to it at all. Why dream of playing a game against the race? How can you hope to gain happiness through deception? Don't be a lone wolf. Publish your results; take the world; yes, take the nation at least in a normal, honest fashion. Your whole conquest and control premise is utter lunacy!"

The Invisible Man interrupted Kemp's retort with his defensive and Unseen Arms extended. "You are Judas personified! You've already betrayed me! Are you Benedict Arnold resurrected? There are footsteps coming upstairs. My sensitive ears hear them!"

"Nonsense, Mr. Griffin. Absurd nonsense."

"Let me see," the Invisible Man said, testing Kemp's loyalty. And Griffin began advancing toward Kemp, his Unseen Right Arm extended, toward the door.

And then, events happened helter-skelter and very swiftly. Kemp hesitated for a second, and then moved to intercept his new-found rival. The Invisible Man started feigning an offensive move, and then suddenly, his partially-naked and invisible form stood still.

"Traitor!" the Livid Voice exclaimed, and without any definite indication, the Invisible Man's dressing-gown opened, and sitting-down upon the office chair, the Unseen began disrobing. Kemp made three swift steps to the door, and Griffin, with his leg quickly vanishing, soon sprang to his feet with a shout, completely invisible, and stark naked, from head to toe, to epididymis. Kemp, out of sheer horror, forcefully flung the door open.

As the portal expanded, there came a sound of hurrying feet along with several unrecognizable voices emanating from downstairs.

With a quick movement, Dr. Kemp thrust the Invisible Man back, sprang aside, and managed to slam the door. In another moment, Griffin would have been alone in the belvedere study, a trapped prisoner, save for one minor detail. The key had been slipped in rather hastily that morning. As Kemp slammed the door, the object fell upon the carpet.

Dr. Darrell Kemp's face became white as sugar. Out of desperation, the prominent Physician tried gripping the door handle with both hands. For a moment, the Professor stood lugging and tugging. Then, the door gave a gap of six inches, and in the intense struggle, Dr. Kemp managed get it closed again.

The second tug-of-war caused the sturdy door to be jerked a foot wide-open, and Griffin's dressing-gown was caught, wedging itself into the opening. The Doctor's vulnerable throat was soon gripped by strong invisible fingers, and Kemp abandoned his hold upon the handle to defend himself from the invisible maniac. The Chemistry Professor was forced back, tripped, and incidentally, pitched heavily into the corner of the landing. The empty dressing-gown was quickly flung over Kemp's head by the incomparable, escaping Invisible Man.

Halfway up the staircase ran Colonel Adye, the recipient of Dr. Kemp's emergency letter, and the official chief of the Burdock police. The no-nonsense Colonel was staring aghast at the sudden disheveled and unkempt appearance of distinguished Professor Kemp, followed by the extraordinary sight of jumping and dancing articles of clothing tossing all around in empty aerial patterns. The high-ranking police inspector had observed his friend Kemp knocked-down, but by no one in flesh form, and then Adye watched the instructor weakly struggling to his feet. The astounded Colonel could not believe what his objective eyes had just witnessed.

"My God!" Kemp cried over to Colonel Adye. "The game's up! Griffin has successfully disappeared and gone from *our* midst!"

Jay Dubya

Chapter 25

"INVISIBLE MAN IS HUNTED"

For a brief interval, Dr. Darrell Kemp was too inarticulate to make Colonel Adye understand the very inexplicable events that had just occurred inside his Burdock residence. The pair stood staring wonderingly upon the landing, with Kemp speaking swiftly and erratically. The remaining grotesque materials of Griffin's bloody swarth still remained on his stained wrist. But presently, Colonel Adye began to finally grasp some of the more essential parameters of the extraordinary situation.

"I can attest that he is the ultimate in madness; yes, and also the absolute authority on human lunacy and cultural revolution," Dr. Kemp claimed to the Burdock Top Cop. "Indeed, pure selfishness magnified to the ultimate level. This Invisible Man Griffin only thinks egocentrically, Colonel, and that's the long and the short of it. Nothing else exists in his twisted mind than his own advantage, survival and safety. In my chosen profession, I've listened to such a convoluted story from him this morning of brutal self-preservation and of total disregard for the rest of humanity."

"My God, Kemp. This Griffin you're describing might he the most dangerous fellow in all of England!"

"As you well-know, Colonel, the Perpetrator, *our* Perpetrator, has already severely wounded several good men around Sussex, and his burgeoning mania for power and vengeance is just getting started. Griffin has no conscience, no common democratic ethics, and no Christian morals. We must prevent him from destroying and corrupting other innocent, decent human beings. He'll create a panic if not thwarted. Nothing can stop him once he transforms into invisibility. Griffin is going out into civilization now, livid and furious! If not captured and imprisoned, he'll soon turn into a diabolical killing machine that'll make London's Jack the Ripper and that infamous long-gone American killer John 'Liver Eating' Johnson look like minor comic strip characters. However, Colonel, this Griffin is an absolute, complete fraud. The psycho is a threat to both you and me, but also to himself. The Invisible Man, although quite accomplished at performing his singular amazing skill, erroneously and actually believes that he is an existential threat to the entire world, when in reality, Griffin can only kill *individuals* one at a time."

"I agree Darrell that the Formidable Perpetrator must be apprehended immediately," Colonel Adye aptly replied. "That is certain after me reading all of the incredible local and London newspaper accounts. And it's my absolute sworn duty and oath to protect the public, and to enforce the principles of law and order here in Burdock."

"But how can your insane scheme be accomplished?" Dr. Darrell Kemp impetuously questioned, as the Doctor's befuddled mind suddenly became a warehouse of constructive ideas. "Colonel, you must begin at once on your pursuit and assemble every available man who knows how to fight, wrestle, and accurately shoot a gun to take-up the chase. The Lunatic must be prevented from leaving this district and causing widespread havoc and mayhem elsewhere. Once this Villainous Felon gets away," Dr. Kemp speculated, "the heartless Fiend will go through the countryside as he wills; killing, destroying, and maiming are his worshipped gods. The Psychopath dreams of a new Reign of Terror! Yes, Colonel Adye; the Crazed Fanatic wants to initiate a British Reign of Terror based on that of the French Revolution, almost a hundred years ago, I tell you. It's all wicked madness personified. Yes, fantasy destruction turned into stark reality."

"What do you suggest I should do to begin with first? Sometimes first is worst!"

"You must set a watch on trains, roads, and shipping routes while we still have standard civilization to maintain. The county garrison must help in assisting you in your endeavor. I recommend that you must immediately wire London for help. The only thing that may keep him here is the thought of recovering some books of important notes Griffin counts of personal value," Kemp explained. "I'll tell you more of that significance later! Right now, Colonel, there is a man in your police station, a certain devious criminal, a youth named Thomas Marvel, whom you might want to further interrogate about this insane potential Killer's inner motivations."

"I know the name," Adye confirmed. "I know a degree of background about those cryptic books you've just referenced, too. But the prevaricating...."

"Says that he hasn't the volumes in his possession. However, Griffin thinks that the tramp Thomas Marvel does know where the notes are hidden. And Colonel, you must prevent this evil Fiend Griffin from eating or sleeping; day and night the countryside must be wary of him and of his prowling threat. This is by far no joke. Food must be locked-up and secured; I mean all food, so that Griffin will have to break his modus-operandi in acquiring it."

"Anything else Kemp?"

The houses everywhere in Burdock must be barred and locked to prevent his diabolical access. Pray that Heaven sends us cold nights and rain to stifle and kill the Bastard because foul weather could slow him down to a mere crawl! The whole country-side must begin hunting and keep hunting this Formidable Enemy to society until the Invisible Man is captured. I tell you, Colonel Adye; this criminal is a danger, a menace, and a veritable disaster-in-progress; unless Griffin is pinned-down and secured, it is frightful to think of the catastrophes that might result. My personal opinion is that this Griffin should be killed first and then, interrogated by Satan himself in hell later!"

"What else can we do Kemp?" Adye wondered and asked. "I must go down at once and begin organizing a search party. Yes, an experienced posse of deputies. But why not come along? Yes, Doctor. I'm asking you to join the search, with you being an expert on how this Crazed Man's mind functions. Come into town, and we'll hold a sort of war council. I'll get Hopps to help in the planning, and also the railway managers' assistance will be indispensable. By Jove! It's positively urgent and absolutely essential. Come along now, Darrell. Tell me all relevant information about this Brute Griffin as we go into town. What else is there we can do? What chaotic mayhem this Berserk Griffin had already caused inside the Jolly Crickets is more than enough evidence for me to hunt-down the dirty Bastard!"

In another moment, Colonel Adye was leading the way downstairs. The front door had been opened, and the two assigned policemen were standing guard outside and were staring aimlessly at empty air. "He's gotten away, Colonel; Harry and I have never seen anything like it. So eerie and frightening it all was. Rushed by us like a zephyr and disappeared into the night like a fleeting vapor!"

"Thanks plenty, Jim. We must go to the central station at once," Colonel Adye decided and commanded. "One of you go on down and get a cab to come-up and meet us. Quickly, I say. And now, Kemp, anything else before we tally-ho?"

"Dogs," Kemp declared. "Get the best hounds in the county. If he's bleeding, his blood will still be seen. The tracking hounds won't see him, but they can smell and detect his evil scent. Get the best dogs in Burdock to track and hunt his whereabouts."

"Good idea," Adye acknowledged. "It's not generally known, but the prison officials over at Halstead know a man with the finest breed of bloodhounds. What else might we need?"

"Bear in mind," Kemp judiciously elaborated, "that his food will show right through his invisibility. After eating, his swallowed food will be visible throughout his digestive system until it is thoroughly absorbed and digested; yes, until it is fully assimilated. So that means he has to hide and shelter after eating. You must keep on beating the Fiend into submission until the wild animal is either knocked unconscious or killed."

"My God Kemp! This Griffin threat sounds like the devil himself!"

"Forget all about justice and a fair and just trial. Remember Colonel what this Griffin had done to your good friend Jaffers over in Iping, and Jaffers is reputed to be the toughest constable in all of

Sussex County. Every thicket, every quiet corner, and every tree must be thoroughly investigated and searched. And put all weapons away," Kemp strongly advised. "Griffin can't carry such heavy things for long because his strength will be diminished in a hurry. And what he can snatch-up quickly, the Rabid Beast will use and strike men with, those utilitarian objects, which must be hidden away from his disposal. The best approach, Colonel, is to mass tackle the Invisible Man, and then beat the Bastard to a pulp until he is rendered unconscious, or better yet, until the Son-of-a-Bitch yields to arrest."

"Good again," Adye commended. "For the sake of public safety, we shall have the Monster yet in custody!"

"And also maintain vigilance on the roads," Kemp continued, and hesitated.

"Yes indeed?" Colonel Adye agreed. "The roads in and around Burdock will be patrolled relentlessly and incessantly."

"Powdered glass will be essential in tracking his footprints," Kemp recommended. "It's cruel, I know. But think of what he may do if he's still maiming and killing on the lam!"

Colonel Adye drew the air in sharply between his teeth. "It's unsportsmanlike, but quite necessary. I don't know. But I'll have powdered glass ready if that's what you suggest. If he goes too far...."

"The Man's becomes grossly inhuman, I tell you!" Dr. Kemp yelled, a bit out of character. "I'm absolutely sure that the Maniac will try and establish a new Reign of Terror around Burdock. Right now, he's probably trying to find some sympathetic confederates and rebellious apprentices as recruits. I predict that as soon as he has gotten-over the emotions of this latest escape, as sure as I'm talking to you, Colonel, our only chance is to be ahead of his self-centered, self-preservation mode of thinking. He has cut himself off from his own kind, and this Menace Griffin must be stopped by all means! The Fiend is a toxic plague to all humanity!"

Jay Dubya

Chapter 26

"THE WICKSTEED MURDER"

The Invisible Man had madly rushed stark naked out of Darrell Kemp's house in a mental state emblematic of blind fury. A little child innocently playing with a doll near Dr. Kemp's gateway was violently caught-up in the wild escape, and maliciously thrown aside, so that the crying girl's ankle had become broken, and thereafter, for some hours, the adamant Invisible Man had successfully passed-out of the visible range of human perception and visual detection.

No one in and around Sussex County specifically knew where the fleeing renegade hid, nor what he had done after leaving Dr. Kemp's Burdock residence. But one can imagine an obsessed Griffin hurrying through the hot June forenoon, scampering up the steep hill and entering onto the open downland, situated directly behind Port Burdock; and the Wandering Ogre's tortured soul was more-than-likely raging and despairing at his intolerable fate, and finding shelter at last, his emotions heated and weary, and with his invisible legs crouching behind bushes like a prehistoric, famished cave man, amid the thorny thickets of Hintondean.

The Fanatical Fugitive's contorted brain was desperately endeavoring to piece together again his shattered schemes against his own "inferior species" being decisively trounced and permanently defeated. That dim prospect seemed to Dr. Kemp and to Colonel Adye to be the most probable and favorable refuge for disappointed, frustrated, on-the-prowl Griffin, for it was the Wanton Fugitive attempting to re-assert himself in a grimly tragic manner, at about two in the afternoon.

One wonders what the *Light Experimenter's* state of mind may have been during that critical transition time, and precisely what ignoble plans the confused insurgent had surreptitiously devised. No doubt, alienated Griffin was sulking and almost-ecstatically exasperated by Dr. Kemp's defensive treachery, and although we may be able to understand the motives that had led to that ascending palpable deceit, we may still imagine, and even sympathize, a little empathy with the fury that the Invisible Man's attempted surprise altercation with Dr. Kemp must have promptly occasioned.

Perhaps something of the stunned astonishment of Griffin's Oxford Street negative experiences may have returned to *his* dysfunctional memory, for the Nefarious Fugitive had evidently counted on Professor Kemp's co-operation with the Psychopath's brutal dream of terrorizing and dominating the entire world. At any rate, the contemporary Human Plague had sensationally vanished from his kin about midday, and no living witness could account for exactly what particular damage the Itinerant Danger had done until about half-past two that same afternoon. It was an unfortunate development, perhaps, for humanity, but for on-the-lam Griffin, it was a fatal and tragic mistake.

During that auspicious time, a growing multitude of yeomen, scattered over the countryside, were busy with their own personal concerns. In the morning, the Prowling Maniac had still been simply a mere legend; a tabloid fable, and also a much-gossiped-about terror; however, by mid-afternoon, and by virtue chiefly of Dr. Kemp's carefully-worded public proclamation that had been documented in the afternoon newspapers, Griffin was depicted and presented as a tangible antagonist, a Brute to be wounded, captured, or overcome, and the countryside native inhabitants began rather proficiently aggregating themselves, coordinating their assets with rare, inconceivable rapidity.

By two o'clock, even the beast-on-the-prowl might still have removed himself out of the district by getting aboard a train rumbling into London, but after two in the afternoon, that singular prospect, with police on patrol at all prospective stations, essentially became impossible. Every London-bound passenger train, along the various connecting lines, had been mapped on a great drawn parallelogram, networking between running routes from Southampton, Manchester,

Brighton and Horsham; all defensive commuter carriages now with locked doors.

And the associated commodity goods' traffic was almost entirely suspended, all because of the roving Invisible Man. And in a great circle encompassing twenty miles around normally-somnolent Port Burdock, brave yeomen, armed with guns and blunt bludgeons, were presently setting-out in groups of three and four, accompanied by fierce-smelling dogs, out patrolling the country roads, forests, and fields for their Human Prey.

Mounted policemen militantly rode along the various transportation lanes, stopping at every cottage and lodge, and warning concerned residents to lock-up their houses, and also, to keep indoors unless the dwellers were fully-ready to do battle. And all of the elementary schools in the vicinity had dismissed by three o'clock, with the children, scared, and kept together in large groups, being hurried or escorted home by their protective teachers.

Dr. Kemp's strongly-worded official proclamation being then signed, authorized, and distributed by Colonel Adye, had been posted onto public reading boards over the whole district, and done by five o'clock in the afternoon. The formal statement that Professor Kemp had written and published clearly indicated that all the conditions of the impending struggle, and the vital necessity of keeping the Invisible Man from obtaining food and sleep, along with the public's need for incessant watchfulness of any evidence of *his* lethal movements, were all paramount to achieving and accomplishing Griffin's imminent arrest.

And as a result, "swift and decisive" was both the action and the watchword of the local authorities, and so prompt and so universal was the belief in this strange and savage creature being a dire curse on local humanity, that before nightfall, an area of several hundred-square-miles had existed, worrying the public in a stringent state of siege. And before nightfall, too, a thrill of horror had penetrated through the wholly-very-nervous and inordinately vigilant countryside. Whispers and gossips were speedily going from mouth-to-mouth throughout the entirety of Sussex County, and swift and certain information, either truth or exaggeration, was being distributed over the entire length and breadth of the region, but the latest news separately passed the knowledge of Mr. Paul Wicksteed.

If the popular supposition that the Invisible Man's refuge had been the Hintondean thickets, then Colonel Adye and Dr. Kemp supposed that, in the early afternoon, the Mobile Fugitive had sallied-out again, bent upon some satanic project that involved the use of a lethal weapon. There were several hearsay reports that an Unidentified Stranger, toting an iron rod in hand, had been seen traversing the area woods before the Crazed Prowler had encountered and confronted Mr. Wicksteed, and soon brutally overwhelmed and decapitated the elderly farmer.

Of course, Colonel Adye and Dr. Kemp knew nothing of the specific details of *that* deadly interaction at the moment of its heinous occurrence. The murder had been enacted on the edge of a gravel pit, only two-hundred-yards from august Lord Burdock's opulent lodge's gate. Everything in the preliminary investigation pointed to a desperate struggle, including the trampled ground, the numerous wounds which Mr. Paul Wicksteed had received, along with the aged farmer's splintered, blood-stained walking-stick; but why the attack had been made, apparently in a murderous frenzy, was still impossible to imagine and assess the precise motive.

Indeed, the theory of heightened madness was almost unavoidable to discredit. Mr. Paul Wicksteed had been a respectable gentleman of seventy-five years of age, and a favorite steward to wealthy Lord Burdock, who was a generous charity benefactor who was both loved and adored by his neighbors and fellow church-goers.

Most certainly, the very last person in the world to provoke such a terrible antagonist to commit violent murder would be the deceased victim.

Concerning Mr. Wicksteed, the police theorized that the Invisible Man probably used a blunt iron rod, which had more-than-likely been pulled and dragged from a broken piece of fence. In exploring the local unfamiliar landscape, it had been hypothesized by Colonel Robert Adye and Dr. Darrell Kemp that the quiet farmer, returning peacefully home to his midday meal, had been viciously attacked, and his feeble defense easily beaten-down. And then, the kind country gentleman had been administered a severe pummeling, and received a thrice broken arm, which immediately felled Wicksteed and caused the aged farmer to involuntarily surrender his soul. And the reprehensible field murder had been gruesomely completed with the victim's skull being smashed into what appeared to be virtual red strawberry jelly.

Colonel Adye addressed Dr. Kemp inside the Burdock Police Station. "Of course, Darrell, Griffin must have dragged that heavy rod out of the fencing before the Sociopath had ever met his unsuspecting victim. Only two details beyond what has already been stated seem to bear on the matter."

"Which two details are you citing?"

"Well, Darrell, detail number one is the circumstance that the gravel pit was not in Mr. Wicksteed's direct path home, but nearly a couple of hundred-yards out of his usual way. The other relevant circumstance is the assertion of a little girl to the effect that, going to her afternoon school session, she saw the murdered man, still in good shape at age seventy-five, 'trotting' in a peculiar manner across a field, heading towards the gravel pit."

"Was the girl humored by this old man Paul Wicksteed jogging across the field near the woods?"

"I think so, Darrell. Her pantomime of his action suggested to my top investigators that a man pursuing his target victim on foot, that is to say Mr. Wicksteed, had been waving a striking stick at the fleeing, elderly farmer. The young girl was greatly amused by *that* irregular scenario, not ever before seeing what she perceived as grown men playing a weird chasing game."

"How old was the girl, and did she actually see the pursuer club Mr. Wicksteed?"

"She is twelve years old, and can be regarded in court as being a credible witness. But Darrell, the girl did not see any violence occur; just the one man chasing the other. And then oddly, the pursuing Man, according to the child's oral testimony, had disappeared, and only the rod itself waving in the air was chasing after the old farmer! That is what the girl, Adrian Meyers, said made her think that the entire ordeal was amusing!"

Dr. Kemp had a few interesting questions and observations to review with Colonel Adye. "Now Bob, one may imagine and assume that Griffin had taken the rod as a weapon indeed, but without any deliberate intention of using it in committing murder. That would be his defense attorney's argument! It's really only circumstantial evidence that we now have."

"Mr. Wicksteed may then have come by the girl's home and noticed this rod inexplicably moving through the air. Without the farmer ever having any remote thought or knowledge of the Invisible Man, for Port Burdock is ten-miles away from the rural murder scene. It is quite conceivable, Dr. Kemp, that poor Mr. Wicksteed, just like little Adrian Meyers, may not even have ever heard of the Vindictive Invisible Man, because of that ten-mile distance from Burdock."

"No doubt, Colonel, that the predatory Invisible Man could've easily distanced and overcome his aged prey under ordinary circumstances, but the position in which Wicksteed's body had been found, according to *your* initial police report, suggests that the farmer had the ill luck to drive his attacker into a corner between a drift of stinging nettles and the aforementioned gravel pit. Rather remarkable feat of strength, wasn't it Bob, for a seventy-five-year-old codger. Wouldn't you tend to agree with *that* assessment?"

"But Darrell; it's way too early in the investigation to make loose assumptions that might turn-out to be pure hypothesis or conjecture. The only undeniable fact is that children like Miss Adrian Meyers are often unreliable witnesses because their world is often based on fantasy stories and nursery rhyme associations that they had learned in their early schooling."

"Then Bob, the major evidence being advanced will be the blood-stained iron club, the bloodied nettles, and the mauled and mutilated condition of Mr. Wicksteed's extremely-abused body. The abandonment of the rod murder weapon by Griffin suggests that in the emotional excitement of the altercation, the club had been abruptly abandoned. The Invisible Man was certainly an intensely egotistical and insensitive humanoid, but at the sight of his victim, his first victim, lying bloodied and pitiful at his feet, may have triggered and released some long-pent fountain of remorse, a weighty guilt which, for a time, may have flooded and neutralized whatever scheme of evil action Griffin may have contrived."

"But Dr. Kemp, the wily and unstable Bastard is still on the loose, and represents a grave threat to every fearful citizen in Sussex County!"

"I agree with your general analysis, Darrell," Bob Adye complimented his new-found associate. "You'd make a good forensics detective, I'm quite sure. After the atrocious murder of Mr. Wicksteed, I guess that Mr. Griffin would seem to have struck across the country towards the downlands. There is a story circulating around Bristol of an odd voice, heard about sunset, listened to by a couple of laborers working in a vegetable field. The strange staccato was alternately wailing and laughing, sobbing and groaning, and ever and again, shouting vulgar expletives. It must've been quite queer hearing those conflicting sounds and noises. The variety of distinct echoes had drifted-up across the middle of a clover field, and died away, going towards the meadows and the hills."

That afternoon, according to Colonel Adye, the Invisible Man must have learned information of the rapid use which Dr. Kemp had made of *his* evil behavior and his singular machinations. Griffin must have found houses locked and secured; or the on-the-lam Fugitive may have loitered about railway stations, and prowled about country inns, remarkably naked, so no one in the area could ever detect his anonymous maneuvering. And no doubt, the possessed and crazed Fiend had read the publicly posted proclamations, and realized something of the nature of the burgeoning campaign being generated against him, and also against his perverted Reign of Terror objectives.

And as the evening advanced towards midnight, the fields became dotted here and there with groups of three or four deputies, and the early crop zones were noisy with the yelping of barking dogs. Those men-hunters had particular instructions from the police in the case of incidentally experiencing a surprise encounter with the unpredictable, Roaming Maniac.

But amazingly-elusive Mr. Griffin, the incomparable and inimitable Invisible Man, had managed to stealthily avoid every hunter and every hound-dog desperately searching in the forests and country farm fields to collar the Renegade Desperado. For that day and night, at least, the pursued lost heart to escape being violently apprehended.

And for nearly twenty-four consecutive hours, save when the Petulant Perpetuator had turned on Mr. Paul Wicksteed, Griffin was still then a hunted savage on the prowl. In the night, the pursued Renegade must have eaten and slept; for in the morning, the Antagonist rose from his nocturnal forest slumber, and was himself active again; powerful; angry, and malignant; with Griffin mentally preparing his brain for his last great battle against the civilized world.

Chapter 27

"THE SIEGE OF KEMP'S HOUSE"

D r. Kemp read to himself a strange missive, which he had recently written in pencil upon a greasy sheet of paper.

June 4, 1896

"You are a complete fraud. You have lost your Reign of Terror power. You are now politically and socially impotent.

I must confess, on the whole, you have been amazingly energetic and clever, although what you stand to gain by it, I cannot imagine. You are against me. You had tried to rob me of a night's rest. But I have had food in spite of you; I have slept in spite of you, and the game is only beginning. Yes, I repeat, the game is only beginning. There is nothing beneficial to it, but only to start the Terror Façade, which has no satisfactory goal or ending.

This letter announces the first day of the New Terror. Port Burdock is no longer under the Queen; tell your Colonel of Police, and the rest of them; Port Burdock now is under my jurisdiction; the New Terror!

In a few short days, the Epoch of the New Invisible Man, replacing your incompetence, will begin. And I am the New Invisible Man the First. To begin with, the rule will be easy. The first day there will be one execution for the sake of example, a man named

Kemp. Death starts for him today. He may lock himself away in his home, hide himself, get guards about him, or put on armor if he likes. Death, the Unseen Death, is coming to Kemp. And to you also, dethroned Invisible Man. To-day Kemp is to die, and you too will feel the weight of my merciless power and wrath.

Anonymous New Invisible Man

Dr. Kemp read his "trap Griffin" letter twice, and reckoned that he could goad the Invisible Man back to *his* home in Burdock, and collaborate with Colonel Adye to collar Griffin in the act of breaking into Kemp's home and effectively, with the help of reliable deputies and vicious bloodhounds, apprehend the Invisible Man in or on Dr. Kemp's property, and then bring the wanted Maniac to British justice.

'This letter is no hoax, but instead, it's an elaborate plan to trap Griffin, and use his strong desire for power, along with his hate for me, to capture the Beast and put him away, either in a jail cell, or in a mental institution. That's his Voice right there captured in written form in the letter he had accidentally left in my home during our little scuffle! And he means to actually kill me, and the Fiend is quite delusional about this bizarre Reign of Terror caprice. In a nutshell, Griffin is an egocentric narcissistic, psychopathic, sociopathic lunatic who, in reality, is suffering from overwhelming schizophrenia. This honest missive is definitely no elaborate scam.'

After assessing and evaluating his 'trap Griffin' letter, Dr. Kemp turned the folded envelope that had fallen out of Griffin's possession during their brief altercation inside the Doctor's home. The Professor turned over the piece of paper and saw on the address side the postmark: Hintondean, and the prosaic detail "5th. to pay".

The fatigued Chemistry Expert got-up slowly from his chair, leaving his lunch unfinished. Dr. Kemp rang for his housekeeper, and told Maria to go around the home at once, examining all the fastenings of the windows, and then closing and locking all the downstairs shutters. From a locked drawer in his bedroom, the Professor took a little revolver, examined it carefully, and put the pistol into the pocket of his lounge jacket. The College Teacher wrote a number of brief notes, one addressed to Colonel Adye, gave them to his female servant to deliver, and provided explicit instructions as to her safest way of leaving the house and venturing into Burdock.

"There is little or no danger to you, Maria. You mail and deliver letters, prescriptions, and memos for me all the time."

Dr. Kemp ate with missing thought gaps meandering between his random ponderings. Finally, the Meditator struck the table sharply and firmly with his fist. "We will have him!" Kemp yelled to himself. "And I am the alluring bait. He will come too far and will overreach."

The Plotter ascended the steps up to the belvedere room, carefully shutting every door after him. "It's a damned mentally insane egotistical game the dirty Bastard's playing, but the chances and odds are all favoring *me,* Mr. Griffin; you'll be soundly defeated in spite of your self-centered, paranoid invisibility. Griffin *contra mundum* ... with a vengeance. Yes, Griffin. Logic and good will ultimately triumph over insanity and evil!"

Dr. Kemp stood at the window staring at the hot hillsides in the distance, and momentarily reflected on reality. 'He must get food every day, and I don't envy him in the least. Did he really sleep last night? Out in the open wilderness like a wild jackal or a neurotic baboon? Yes, I think so, somewhere being fairly secure from collision with wayward villagers and clashing with structured civilization. I wish we could get some good cold wet weather instead of this heat, which would give Griffin a terrible cold, and perhaps kill the no-good Asshole.'

'The Invisible Man may be watching me right now, thinking that I don't suspect him doing the observing. Insecure people always think that others care to spy on them, but conversely, insecure people are the first ones to spy on other people.'

Dr. Kemp stepped closer to the window. Something had rapped smartly against the brickwork over the frame, and the sound made the Man start violently back.

'I'm getting a trifle nervous,' Kemp reckoned. 'It must've been a disoriented sparrow.'

Presently, the Chemistry Professor thought he had heard the front-door bell ringing, and soon hurried downstairs. Kemp unbolted and unlocked the door, examined the chain, put it up, and opened the hinges cautiously, without showing the person on the other side himself. A familiar voice hailed and greeted the resident.

"Your servant's been aggressively assaulted, Kemp," Colonel Adye announced, coming around the partially-open front door.

"What!" Kemp exclaimed. "You must be joking, Bob. Maria delivers mail and telegrams for me all the time without a hitch."

"She had that note of yours taken away from her, I understand. He's close around here. Griffin is closing-in on your affairs. Let me in, damn it."

Kemp released the chain, and Colonel Adye entered through as narrow an opening as was possible for a man of his large size. The Police Inspector stood in the hall, looking with infinite relief at Kemp, awkwardly attempting to refasten the door. "Your note had been snatched out of her hand. The incident horribly scared the wits out of your girl. She's down at the station, crying hysterically. Griffin's close here. What was it all about? Why all the secrecy?"

"What a fool I was," Kemp admitted. "I might have known some interfering bullshit could happen."

"I don't follow your train of thought!"

"Look here, Colonel!" Kemp indicated by signaling and waving his hand up towards the combination study and office room. "Come upstairs and we'll talk."

In the study, the Amateur Plotter handed Colonel Adye the Invisible Man's envelope that Griffin had accidentally dropped and left behind. Adye read the sending address and whistled softly. "And you Doctor? How did you respond, if you did respond?"

"I stupidly proposed a dumb-ass trap, like any damned fool would do," Kemp regretfully disclosed. "I presumed that the envelope had been addressed by Thomas Marvel to Griffin, or perhaps from Griffin to Marvel, but not knowing the\differences between their handwritings, I took a long-shot in the dark. Either way, I believe that my plan has drastically failed quite miserably, now that Maria has been assaulted. And so, Colonel, I sent my proposal out by my maid servant. I think my reasoning was to get Griffin to return to this home in Burdock, and to coordinate with you and the jail police to arrange an orderly arrest."

Much to his host's surprise, Colonel Adye followed Kemp's commentary with a rather glib profanity. "Never fuck with dangerous fuckers! That's my sacred rule number one. We can't procrastinate a minute longer! Griffin's been sedentary around Burdock for too long now, without trying something majorly evil," Colonel Adye told Kemp. "The delirious scourge is excessively incorrigible!"

"I had the Local Menace figured-out right from the start," the Doctor claimed to the Top Cop. "I recognized that Griffin was really an emotionally-underdeveloped, anti-social ingrate possessing a warped sense of self-importance *above* everyone else. I would try to entertain and amuse the Invisible Man by telling him goofball and zany jokes and puns such as: 'I play golf in the mid-80s; if it gets any warmer, I stay home'; or Colonel, 'there're two ways to play golf; the unethical way and the fair-way'! or, 'you must think you're a dozen eggs because you're always scrambling-around evading the law; or stand, walk and screw erect.'

"And what was the purpose of those asshole jokes?"

"I had heard that Thomas Marvel was already in your Burdock Jail, so Bob, I figured if I could win immature Griffin's confidence and trust with a litany of cornball jokes, then I could convince the Plague to interview Thomas Marvel inside his jail cell to learn the whereabouts of his three cryptic notebooks, and then after Griffin would enter the confined enclosure, you and I would slam the iron gate shut, trapping both Marvel and Griffin inside!"

A resounding smash of glass was heard originating from downstairs. Colonel Adye had a silvery glimpse of a little revolver half out of Kemp's pocket. "It's a broken window; Kemp. What the hell else could it be!"

As the men reached the middle of the steps, there came a second and third smash while the baffled pair were still standing and conferring on the staircase. When the duo hastily reached the upstairs study, the amateur and the professional sleuth found two of the three windows smashed, half the room littered with splintered glass, and three enormous flints lying upon the writing table.

The bewildered men abruptly stopped and contemplated the wreckage that had been intently wrought. Kemp swore again, and as he did so, the third belvedere window had rendered a loud snap, sounding like a pistol being shot. Large pieces of glass circulated around the ceiling, and then collapsed in jagged, shivering triangles onto the study's floor.

"What's this for?" Adye wanted to know. "Do you suppose that's Griffin out there throwing rocks, flint, coal or whatever?"

"It's a beginning," Kemp vaguely answered. "He does have revenge instincts."

"There's no way of climbing up here, is there?"

"Not for a gaunt cat or a skinny squirrel," Kemp replied. "For a human, though, it would be an arduous challenge. But Colonel, we aren't quite safe up here from heavy rocks and shattering glass."

"No shutters?"

"Not here in this room. I never had them installed, and now I regret my thrifty nature. Anyway Colonel, the drain pipe's too steep and too narrow to support the weight of an average-sized man. All the downstairs rooms, hello! What the hell was that?"

Smash and crash, and then a loud whack of boards being hit hard came from downstairs. "Confound him!" bellowed Kemp. "That must be, yes, it's one of the downstairs bedrooms. He's going to do all the house. But he's a fucked-up, Delirious Fool. The ornamental shutters are up downstairs, and I believe that some of the glass will fall outside. Being barefoot and naked, he'll cut his bare feet to shreds."

Another downstairs window loudly proclaimed its immediate destruction. The men stood on the landing with perplexed and helpless expressions evident upon their faces.

"I have it!" Adye nebulously remarked. "Let me have a stick or something heavy and firm, and I'll go down to the station and get the bloodhounds put on his trail. That ought to settle him good! They're standing by, not but ten minutes—"

Another downstairs window went the way of its already-demolished peers.

"You have a revolver?" Adye asked.

"That's alright, Colonel. Thanks for offering me yours. But if you're heading back to the barracks, you'll need it more than me."

"I hope I can remember after dealing with this loony, invisible, Naked Fool on the prowl. But until I return with more help and guns, I believe that you'll be safe here. The entire completion should take less than ten-minutes."

Kemp, ashamed of his momentary lapse from truthfulness, and even though the Colonel had amassed thirty-years of valuable police experience, the Top Cop realized that he had just been outdone and outsmarted by an invisible, naked, belligerent, Loony Fiend.

"Now for the door," Colonel Adye remembered and related to his newest police colleague. "I need to get help from the station without delay. Don't worry my friend, and keep the faith. I'll be back soon with a large trained posse, and also with some mean-ass vicious hounds that'll make naked Griffin crap the pants that the invisible scumbag isn't wearing!"

As the two colleagues stood, hesitating in the hall, the pair heard the last of the first-floor bedroom windows crack and crash. Kemp went to the door and began to slip the bolts as silently as possible, with his face being a little paler than usual.

Jay Dubya

"Colonel Adye; you must step straight-out," Kemp instructed. "Don't be reluctant or hesitate! Now good luck in your escape."

"I learned many years ago," the Colonel informed the Doctor. "If you're good, then you don't need luck!"

In another moment, the Police Inspector was on the front doorstep, and the metal bolts were dropping back into the staples. The head policeman of Burdock hesitated for a moment, feeling more comfortable with his back against the door. Then the Top Cop marched, upright and square, down the steps, next crossed the lawn, and then approached the gate. A light breeze seemed to ripple over the grass. Something moved near him. "Stop a bit," a Voice recommended, so Adye halted dead, and his hand tightened on the revolver.

"Well?" the Colonel questioned, his face white and grim, and with every nerve tense and strained.

"Oblige me by going back into the house," the Imperative Voice demanded as tense and terse as Adye's.

"Sorry, my Man," the Chief Inspector said a little hoarsely, and moistened his lips with his tongue. 'The Voice is on my left flank,' the Police Commander thought. 'Suppose if I were to take my luck with the revolver and make a shot?'

"What are you going for?" the Skeptical Voice imperatively stated, but soon there was a quick movement of the two debaters, and a flash of sunlight gleamed from the open lip of Adye's pocket.

Colonel Adye desisted, and deeply thought-out the entire sequence of events that had been occurring in the last half-hour. "Where I go," the Barracks Commander sternly and slowly replied, "is my own damned business." The final two words were still on the speaker's lips, when an invisible arm wrapped around his neck; his back felt a stiff knee, and Burdock's Chief Policeman was sent sprawling backward. The elderly Chief Cop clumsily drew his pistol and absurdly fired, and in another precious moment, the Top Cop had been struck in the mouth by a clenched fist; several teeth were cracked, and the revolver strenuously wrested from *his* grip. The

Colonel made a vain clutch at a slippery invisible leg, tried to struggle-up, but fell back onto the wet turf.

"Damn!" Colonel Adye exclaimed, examining blood from his mouth inside his open left palm. The Voice incessantly laughed, indicating being highly amused. "I'd kill you now if it wasn't the waste of a bullet," the 'invisible satanic ghost' yelled and cackled. Thinking quickly and wisely, the creative-but-outsmarted Law Enforcement\Officer keenly noticed that the fully-loaded revolver had been suspended in mid-air, six-feet above the lawn's turf, and hovering above *his* bald head.

"Well?" Colonel Adye grunted sullenly, sitting-up, staggering to his feet, and then dusting himself off.

"Attention ancient Fuck," the Voice austerely ridiculed the high-ranking Law Enforcement Officer. "Don't try any asshole lethal games with me. Remember; I'm ruthless, and I can see your face, but you can't see mine. You've got to go back into the house as my hostage prisoner. Get the hell back inside, or else you might not live to see the sunshine, nor drink moonshine tomorrow! You fuckin' lush!"

"He won't let me inside," Adye argued. "He just kicked me the hell out."

"That's a real damned pity," the argumentative Invisible Man maintained. "Personally, I've got no particular quarrel with you, but now, your Dr. Kemp is destined to soon die at *my* discretion. His house will be his coffin!"

Chief Officer Adye again nervously moistened his lips with his tongue, overtly exhibiting the mounting pressure. The experienced and perspiring "Relic Cop" glanced-away from the revolver's barrel, and his wide-open eyes looked west and recognized the far-off sea, very blue and dark, reflecting and shining under the strong midday sun; and to the east *his* pupils perceived the smooth green down; the white cliff of the Head, and the multitudinous local hillside towns. Then suddenly, Colonel Adye felt that life was very sweet and worthy of preserving. His eyes came back to the little metallic six-shooter wavering just above his head, but then, approximately six-yards-away. "What am I to do?"

"What am *I* to do with you would be the more accurate terminology to express?" the Invisible Man clarified to his adversary rising-up from the turf. "You'll try to get help if I mercifully release you from *my* custody. How terribly ironic! I'm going to release the Head Cop from *my* custody! Ha, ha, ha. The only solution is for you to go back into the house. Otherwise, it's coffin time without you coughin' any more, ha, ha, ha!"

"I'll try to convince him to let me back inside, and if I can't persuade Dr. Kemp to relent, then I'll have to beg, borrow and steal my way inside there! If the Doctor consents and lets me enter, will you promise not to rush the door?"

"I've got no special quarrel with you, although personally, I positively despise your smelly guts," the Voice nastily chided. "But in a few days, after my Reign of Terror commences, you'll be working for me, Fat Boy. But first I have to intimidate and tame everyone in Burdock to obey my supreme authority. Once everyone fears my invisible powers, which the uneducated idiots will perceive as black magic and not advanced science, then I'll be in full control of Burdock, including *you,* and the local yokels will immediately work and constructively-contribute to *my* central government."

In the meantime, Dr. Kemp had hurried upstairs after letting Adye out, and now crouching among the broken glass shards, and peering cautiously over the edge of the study's window sill, the Doctor realized that Colonel Adye had been engaging in an impromptu negotiated parley with the Unseen Griffin. 'Why doesn't *he* fire?' Kemp wondered. 'Maybe he's growing a conscience after all! Surely Adye has surrendered the revolver. It's fuckin' floating over the Inspector's noggin!'

"I promise not to rush the door," Adye was saying and repeating. "Don't push a winning game too far. Give a man a decent chance. If the tables were reversed, I'd give you a second one. And if you shoot and kill me, your Reign of Terror campaign will most-certainly perish with you, because every cop and hunter in all of England will chase your ass down, and want to collect the handsome reward money!"

"You go back to the house. I'm tellin' you flatly. I will not promise you or anyone else anything. Now walk to the front door!"

A loud pounding and knocking at the front door soon ascended in magnitude. This ongoing household incarceration of Dr. Kemp, and possibly also Colonel Adye, was followed by a period of total silence.

Dr. Kemp sat listening intently in the upstairs belvedere room, and then began peering cautiously out of the three empty window frames, one after another. Developing a degree of false courage, Kemp hastened to gaze-down upon the front lawn,

Chief Officer Adye lay motionless over the edge of the gravel, just as when he had fallen. Coming along the road approaching the hillside villa were Maria and two on-a-mission patrolmen, nearing the scene of recent conflict. Then, the blows of the confiscated garden axe, with its repetitive splitting and smashing were resumed, and all hell broke loose as shattered splinters, glass, wood and other materials flew in disharmony with discharged errant police bullets flying across the front lawn in a spectacular raging battle.

A wild pounding came at the front door. It was the two intimidated policemen seeking temporary shelter from an alien-style Invisible Man ambush. Hearing the out-of-control racket, Dr. Kemp ran into the hall, put up the main entrance door chain, and clumsily drew the bolts. The Doctor made Maria speak for identification purposes before he dropped the chain, and the three survivors of the external battle with the Invisible Man blundered into the house, landing in a heap of bodies, and Kemp instinctively slammed the door shut.

"The Invisible Man!" Kemp exclaimed, all out of breath. "He has the Colonel's revolver, with two shots left I believe. He's probably already killed Adye. Shot him anyhow. Didn't you see him lying on the lawn? He's lying there."

Jay Dubya

"Who?" asked the first policemen, a rank rookie private. "Who is lying on the front lawn?"

"Your superior, Colonel Adye!"

"What's that smashing I hear?" the second frightened policemen, a skinny corporal asked.

"He's in the kitchen, scouring for food and scraps, or Griffin soon will be," Dr. Kemp spoke-out. "I think he's found an axe in the rear garden that, in my haste, I had forgotten to take the tool into the house and store-away to keep the Insane Bastard from stealing and using it as a deadly weapon on Maria and me."

Suddenly, the house was full of the Invisible Man's resounding blows and facial punches. Maria stared towards the pantry, shuddered in horror, and swiftly retreated further back into the dining-room, crawling and bawling under the large table.

Next, Dr. Kemp and the two non-veteran cops heard the kitchen door give way, which meant that the Unseen had gained access to the food pantry inside.

"This way," Kemp lowly indicated, waving his hand and crouching-down to almost a mongrel dog's skulk.

"Whup!" said the younger policeman, who following the Doctor's fine example, ducked-down, and caught the axe upon his extended poker. The pistol snapped its penultimate shot and ripped-through a valuable Sidney Cooper farm landscape painting.

The second distraught policeman brought his poker down on the physically absent Invisible Man. Kemp then felt a hard blow given to the nape of his neck, and the bad-luck Professor fell straight to his knees. The rookie cops quickly realized that the full-scale, surreal melee had been involving the Invisible Man against three opponents, so the corporal began swinging the poker that the Doctor had handed him, just before the wild and crazy dining-room donnybrook had erupted.

And next, the lowly private picked-up an available chair, lifted the seat over his head, and waited for the first propitious opportunity to crash-down the exquisite piece of furniture upon the Invisible Man's invisible skull, once Colonel Adye's three-dimensional

244

service revolver would be seen dangling and dancing about inside the Unseen Man's invisible hand.

The Invisible Man was by then energetically twirling his new-found garden axe around his invisible head, as if the weapon were a medieval knight's cudgel. The Unseen's axe and the rookie cop's poker clanged in a primitive dueling battle, and after five colliding impacts, the Invisible Man's invisible head had been incidentally scratched. The Unseen, afraid of his form being detected while bleeding from his injury, and also from becoming visible expending energy, abandoned his recalcitrance.

The heavy axe dropping was seen by Kemp, by a screaming and delirious Maria, and by the two excessively petrified greenhorn policemen, who were fearfully retreating to safety inside Dr. Kemp's kitchen.

"Stand away, you two," Griffin screamed at the already-coerced novice officers. "I don't want you two clowns. I only want to kill that total loser Kemp."

"We want you!" the first policeman intrepidly boomed, making a quick step forward, and recklessly swiping with his poker at the queer-sounding Voice. The Invisible Man started back, and his invisible frame blundered into the corner umbrella stand.

Involved in a live-or-die crisis, the young private wanting to live another day, initiated a desperate swipe with his borrowed black fireplace poker, and amazingly, his weapon made solid contact with invisible flesh, hitting something soft that snapped. There was a loud and sharp exclamation reflective of excruciating pain, and then, the heavy garden axe fell to the pantry floor. The policeman swiped again, but this time at vacancy, and his futile swing hit absolutely nothing.

The two exceptionally-tired policemen, Dr. Kemp, and Maria heard the dining-room door open, and a quick rush of feet rumbled within.

"Where the hell is he? Where is the dirty Bastard?" Dr. Kemp wanted to know, getting-up off the dining-room floor and brushing-off an abundance of excess debris and dust from his trousers. "Griffin had used the garden axe to break all of the downstairs shutters and windows."

"Don't know. I do think I've hit him, sir," the perspiring cop holding the black poker proudly reported. "I think he's standing somewhere in the hall, or perhaps he's in the pantry, or maybe he's fled the house and has left the premises altogether. Unless he's luckily slipped past you. Doctor Kemp—er, sir."

The second policeman began struggling to his feet. Suddenly, the faint pad of bare feet upon the kitchen stairs could be heard.

"Yap!" cried the first policeman, who wildly flung his poker towards the sound which the officer presumed was the exact location of the ever-mobile Invisible Man. The errant poker only collided with the dining room floor, landing on the opposite side of the chamber.

"Doctor Kemp. Where the hell is Dr. Kemp?" the poker hurler asked.

"Doctor Kemp's missing-in-action, along with his girl servant," the second cop noticed and reported. "But where the hell did the two disappear to?"

A sudden rapping on the front door produced a rather welcomed sight.

"Sorry to bother you good policemen," Colonel Adye greeted. "But I was feigning being shot dead out there on the front lawn!"

Chapter 28

"THE HUNTER HUNTED"

Mr. Silas Heelas, Dr. Kemp's nearest neighbor among the villa estate holders in rustic Burdock, was asleep in his "across the lane" summer house when the siege of Dr. Kemp's residence began. Mr. Heelas was one of the 'sturdy minority' who refused to believe "in all this nonsense" about an Invisible Man causing massive community chaos among the local citizenry.

The old curmudgeon's wife, however, as Old Silas was subsequently to be reminded, did place ample credence in the criminal and evil activities of one Mr. Griffin. Mr. Heelas insisted upon walking about his garden just as if nothing of consequence was the matter, and the self-appointed fool went to sleep in the afternoon in accordance with the custom of elderly years accumulating. The ancient fogey slept through the smashing of the windows, and then woke-up suddenly with a curious persuasion that something was drastically wrong and "out of sorts" in the ordinarily peaceful Burdock neighborhood.

The obnoxious geezer looked across the lane at Dr. Kemp's wrecked house, rubbed his eyes, and looked again. Then, almost-blind Mr. Heelas put his feet to the ground, and sat listening. The daft old man said he was "damned", but still the strange sight seen across the road was highly visible. Dr. Kemp's house looked as though it had been deserted for weeks after it had endured what appeared to have been a major violent riot. Every expensive window in the residence across the lane had been broken and egregiously vandalized.

"I could've sworn it was all right and in excellent condition just yesterday!" Silas recalled as the Old Fart glanced-down and peered at his broken wristwatch. "Twenty-minutes-ago, that house across the street was my favorite in all of Burdock."

Mr. Heelas became abundantly aware of remembering a measured dissonant symphony concussion, and the attendant clashing of glass, occurring far away in the distance. And then, as the farting asshole sat open-mouthed and passing gas as if on his death bed, came a still more wonderful remembrance swimming into his rapidly-disintegrating cerebrum. The shutters of the drawing-room window had been violently flung-open, and Maria Torano, Dr. Kemp's loyal housemaid, dressed in her outdoor hat and fluttering garments, appeared struggling in a frantic manner to throw up the accompanying sash.

Suddenly, as Dr. Kemp appeared beside her, helping the maid perform her arduous task, in another moment, the window was open, and the servant was again laboring to perform her household duty. Maria pitched forward and seemingly fell and vanished among the rhododendron and hydrangea shrubs.

Mr. Silas Heelas stood-up, exclaiming vaguely and vehemently at all those fabulous events transpiring before his nearly-blind eyes. The senile gentleman saw Dr. Kemp standing on the sill, spring from the window, and like a circus acrobat, incredibly reappear almost-instantaneously, and next running along a path in the shrubbery, and stooping as he ran, like a man wanting to evade public observation.

The Doctor soon vanished behind a laburnum, and appeared again, ambitiously clambering over a fence that abutted onto the open down. In a second, the human contortionist had tumbled-over, and was running at a tremendous pace down the slope towards addled, bewildered, and absolutely senile Mr. Silas Heelas.

"Lord!" Mr. Heelas hooted, being struck with a rare idea. "It's that Invisible Man Brute! The fuckin' London newspapers that my wife reads to me have been right all along! Yes sir, it's all been right about him, after all!"

Mr. Heelas' cook was watching him from the top window, and he was amazed to see the 'human dynamo' come pelting towards the house at a good twelve miles-an-hour. There was a slamming of doors, a ringing of bells, and the voice of Mr. Heelas bellowing like a raging bull being castrated. "Shut the doors; shut the windows; shut everything!"

"Shut the fuck up!" the cook yelled-over. "Why the hell didn't you die yesterday, you fucked-up cretin!"

"The Invisible Man is coming! The Invisible Man is coming!" parroted old Silas during his major mania bout.

Instantly, the Heelas house was full of screams and myriad erratic directions, and scurrying feet were discerned all over the modest residence. Old Mr. Silas Heelas ran all by himself to go and shut the French windows that had opened onto the prehistoric fart's cherished veranda. As he did so, Dr. Kemp's head, shoulders, and knees appeared over the edge of the garden fence. In another moment, the sprinting Doctor had plowed-through the asparagus plants, and was presently doing a right-angle detour, running across the tennis lawn toward the old coot Silas Heelas's house.

"You can't come in," boisterously screamed Mr. Silas Heelas, accidentally and miraculously remembering how to shut the bolts. "I'm very sorry if he's after you, but you can't come in! Even if you keep-a-knockin', you can't come in!"

Running Dr. Kemp appeared with terror shown upon his face, rapping and then shaking frantically at the neighbor's French window. Then, seeing his efforts were vainly useless, the Doctor ran alongside the veranda, vaulted the end, and went to hammer his fists at the side door. Next, Kemp dashed around by the side gate to the front of the house, and so briskly hustled into the hill-road.

And Mr. Heelas, staring from his window, noticing with an astonished face of horror, had scarcely witnessed Kemp vanish into thin air, but the asparagus plants were being trampled this way and that, by Unseen pursuing feet. At that extraordinary phenomenon, thinking that his ninety-nine-year-old wife and rebellious cook would institutionalize his ass, Mr. Silas Heelas precipitately fled upstairs, and the rest of the fucked-up chase became beyond his purview. But as the hoary dumb-fuck passed the staircase window, Silas heard the side gate slam.

Emerging into the hill-road, Dr. Kemp naturally took the downward direction, and so it was that the runner came to duplicate, in his own person, the very same race route he had watched with such critical eyes from the belvedere study, only four days before.

Dr. Kemp ran that marathon very well for a man out of training, and although his face was white and wet, his wits were cool to the last. The Professor industriously dashed with wide strides, and wherever a patch of rough ground intervened, and wherever there came a patch of raw flints, or a shard of broken glass shining and dazzling in the morning sunlight, Dr. Kemp crossed it, and left the markings of bare-invisible-feet, which trailed-behind to take what line the footprints would mimic, and then instantly disappear behind the hustling Physician's forward progress.

For the first time in his life, Kemp had discovered that the hill-road was indescribably vast and desolate, and that the beginnings of the town far below, at the hill's foot, were strangely remote. Never had there been a slower or more painful method of progression than running *that* same daily distance, perpetually over and over again, an unlucky seven times each day.

All the gaunt villas, sleeping in the afternoon sun, looked locked and barred; no doubt the various abodes were locked and barred by *his* own orders. But at any rate, the homes might have kept a lookout for an eventuality like this daily one, as authorized by the singular Invisible Man.

Burdock was rising-up now for much-needed rebellion; the sea had dropped-out of sight behind the village, and people down below were stirring and restless as usual. The restive population was awakening to a train's whistle at the station platform, just arriving at the hill's foot. Beyond that developing Burdock scene was the all-too-familiar police station.

The people below were casually staring at Dr. Kemp's daily marathon sprint, and his breath was beginning to irritate the vulnerable tissue inside his throat. The tram was quite near now, and the "Jolly Crickets" lounge was noisily barring its doors.

Beyond the tram were posts and heaps of gravel, representative of the village drainage works. Dr. Kemp had a transitory idea of jumping into the tram and slamming the doors, and then the "New Fanatic" resolved to turn direction and head for the police station.

In another moment, the perpetual Sprinter had passed the door of the "infamous and risqué "Jolly-Crickets Inn", and now continuing on his daily circuitous route, the indefatigable jogger was in the blistering fag-end of the street, and still enthusiastically pursuing his ongoing seven-times-a-day enterprise.

The tram driver and his helper, arrested by the sight of Dr. Kemp's furious haste, stood staring with the tram horses unhitched. Further on down the line, the astonished features of various railroad paraphernalia appeared above the mounds of gravel, and then soon each one separately flashing, and then almost-magically disappearing in sequence.

Dr. Kemp's pace lightened a little, and soon the relentless Sprinter heard the swift pad of his rabid pursuer, and the scared-shitless runner leaped forward again. "The Invisible Man!" neurotic Kemp cried and shrieked to the railroad workers with a vague indicative gesture, and by an inspiration, the dashing young man leapt the excavation and placed a long distance between himself and the adamant marathon pursuer.

Then, abandoning the idea of entering the police station, the sweating Hustler frantically turned into a narrow side street, rushed by a green-grocer's cart, hesitated for a tenth of a second at the door of a "sweet-stuff shop", and finally made haste for the mouth of an alley that again ran back into Hill Street.

Two or three little children were playing with marbles there, and the Professor's approach frightened the tiny tots, who shrieked and scattered at *his* apparition, and doors and windows opened, and excited mothers revealed their hearts concern for their offspring's safety.

Out of the crowd of hysterical bystanders ran Dr. Kemp, zipping into Hill Street again, three-hundred-yards from the tram-line's end. And immediately, Kemp's sensitive ears became aware of a tumultuous vociferation, along with the wild stampede of excited Burdock residents.

Dr. Kemp glanced-up the street towards the hill. Hardly a dozen-yards off ran a huge railroad worker, cursing in a litany of expletives, and slashing viciously with a spade, and hard behind him came the tram conductor with his huge fists clenched. Up the street, others followed these two militant aggressors, striking and shouting zany vulgarities. Down towards the town center, men and women were also running, and as usual, Kemp noticed clearly one-man coming-out of a shop-door with an enormous stick in his hand. "Spread out! Spread out!" someone beckoned.

Dr. Kemp suddenly grasped the altered condition of the daily chase. His legs stopped, and as the Researcher looked around panting, in a shocked state of mind insanely hollered, "He's close here! Form a line across for protection. He's now getting close to here!"

Without any notice, the now-unemployed Chemistry Professor was hit hard under the ear, and his body went reeling while trying to face towards his Unseen Antagonist. The daily victim of such abuse just managed to keep his feet, and Professor Kemp struck a vain counter in the air. Then, the martyr was hit again under the jaw, and his body soon was sprawling headlong onto the ground. In another moment, a knee compressed upon the Doctor's diaphragm, and a couple of eager hands gripped his throat, but the grasp of one palm was weaker than the other.

Kemp's hands pulled the Aggressor's wrists, and the Fired University Physician heard a cry of pain emanating from his assailant's throat, and then the spade belonging to one of the railroad laborers came whirling through the air above the Doctor's head, and the shovel struck a metal pole with a dull clang.

Dr. Kemp felt a drop of moisture land upon his face. The grip at his throat suddenly relaxed, and with a convulsive effort, the Renegade Physician loosened himself, grasped a limp shoulder, and rolled uppermost. The exhausted victim tugged the Unseen's elbows near the ground. "I've got him!" Kemp screamed. "I've finally got him. Help! Help me somebody! He's down!" the Doctor pleaded in vain. "Hold his feet and keep him pinned to the turf! Please help me somebody!"

In another second, there was a simultaneous rush upon the ongoing altercation, and a straggler coming into the road suddenly might have thought an exceptionally savage game of Rugby was in progress. And there was no redundant shouting after Kemp's pathetic and desperate cry, but only a sound of blows, kicks, punches, and heavy breathing.

Then came a mighty effort, and the Invisible Man threw-off a couple of his muscular antagonists and rose to his invisible knees. Kemp clung to his adversary in front like a bloodhound to a stag, and a dozen hands gripped, clutched, and tore at the Unseen's Invisible Body. The hysterical tram conductor suddenly got a hold of the Invisible Man's neck and shoulders, and lugged Griffin backwards in a strenuous stranglehold.

Down went the heap of struggling men again, and the pile rolled-over in a human cluster. There was an abundance of savage kicking being enacted. Then again, very suddenly, a wild scream of "Mercy! Mercy!" that instantly swelled and swiftly died-down to a dull sound, resembling that of choking.

"Get back, you miserable Fools!" Kemp's muffled voice begged. And next, there was a vigorous shoving back of a myriad of stalwart human and ghostly forms. "He's hurt, I tell you. Stand back! At last, he's hurt!"

A brief fracas ensued in order to clear a space, and then the circle of eager faces witnessed the Brave Doctor kneeling, as it seemed, fifteen-inches into the air, and him holding and squeezing a pair of invisible arms to the ground from *that* height. Behind the preoccupied Doctor, a young constable was assiduously gripping and pulling invisible ankles.

"He's not shamming," the Doctor yelled, cautiously raising his knee. "And I'll hold his ass down until more help arrives."

Scads of patrons were exiting the "Jolly Crickets" and stood watching the frenetic scene evolve. Kemp felt about with his free hand, his fingers seeming to pass through empty air. "He's not breathing," someone shouted in reference to the Invisible Man. I think he's expired!" And then, "I can't feel his black heart beating. Yes, thank God he's fuckin' finally expired."

Suddenly, an old woman, peering under the arm of the muscular railroad laborer, sharply screamed. "Looky there!" she bellowed, and thrust-out a wrinkled finger.

And looking where she had pointed, everyone saw, faint and transparent as though the image was made of glass, distinctive and distinguishable veins, arteries, bones, and nerves, and also the outline of a hand that was both limp and prone. The flesh grew clouded and opaque, even as the stunned bystanders incredulously stared and gawked.

"Hello!" the constable gleefully yelped. "Here's his cold feet a-showing!"

And so, slowly, beginning at his hands and feet, and methodically creeping along *his* limbs to the vital centers of *his* lacerated body, that strange transformational change evolved and continued. It was like the slow spreading of a most-lethal poison.

First came the little white nerves; next a hazy grey sketch of a limb; then the glassy bones and intricate arteries; next the flesh and skin; and finally, the whole form growing and becoming dense and opaque. Presently, the mesmerized Burdock viewers could see *his* crushed chest and *his* badly bruised shoulders, and also the dim outline of *his* drawn and battered features.

When at last the crowd made way for Dr. Kemp to triumphantly stand erect like a victorious Roman gladiator over his vanquished opponent, there lay, naked and pitiful upon the dry ground, the abused and broken body of a Young Man about thirty years of age. His hair and dwarfish brow were snow white, but not grey with age, but white with the whiteness of albinism. And most notably, the deceased had eyes that were still shining like garnets. The former Invisible Man's hands were still tightly clenched; his blurred eyes remained wide open, and his facial expression was one of total anger and dismay.

"Cover his face!" a disgusted man demanded. "For God's sake, cover that damned devil's face!" And three little children, pushing forward through the crowd, were suddenly twisted around and sent packing-off, again to play marbles.

Someone brought a tablecloth sheet from the "Jolly Crickets", and having dully covered *his* final remains, the relieved crowd of humane pallbearers carried *his* corpse into that bawdy house of amusement and frivolity.

And there the cadaver was laid upon a shabby bed in a tawdry, ill-lighted back bedroom, surrounded by a throng of ignorant and petty people, with *his* nude form broken and wounded, betrayed and unpitied. Griffin, the first of all men to make himself invisible, and possibly the most gifted physicist the world has ever seen besides Dr. Darrell Kemp, had ended his earthly existence in infinite disaster, which terminated his artificial life upon this frail and fragile Earth.

Dr. Darrell Kemp had one last ethereal thought regarding the menace he had known as "the Fiend Griffin". 'The Invisible Man had doomed himself to a plagued life of redundant recidivism. If it weren't for the Invisible Man's remarkable ability, if that unique factor would be stripped-away from him altogether, then what simply remained was an egocentric, immature, ingrate, no better than the irresponsible imp Mr. Thomas Marvel, and in terms of responsible public behavior, Tom Marvel and Griffin, the inimitable Invisible Man, could actually be two almost-identical kindred stooges, acting in concert like genetic twin brothers.' Thus ends the totally weird and strange story of Griffin, Sussex County, England's incomparable Invisible Man.

About the Author

Jay Dubya is author John Wiessner's pen name. John is a retired New Jersey public school teacher, having diligently taught the subject for thirty-four years. John lives in Hammonton, New Jersey.

Counting *Poe: Pelted, Pounded, Pummeled and Pulverized*, John has written and published sixty-two total books. *Pieces of Eight, Pieces of Eight, Part II, Pieces of Eight, Part III* and *Pieces of Eight, Part IV* all contain short stories and novellas that feature science fiction and paranormal plots and themes. *Nine New Novellas, Nine New Novellas, Part II, Nine New Novellas, Part III, Nine New Novellas, Part IV, One Baker's Dozen, Two Baker's Dozen, Snake Eyes and Boxcars* and *Snake Eyes and Boxcars, Part II* are short story collections all written in the spirit of the *Pieces of Eight* series.

Other Jay Dubya adult-oriented fiction are the works *Black Leather and Blue Denim, A '50s Novel*, and its exciting sequel, *The Great Teen Fruit War, A 1960' Novel. Frat Brats, A '60s Novel* completes the action/adventure trilogy. Jay Dubya also has produced two irreverent Biblical satires, *The Wholly Book of Genesis* and *The Wholly Book of Exodus*. A third satire *Ron Coyote, Man of La Mangia* is a parody on Miguel Cervantes' classic novel, *Don Quixote* published in 1605. *Thirteen Sick Tasteless Classics, TSTC, Part II, TSTC, Part III* and *TSTC, Part IV* are satirical works that each corrupt thirteen classic stories from American and British literature and from Greek mythology. *Fractured Frazzled Folk Fables and Fairy Farces* and *FFFF & FF, Part II* satirize and corrupt famous children's literature stories. *Mauled Maimed Mangled Mutilated Mythology* is another popular adult-oriented satirical/parody work that pokes fun at twenty-one famous classical myths. *O. Henry: Obscenely and Outrageously Obliterated* is another satirical adult rewrite. Finally, *Shakespeare: Slammed, Smeared, Savaged and Slaughtered* and *Shakespeare: S, S, S and S. Part II* poke fun at the famous works of the great playwright.

The author has also penned a young adult fantasy trilogy: *Pot of Gold, Enchanta* and *Space Bugs, Earth Invasion. The Eighteen Story*

Gingerbread House is a collection of eighteen new children's stories. And last but not least, two non-fiction works are *So Ya' Wanna' Be A Teacher* and *Random Articles and Manuscripts.*

Jay Dubya really likes '50s music and he also listens to songs by the Beatles, *ELO*, the Carpenters, the Beach Boys, Fleetwood Mac, the Eagles', the Rolling Stones, John Mellencamp and John Fogerty.

Jay Dubya

Author Biography

Born in Hammonton, NJ in 1942, John Wiessner had attended St. Joseph School up to and including Grade 5. After his family moved from Hammonton to Levittown, Pa in 1954, John attended St. Mark School in Bristol, Pa. for Grade 6, St. Michael the Archangel School in Levittown for Grades 7 and 8 and then Immaculate Conception School, Levittown, Pa. for Grade 9. Bishop Egan High School, Levittown Pa was John's educational base for Grades 10 and 11, and later in 1960, the aspiring author graduated from Edgewood Regional High, Tansboro, NJ. John then next attended Glassboro State College, where he was an announcer for the school's baseball games and also read the nightly news and sports over WGLS, GSC's radio station.

John Wiessner had been primarily an English teacher in the Hammonton Public School System for 34 years, specializing in the instruction of middle school language arts. Mr. Wiessner was quite active in the Hammonton Education Association, serving in the capacities of Vice-President, building representative and finally, teachers' head negotiator for 7 years. During his lengthy teaching career, John had been nominated into "Who's Who Among American Teachers" three times. He also was quite active giving professional workshops at schools around South Jersey on the subjects of creative writing and the use of movie videos to motivate students to organize their classroom theme compositions.

John Wiessner was very active in community service, being a past President of the Hammonton Lions Club, where he also functioned for many years as the club's Tail-Twister, Vice-President and Liontamer. John had been named Hammonton Lion of the Year in 1979 and in 2009 received the prestigious Melvin Jones Fellow Award, the highest honor a Lion can receive.

John also was a successful businessman, starting with being a Philadelphia Bulletin newspaper delivery boy for two years in the late 1950s in Levittown, Pennsylvania. After his family moved back to New Jersey in 1959, John worked at his grandparents and his

258

parents' farm markets, Square Deal Farm (now Ron's Gardens in Hammonton) and Pete's Farm Market in Elm, respectively. He later managed his wife's parents' farm market, White Horse Farms in Elm for three summers.

Also, in a business capacity, for 16 summers starting in 1966 John Wiessner had co-owned Dealers Choice Amusement Arcade on the Ocean City, Maryland boardwalk and also co-owned the New Horizon Tee-Shirt Store for eight summers (1973-'81) on the Rehoboth Beach, Delaware boardwalk. In addition, "Jay Dubya" was a co-owner of Wheel and Deal Amusement Arcade, Missouri Avenue and Boardwalk, Atlantic City. And then, for 18 summers beginning in 1986, John had been the Field Manager in charge of farm crew-leaders for Atlantic Blueberry Company (the world's largest cultivated blueberry farm), both the Weymouth and Mays Landing, New Jersey Divisions.

After retiring from teaching in 1999, writing under the pen name Jay Dubya (his initials), John Wiessner became the author of 62 books in the genre Action/Adventure Novels, Sci-Fi/Paranormal Story Collections, Adult Satire, Young Adult Fantasy Novels and Non-Fiction Books. His books exist in hardcover, in paperback and in popular Kindle and Nook e-book formats.

In January of 2022, John Wiessner (Jay Dubya) was nominated into Marquis Who's Who in America, and in April of that same year, was one of nine distinguished Who's Who in America members honored with Lifetime Achievement Awards, all nine sharing an article of recognition appearing in the Wall Street Journal.

Google: Jay Dubya books
Google: Walmart, Jay Dubya